CONTEMPORARY EUROPE AND SOUTH ASIA

About The Editors

B. Vivekanandan, M.A., Ph.D (JNU), is Professor and former Chairman, Centre for American and West European Studies, School of International Studies, Jawaharlal Nehru University, New Delhi. He has written, edited or contributed to 25 important books on international affairs, European affairs, and India's Foreign Policy. Some of his important books include: *International Concerns of European Social Democrats; Pathfinders: Social Democrats of Scandinavia; The Shrinking Circle: The Commonwealth in British Foreign Policy, 1945-74; Building on Solidarity: Social Democracy and the New Millennium, ed.;* and *In Retrospect: Reflections on Select Issues in World Politics, 1975-2000.*

He has also contributed to the leading international journals like *Round Table, Orbis, Asia Pacific Community, Asian survey, International Studies, India Quarterly* and *Indian Journal of Political Science.* He is research supervisor of several Ph.D students doing research on Europe.

A widely travelled person his research visits abroad include the following countries: Australia, Austria, Belgium, Canada, Denmark, Finland, France, Germany, Greece, Italy, Norway, Portugal, Soviet Union, Spain, Switzerland, Sweden, The Netherlands, United Kingdom, and United States.

D.K.Giri, M.A, M.Phil, Ph.D (JNU), Ph.D (Hull, UK), is Senior Research Fellow at the Institute of Social Sciences, New Delhi. He was associated with the Centre for Developing Area Studies, and the Centre for European Studies at the University of Hull, United Kingdom.

He has had a consistent academic record – first class and merit scholarships throughout. He taught at Jamia Millia Islamia, New Delhi and has guest-lectured at universities in India and abroad. He has contributed number of articles to the leading journals on a wide range of subjects with specialisation on developmental issues. He is the author of *European Union and India: A Study in North-South Relation.*

Dr. Giri has widely travelled for research and other academic purposes. The countries he has visited include: United Kingdom, France, The Netherlands, Germany, Belgium, Luxembourg, Sweden, Finland, Spain, Denmark, Portugal, Ireland, Soviet Union, Afghanistan, and Poland.

CONTEMPORARY EUROPE AND SOUTH ASIA

Edited by

B. Vivekanandan
Professor of European Studies
Centre for American and European Studies
School of International Studies
Jawaharlal Nehru University
New Delhi

Dr. D. K. Giri
Senior Research Fellow
Institute of Social Sciences
New Delhi

CONCEPT PUBLISHING COMPANY; NEW DELHI-110059

ISBN 81-7022-903-0

First Published 2001

Published and Printed by
Ashok Kumar Mittal
Concept Publishing Company
A/15-16, Commercial Block, Mohan Garden
New Delhi-110059 (India)
Phones: 5648039, 5649024
Fax: 091-(11)-5648053
E-mail: publishing@conceptpub.com

Preface

On 18th May 1498 Vasco da Gama reached India's port town Calicut on the Malabar Coast. This marked, as it were, the beginning of the opening up of the greater Indian region to European influence. In many ways, this was an episodic development, with far reaching consequences, for South Asia, in particular, and the rest of the world in general. Vasco da Gama's voyage to the 'Indies' was of course part of a larger design to secure an effective control over the East Indies trade and, particularly, the lucrative trade in spices.

The characterisation of the 16th century as the Vasco da Gama epoch is suggestive of the significance of the Portuguese and later on, the European, (the Dutch, the French, the Danish and the English) impact on the economic, social, cultural and political life of the South Western Coast of India and the entire South Asia. Five hundred long years have passed since this momentous event. It would, at this stage, be pertinent to look back and critically assess the complex developments from the people's perspective. There was more than ever before a compelling need to evaluate and critically assess more closely the historical and long term process of global integration and the structuring of a certain dependent pattern of development. The current interest and importance of the process of 'globalisation' and 'liberalisation' underscored the need for this enquiry and evaluation.

In order to deliberate on these and other related issues, the Institute of Social Sciences organised a conference from 16 to 20 May 1998, at the historic cities of Calicut and Cochin.

Besides providing a common platform for scholars from Europe and South Asia of different disciplines, it also brought together thinkers, academics and political leaders to exchange ideas on the forces of history unleashed by colonialism, and its consequences. There is, of course, renewed interest in investigating the phenomenon in its entirety. The conference was a unique opportunity to achieve a deeper understanding to combat domination and dependency with a view to working towards a New World Order. Renowned scholars working on Indian, Portuguese, Dutch, French, English and Danish history and culture, international relations, and global political economy participated in the conference.

The conference consisted of three symposia: Human Geography and Environment, Dependence and Domination, Science and Technology, and had eight working sessions: Cultural Process, Political Economy, National Identity in South Asia, Globalization, Religion, Education, Trade and Commerce, and Contemporary Europe and South Asia.

About 150 papers were presented at the Conference, both in symposia and in working sessions, spanning over 60 hours' discussion. Scholars from European and South Asian countries discussed the issues, past and present, and explored the future relations. A collective opinion emerged at the end of the conference to continue studies and exchanges to strengthen the relations. It was then decided to bring out three volumes for wider dissemination of papers deliberated at the conference. The present volume is on the working session on Europe and South Asia dealing with various facets of the relation. It is being brought out as a companion volume, delinked from the other two volumes under preparation, which deal with forces of colonization, decolonisation and recolonisation. European Union, untainted with a colonial image, is a new entrant in international relations, with the promise of introducing a new politics based on concerns for democracy, human rights and social justice. I thank Prof. B. Vivekanandan and Dr. D.K. Giri for working on this volume. Our thanks of course go to the contributors who showed promptness and enthusiasm in responding to out invitation to write for and participate in the conference.

I must place on record my appreciation to all my colleagues in the Institute who successfully rose to the challenge of organising such a big conference in Calicut and Cochin, and coordinated from three centres — New Delhi, Brussels, Kottayam. Even the political tremors of the nuclear explosion felt in and outside the country and the heavy rains just on the eve of the conference did not dilute the determination, nor did it dampen the spirit of the organisers and young volunteers of local colleges in Kerala. We will feel amply rewarded if the publication contributes to the building of Euro-South Asian relations in a meaningful way.

George Mathew
Director
Institute of Social Sciences

New Delhi

Contents

Editors' Introduction

Europe and South Asia have behind them five hundred year's lively interaction. It has produced a plethora of experiences which made tremendous impact on life and politics on both sides. Their relationship has passed through an imperial and post-imperial phase. Vasco da Gamma's landing in Calicut (Kerala) was followed by a prolonged period of Portuguese colonialism. Tagging Vasco da Gama, other European imperial powers like the Dutch, the French, the Danes and the English had also descended to South Asia and established colonies.

The age of imperialism, though worked for the benefit of the imperial powers of Europe, was debilitating for South Asia. This was because at that point of time, in terms of the level of development, South Asia was more or less on a par with Europe. But, under the impact of imperialism while the resource flow from South Asia to Europe was steady and substantial, which partially assisted Europe's industrialization and development, South Asia's industrialization was stifled first and was put on a reverse gear through deliberate policies. The clock of industrialization of South Asia was stopped effectively for about two hundred years, widening the gap between Europe and South Asia.

That phase of imperial relationship between Europe and South Asia ended in the aftermath of the Second World War. Britain relinquished its imperial possessions in South Asia in 1947-48, France in 1954 and the Portuguese possessions were liberated in 1961, which together has put the relationship between Europe and South Asia on a new basis of cooperation.

At the cultural and intellectual levels the interaction between Europe and South Asia was fruitful. European scholars like Maxmueller came to India to learn Indian philosophy and thought. At the same time new liberal ideas like liberty, equality, fraternity and democracy which germinated in Europe made their impact on South Asia's Political thinking. In the realms of political institutions, bureaucracy and the development of a *lingua franca* for the region, the British impact was more pronounced. Europe's contribution to the development of a mosaic culture in South Asia is also significant.

In the post-war period, Europe and South Asia embarked upon different experiments. The aggressive nationalism practised by European nations for centuries together had reduced Europe into an arena of internescine quarrels and destruction. The second World War took the level of damage to a point of total exhaustion. The continent had to turn to a former British colony, the United States for assistance through the Marshall plan, to take Europe to the road of recovery. At the brink of total destruction, wisdom dawned in Europe that there should be another way for the management of peace and development in Europe. They came to the conclusion that instead of pursuing the path of aggressive nationalism the European nations should join together under a community framework, in a spirit of cooperation, in order to ensure peace and development for the benefit of all. The establishment of the European Economic Community, which has now evolved into a 15 member European Union, is the fruition of that aspiration. That, indeed, is the most positive development in Europe in the post-war period.

The success of that experiment in Europe which assured peace, security and prosperity in the continent since 1945 has inspired countries of South Asia to emulate the approach followed by the leader of European nations. The establishment of the South Asian Association for Regional Cooperation is a small beginning, the countries of South Asia have ventured to promote cooperation, peace, and prosperity in the region. However, it will take some more time before the SAARC countries could fully grasp the potential of a community approach and the new opportunities it would provide to elevate the entire South Asia as a region of peace and prosperity. It is high time that South Asia moves away from petty quarrels and moves up in a community spirit.

There are certain developments in Europe which deserves our special attention. It concerns the economic relationship between Europe and South Asia. The trade policies which have been pursued by the European Community are showing an increasing tendency of slamming its doors against Class 2 imports from the developing countries where as the Community presses for more opening of the domestic markets of the developing countries for developed countries exports in the name of free market, globalization and liberalization. This approach obviously runs counter to equity and a balanced development of world trade and will lead to further impoverishment of the developing countries. This needs review. Trading environment in Europe is increasingly attuned to protectionism against exports from the developing countries, including countries of South Asia. To promote relationship between Europe and South Asia, there is need of a more liberal approach from the European Union. The rise of non-tariff barriers against South Asian exports to European Community should be withdrawn. The European Union's tendency to liberally use non-tariff barriers against the countries of South Asia is an old framework which promoted inequality in the world and is not conducive for building up of a humane world community based on equity. New parameters need to be clearly drawn. While India's imports from European Union have increased substantially, there is no similar enhancement of India's exports to the European Union. This is upsetting the balance of payment and is not sustainable. Liberalization has worked in favour of the developed countries.

The European Union countries are attracted by the World Bank's assessment of the market potential of South Asia. According to World Bank's assessment South Asia and East Asia would account for more than 50 per cent growth in world economy. It is estimated that by the turn of the century about one billion people of the region would have substantially increased their purchasing power, of which at least 400 millions would have the spending capacity of any American or European. The prognosis has made many European companies to position themselves in these growth areas well in advance.

However, it would be better for the world if the developed countries of the West moved away from a survival of the fittest framework under the globalization-liberalization-free market framework. A more healthy and sustainable framework would be globalization based on international solidarity which can promote a just world order. Europe and South Asia could be partners in that endeavour.

The relationship between contemporary Europe and South Asia has been examined by eleven eminent scholars drawn from Europe and South Asia. They have examined its different facets from various angles. All the papers were presented at the "International Conference on Europe and South Asia: 500 Years' held in May 1998 at Calicut under the auspices of the Institute of Social Sciences, New Delhi. The papers, which constitute this volume, are the revised versions of the papers presented at the international conference.

In this volume, though each essay has its own distinction and thematic completion, together they present a picture of mosaic which characterises the features of relationship between contemporary Europe and South Asia in general and India in particular, with greater emphasis on the post-war scenario. The backdrop is provided by Tom Burden of the Leeds University, Britain, who analyses the linkage between Victorian capitalism and the British legacy in India. He has examined how social change and development of ideologies in Britain in the nineteenth century had affected India. His main argument is that the complex relationship between Benthamism, conservatism and liberalism in the British political life had a direct impact on Britain's important relationship with India. It helped the development of political debate in India and influenced the moderate character of Indian nationalism.

Hartmut Elsenhans of the Leipzig University, Germany, has focussed on the issue of Europe's development and South Asia's under development and underlines the contemporary relevance of a new interpretation of this phenomenon. This, he has analysed in the context of the changing patterns of globalization and the role of the state. He has focussed on the popular perception that poverty and underdevelopment in South Asia was caused by European imperialism, which allowed a backward Europe to overtake a more advanced South Asia, and that Europe's industrial revolution was nurtured by the resources drained out from India through exploitation. While Elsenhans has not totally refuted this popular perception, he tries to point out the deficiency in it. He argues that "the same mechanism which allowed Europe to use South Asia in support of its own industrial revolution can now a days be turned into support for a rapid catching up of South Asia if globalisation of international economic relations is intelligently complemented by state interventionism in South Asia and if the industrially leading countries play their role of locomotives with expanding internal markets at least for a longer transition period. He underlines the importance of a two-way relationship between

Europe and South Asia.

Paul Sutton, University of Hull, UK, has analysed the new directions in the European Unions' development policy. This he has done by examining the "first generation" development policy of the European Union and the circumstances that led to the introduction of "second generation" development policy,. which has considerably changed the character of the EU's relationship with the developing countries. It gives special emphasis on how EU's development policy is likely to affect its relations with South Asia. Sutton points out that the rationale for construction of the single European Market was based on internal reasons and its impact on outside world, including developing countries, received little thought. Yet, there were considerable consequential effects on trade with the developing countries. Sutton analyses these effects and points out what they would mean for South Asia.

European Union's external relations pertaining to South Asia is the focus of Purusottam Bhattacharya's paper on European Political Cooperation (EPC) and South Asia. It may be noted that political cooperation was not part of the Treaty of Rome which established the European Common Market in 1958. It was set in motion in 1970. Bhattacharya discusses the EU-South Asia relations in the context of European political cooperation and then through the dialogues between EU troika and its Indian counterpart after the troika got institutionalized in the European Union. He begins by investigating into EU's approach to South Asia in general and focuses on the areas of existing political relations between EU and South Asia. According to Bhattacharya the EU attention in the EPC context focussed primarily on three issues - Kashmir and India "Pakistan Relations; Democracy and human rights in South Asia, and nuclear non-proliferation in the region. He has examined future prospects of EU-South Asia relations as well.

Extending the analysis of EU-South Asia relationship, Nimmi Kurian's paper deals with India-EU Economic relationship and focuses on the problems and prospects of that linkage. In it, she has given an overview of the main components of that relationship — investment links, the aid flows, and the trade ties. In the trade ties, she looks at the-way trade flows, the commodity composition of India's trade with the European Union in the 1990s, registered rapid expansion in the wake of the liberalisation process India had initiated. In the paper,

Dr. Kurian examines the EU trade policy in some detail since it has far reaching implications for India's exports to the EU. The European Union's protectionist measures, with special focus on prominent non-tariff barriers employed against India, has also been analysed for its deleterious, trade impeding effects. The paper critically examines the prospects of India-EU trade ties and the policy measures necessary to transform the present asymmetrical relationship to a more balanced one.

O.P. Sharma's has focussed his analysis on Indians' export performance in manufactured goods to the United Kingdom during the period of economic reforms. The paper examines India's performance in this context at aggregate level in the British market, which is one of India's major traditional and highly competitive markets in the European Union. It also examines the trends in EU-UK foreign direct investments, which have a bearing on India's export of manufactures. According to Sharma, the emergence of Single European Market and the establishment of the WTO have changed the basic perception of Indo-EU and Indo-UK trade relations. In view of these changes, there is need to re-examine the conventional wisdom of North pulling the South. He says if the developing countries continue to grow by 6 percent and the developed countries by 2-3 per cent per annum, by 2004 the share of global output provided by the developing countries would surpass the share provided by the developed world.

Ankush B. Sawant examines the relevance of Indian experience with a quasi-federal structure as a model for structuring future political union of Europe. According to him the Indian model suits well for political structuring the European Union, which also has all the diversities that are present in India.

In the era of globalisation, non-state actors have assumed new roles and significance. Mick Wilkinson of the Linconshire and Humberside University, Britain, discusses the role of Non-Governmental Development Organisations (NGDOs) in the promotion of EU-South Asia relations. According to him the Northern NGDOs can help bridge the gap between the North and the South. They have the expertise to influence the financial powers to facilitate the less powerful grassroots negotiators in the south. He points out that more than one-fourth of world's NGDO community conducts their operations in South Asia and hence they will be a significant influence in strengthening relationship between Europe and South Asia. He concludes: "If history is not to record globalisation as merely one more avenue for exploitation in the process of neo-colonialism, the NGDO community in North and South must take advantage of the globalisation of modern communication systems in order to press their case for a more equitable and transparent economic order based on principles of solidarity and equity"

D.K. Giri discusses the position, problems and the role of Indian diaspora in Europe. He traces the history of migration of Indians to European countries, its different phases, patterns and conditions. He has analysed the causes of these migrations which, according to him, were the 'push' and 'pull' factors, and examined the problems of integration of migrants into their host societies. The process of a large number of people of Indian origin, especially in Britain should be a factor in shaping EU attitude towards India as this diaspora continues to maintain interest in politics back home. In addition, along with the freedom of movement of people across the European Union, the law on migration and its enforcement are going to be stringent. It may affect a major source like India. Therefore, a better understanding and interactions between EU and India on the movement of professionals is required, Giri argues. The new visa rules for South Asians, hastily proposed recently and withdrawn instantly under protest by the United Kingdom, and the recent call by Germany to Indian professionals to migrate illustrates the concerns expressed by Giri in his paper.

Mario Telo deals with regional and multilateral approaches to shaping international relations and analyses Europe-South Asia relations in these frameworks. He begins by a theoretical investigation of the main trends in international relations with reference to the concept of what he calls "asymmetrical multilateralism". This is followed by a critical analysis of the development in the European Community, mainly the evolution of the European Union as an international actor stressing its 'civil power'. Telo provides a comparable analysis of regionalism in South Asia and Latin America, two important parts of the developing world. He concludes by giving his critical thoughts on the nature of international relations as it unfolds in the post-cold war era.

In the final chapter, Vivekanandan talks of the West viewed by Indians, academics and policy makers. West, according to

Vivekanandan, is largely represented in civilisational and political terms, by Europe, which has remained the epicentre of the West. Admittedly, European political values, technological advancement and ways of life have become models for the rest of the world although in the developing world of Asia, Africa and Latin America, they compete with the native cultures and systems. India has had a long contact with Europe ever since Vasco da Gama landed in South India in 1498 and subsequently, during 300 years of British colonialism in India. Vivekanandan in a way complements Tom Burden's analysis in chapter I and sums up the concerns expressed in other chapters on Europe and South Asia relations. He welcomes the new inspiring resurgence in Europe as it integrates into a Union, but reminds that the resurgence is only regional. Globally, especially for developing countries, European Union is seen to be indifferent and at times exploitative. This does not bode well for South Asia or for Europe. He underlines at the absence, in today's Europe, of the calibre of visionary leaders, like Willy Brandt and Bruno Kriesky, who could rise above provincialism and pan-Europeanism and look beyond the European borders in order to help to bridge the gap between the North and the South, rich and poor, and the developed and developing.

Europe and South Asia, given their historical links and comparable developments towards regional integration, should have a close and cooperative relations in the new millennium. But this is not automatically happening and South Asia continues to be on the margin of EU's priorities. This book moves beyond the traditional approaches to bilateral trade relations between Europe and South Asia. The emerging pattern of international relations demands a rethinking of North-South relations — European Union as a powerful representative of North and South Asia with most characteristics of the South. This book contributes to the process of the rethinking.

New Delhi

B. Vivekanandan
D.K. Giri

1

Victorian Capitalism and the British Legacy in India

TOM BURDEN

The purpose of this paper is to explore some of the major ideological consequences of the relations between Britain and India in the nineteenth century. The main focus will be on the way in which social change and developments in ideology in Britain affected India in varied and contradictory ways. In particular we will examine the complex relationships which developed in British political life between Benthamism, Conservatism, and Liberalism and how this affected India. The underlying argument of the paper is that some central features of the British impact on India developed in the second half of the nineteenth century and that these were substantially coloured by the changing relationships in Britain between these ideologies. Finally, we will identify some of the significant features of the British legacy which resulted from the contradictory processes of nineteenth-century British imperialism due to the conflict between and within these three traditions of thought.

The Ideology of the New Middle Classes

British imperialism was strongly affected by the Industrial Revolution. The Industrial Revolution led to the emergence of a new strata within the class structure. What was to become particularly important for the purpose of understanding Britain's relations with India, was the emergence of a new managerial and professional middle class. Parts of this new middle class was opposed to the whole existing organisation of society and sought to reform it. They opposed 'old corruption' at home and the 'old colonial system' abroad. However, the process of reform involved a long and partially unresolved conflict between reformers and defenders of the old order.

Opposition to reform was centred in the range of institutions which had solidified under the eighteenth century system of 'old corruption'. The continued political importance of 'old corruption' was ensured both by the system of Parliamentary representation involving a very restricted franchise and by the system of access to public office through corruption, purchase and patronage. Old corruption was closely linked to the old colonial system based on conquest and plunder along with the system of monopolistic state-sponsored Chartered companies in overseas trade.

The emergence of this new middle class was associated with a number of significant ideological developments. This new class became the main carrier of a number of new components in British culture which aimed to produce a more regulated and rational society. These were based on free trade, Benthamism (utilitarianism) and a revival of conservative thought in the form of evangelicalism. These came to be three key components of Victorian ideology. These ideas played a major role in the influence British ideas exercised on India.

Free Trade

In Victorian society economic thinking became dominated by liberal thought in the form of classical political economy. This provided strong arguments in favour of private property, free markets and for the superiority of the capitalist mode of production. Believers in a liberal world order supported free trade and free relations between independent self-governing nations and were strongly opposed to imperialism.

In the half century after 1780 Britain substantially abandoned the old colonial system of regulated trade based on the Navigation Acts and the trading activities of the Chartered companies and moved to a system based on free trade (Hobsbawm). Free trade implied that the use of force to secure foreign possessions had no real economic justification. On these grounds, Adam Smith, the founder of classical political economy, attacked the East India Company. India began to move from being a source of plunder and tribute to being a possession in which the establishment of order and economic development created the conditions for it to become a great colonial market for British manufactures. The increased political influence of industrial interests supporting the principles of laissez faire was illustrated in 1813 when the East India Company was deprived of its monopoly of Indian trade and the market was opened up to Lancashire cotton. Paradoxically, however, while the East India Company had been a key support of the old colonial system, it was to become the leading edge of Benthamite influence on imperialist policy and practice in India.

Benthamism

The intellectual centre of the middle class reform movement in Britain was Bentham and his circle. Bentham's views were based on the philosophical system known as utilitarianism. The utilitarians viewed the role of government as to promote 'the greatest happiness of the greatest number'. Benthamism also accepted the arguments of classical political economy that the removal of restrictions on private property and the market would secure efficiency in the economic sphere. His views therefore, supported economic liberalism since they implied a minimal role for the state. They could also be seen a implying democracy since the state was to work to further the interests of the majority. This allowed Benthamism to be adopted by those who sought a liberal and democratic state.

However, there was also an authoritarian strand in Benthamism (Hume). This had a number of sources. Benthamism drew on the Hobbesian legacy in which law and not liberty was the basis of society. Some utilitarians argued that the complexity of policy which was required in order to implement the great happiness principle meant that government should be undertaken by experts. In the case of India, it would often be argued that British rule was justified because of the high level of governmental and administrative expertise which this permitted. Many Benthamites also believed that the power of the state should be used to force people to conform with the requirements of the capitalist free market economy. This authoritarian element in Benthamism helped to make it consonant with conservatism with which, at first sight, it seemed incompatible.

The utilitarians were intimately connected with the East India Company (Lawson, Phillips). James Mill was admitted to the company in 1819 and JS Mill in 1823. James Mill was the author of a six volume *History of British India* published in 1818. He saw India as a country corrupted and debased by political and religious despotism. Bad government was the source of the problem of India and so it needed to be reconstructed. However, Mill rejected the democratic solution of representative government for India. He recommended 'light taxes and good laws' and improvement would follow. Bentham's ideas were also propagated at Haileybury, the training school for servants of the East India Company.

Evangelicalism

Evangelicalism formed a bridge between traditional conservatism and the reformers. It was a high-minded attempt to civilise the emerging industrial working class in conditions in which traditional conservative paternalist forms of social control based on the squire and the parson had broken down because of the rapid development of urban industrial living. Evangelicalism sought to remake society on a moral basis in which the social hierarchy was reinforced by a clear sense of duty on the part of the higher orders of society. Evangelicalism was a modernising version of conservatism combining elements of technocracy with paternalist rule by a traditional conservative elite.

Evangelicalism emphasised principles of morality and rectitude which were also common amongst the reforming middle classes. One way in which evangelicalism and the reform-minded utilitarians were able to combine was through the Victorian conception of the Christian gentleman. This provided a social type through which the rising classes associated with industrial capitalism could forge a common identity with members of the traditional ruling groups.

In relation to colonialism, Evangelicalism was associated with the idea of the civilising mission of British rule. In India, the traditional conservative solution under the old colonial system had been to govern in the Moghul tradition providing security without attempting to transform Indian society. Evangelicals, however, had a strong desire to impose their version of morality and order. They were opposed to whatever they saw as cruel or superstitious and sought to create what they viewed as a civilised Christian society.

The Reform Coalition

The reform movements of the late eighteenth and early nineteenth century united a range of groups and interests including radical artisans, middle class professionals, and some members of the Tory gentry. Many proponents of reform were motivated personally by evangelical or non-conformist religious views as well as the desire to secure a more 'rational' organisation of the business of the state or a strong commitment to the ideals of free trade. Regardless of their motives, however, the effects of their plans were to increase the rational purposiveness of state organisations and to expand the scope of state regulation.

In practice utilitarianism and evangelicalism appeared easily to be able to operate together in the context of both Britain and India. Each of these ideologies shared a strong conviction of their own rectitude and a belief that practical changes should be instituted in line with their values. This combination of self-belief and intolerance of practices with which they disagreed allowed each to give enthusiastic support to wide-ranging schemes of reform. Both these ideologies were linked to the self-conceptions of the rising and expanding middle classes of industrialising England. Many free traders also held to utilitarian beliefs and wished to introduce social, cultural and administrative reforms in India in common with the evangelicals and Benthamites.

Reform of the British System of Administration

From the late eighteenth century reformers sought to establish a bureaucratic administration in every sphere of British government at home and abroad. The process of bureaucratisation of the administrative arm of the state apparatus involved the replacement of 'offices' by state employment, of patronage by appointment on merit, and of fees by salaries. These changes proceeded unevenly and incompletely but the general movement was in the direction of bureaucracy in the Weberian sense.

In the 1780s the Economical Reform movement promoted reforms which began to erode the system of 'old corruption' and place some restrictions on the use of public office for personal gain. Some sinecures were abolished and MPs could not be government contractors (Chester). In 1809 the buying and selling of offices was prohibited, though exceptions were allowed for the army, where the purchase of commissions and promotions, except in the Scientific Corps, was allowed to continue.

The first part of the state apparatus to be fully constructed along the lines proposed by the reformers was the administrative structure in India. This came about because in 1806, the East India Company, under strong Benthamite influence, established Haileybury College as a training school for its administrative staff. The College developed a curriculum which included technical and vocationally relevant subjects. This helped to produce a rationalised colonial administration in India.

The reformers shared a belief in some degree of democratisation although not many were thoroughgoing democrats. However, they all opposed the corrupt system of electoral politics in national and local elections in Britain. The 1832 Reform Act increased the electorate from less than 9 per cent to about 14 per cent of the adult male population. The Act gave the vote to the entrepreneurial and professional urban middle classes and the 'shopocracy'. It abolished some 'rotten' Boroughs in which a Parliamentary seat was controlled by a handful of voters although the absence of secret voting still allowed considerable scope for bribery and corruption.

The system of local government was also reformed. The Corporations which governed towns were often used for the personal enrichment of the 'freemen' who exploited Corporation property and sold offices and contracts. The holders of local public offices did not receive regular salaries though they might be eligible for fees. For example many criminal statutes gave Constables a fee or a share in a fine when a conviction was secured. The Municipal Corporations Act of 1835 established a uniform franchise for the election of urban local authorities. The Act gave the urban bourgeoisie control of the new industrial cities.

The process of bureaucratisation and the advance of the reform movement was epitomised by the reform of the Poor Law undertaken in the Poor Law (Amendment Act) of 1834. Central control was undertaken by a Poor Law Board using circulars and instructions to local Guardians, and through an Inspectorate. The Poor Law Board was an early example of bureaucratic organisation in the state. It employed a 'rational' form of administration based on statistical returns and careful monitoring of the effects of policy. The design of the Poor Law administration became something of a template for future organisational changes in the state administrative structure. The Act was based on the report of the Commission of Enquiry into the Poor Laws which embodied the ethos of the reformers. Its two main authors were Chadwick, a leading Benthamite and the economist, Nassau Senior.

A general reform of the civil service was also introduced. For many reformers the Indian administration provided a model for the reform of recruitment and training in the home civil service. Civil service reform because the subject of considerable debate in the 1830s and 1840s. After the widely publicised disasters of the Crimean campaign in the winter of 1854-5 there were demands for drastic changes in the civil service. Groups such as the Administrative Reform Association wanted examinations based on technical subjects. The programme of civil service reform was based on the Northcote-Trevelyan reforms named after the report of 1854.

In reality these reforms were far less radical than they have often been portrayed. They attempted to establish a system which would perpetuate the gentlemanly character of the senior civil service dominated by upper middle class Oxbridge graduates and avoid the alternative Benthamite model of civil service reform based on the separate education of a technically competent administrative elite (Gowan). The competition for posts was also limited to those with the kind of liberal education received in the public schools and the ancient universities. A similar system of eligibility was later applied to Indians seeking advancement in the Indian Civil Service. The extent of bureaucratisation was thus modified by an attachment to the gentlemanly ethos which limited moves towards the construction of a 'legal-rational' bureaucracy on the Weberian model. The English state never developed a clear notion of the role of expertise: instead it clung to the notion of the 'educated gentleman' with all-round abilities.

Ideology and British policy in India

The Developing Pattern of British Rule

Up until 1858 Britain ruled India through the East India Company rather than by governing directly. Liberal principles were evident in the provision of the Charter of 1833 which said that discrimination on the basis of religion, place of birth, descent, or culture, should not be used to exclude Indians from holding offices in the East India Company. Bentinck, who was Governor General of India from 1828 to 1835, was a Benthamite radical. He undertook reforms to the system of land tenure and the judicial administration. A significant symbolic moment in the attempt to impose the principles of Western rationalism on Indian society was the prohibition of Suttee in 1829.

Benthamism was also the basis for reform of the law in India. Benthamism viewed legal reform as an essential pre-condition of economic advance. Property ownership needed to be individualised and formalised while communal and customary practices were seen as a barrier to economic freedom. Complex feudal arrangements needed to be replaced by simple landlord-tenant relations and various forms of labour servitude by free wage labour. In the reform of the Indian legal system Benthamite principles were apparent in the criminal code produced in 1835, and enacted in 1860. This code was in line with the classical criminological conceptions based on the assumption of individual rationality characteristic of classical political economy. This process of reform went so far as to involve the building of a panopticon (Stokes p.150). However, the civil law was not properly codified due to the complex and contradictory legacy of Hindu and Muslim customary law.

Further cultural domination was encouraged through the establishment of English as the language of administration and education for Indians in 1835 by Macauley, the President of the Committee of Public Instruction. Knowledge of English was deemed necessary for any Indians who wish to secure employment in the government service. Subsequently a Bengali elite began to develop which was characterised by a strong admiration of Britain and of English ways of life. By the time of the 'Mutiny' an English educated administrative and professional stratum was present though it was confined to Western Bengal and the three presidency towns of the Madras, Bombay and Calcutta.

The 'Mutiny' of 1857 was a major shock to British conceptions of the solidity of their rule in India (Metcalf). The 'Mutiny' was a general uprising against British rule largely provoked by the Westernising policies pursued by the East India Company. Sepoy troops mutinied and occupied Delhi. The uprising was put down with enormous savagery over a period of about a year and a half. While the 'Mutiny' was not a nationalist popular uprising it did reflect many of the strains affecting Indian society as a result of the changes brought by British rule.

Following the mutiny, rule by the East India Company was replaced by a unified administrative structure. By the mid-century many English traders and settlers viewed the Company as unsympathetic to their economic interests and as pursuing policies which appeared designed to benefit India and Indians rather than themselves. A new administrative structure was established with a Secretary of State for India advised by a new Council of India, and a Viceroy. The reforms meant that the servants of the East India Company became civil servants.

British policy as it developed after the 'Mutiny' was subject to contradictory impulses. A combination of conservative and Benthamite policies was pursued. The new administrative structure appeared to be based on the principles of Benthamism and meritocracy. Provisions stating a principled opposition to discrimination against Indians in access to public office were contained in the 1858 legislation establishing the Indian Civil Service. However, Indians would only become eligible for these posts if they travelled to England to take the examinations. The key subjects in examinations were mathematics and classics and from 1865 the maximum age of which these could be taken was 21. In 1876 the maximum age was lowered to 19 making it even more difficult for Indian candidates to secure a position. Indians who were able to obtain entry to the Indian Civil Service were mainly from wealthy families. The Indian Civil Service largely remained the preserve of well educated middle and upper class British men. In India, as in Britain, for many members of the middle class the aristocracy was a social model to be emulated (Wiener). This contributed to an aristocratic and conservative approach to the government of India. This was given further support by policies enabling prominent Indians to participate in the legislative councils, allowing some Indian landowners to exercise judicial powers, and maintaining the rule of the Princes in many parts of India.

The decision to maintain the rule of the princes in a third of the country established a powerful conservative interest which generally operated as a barrier to social and political progress. Britain frequently pursued a policy of attempting to reinforce the power and position of these hereditary rulers. Other successful institutions from Britain were adopted to further support the Indian upper class. For example, Britain encouraged the establishment of Indian public schools designed to educate the sons of the Indian aristocracy.

British policy in India was subject to important strains and conflicts in the second half of the nineteenth century. British rule had to adjust both to changes in India due to the growth of nationalism and to changes in the domestic context of British rule which occurred due to the growth of democracy and a mass electorate in Britain. British control of India and the dilemmas and challenges which this posed played a major role in the development of the policies and ideologies of the Liberal and the Conservative parties.

The Liberal Party

The Victorian Liberal Party was a complex and shifting amalgam of different interests and ideological currents. In the second half of the nineteenth-century these developed rapidly under the pressure of democratisation and of the challenges posed to existing policies by new situations. The Indian mutiny, for example, raised difficult issues for the party and forced the different tendencies within it to clarify their position on the question of imperialism. It is useful to distinguish three strands in liberal thought and policy.

The first strand was the Whig tradition which rested on the eighteenth century Whig principles of civil liberties, the rule of law, an independent judiciary, the freedom of the press, and parliamentary government. It was opposed to democracy and viewed parliament as the arena in which the key interests, meaning property interests, in society should be represented. It opposed the extension of the vote to the lower orders of society because this would damage moral and intellectual freedom. In practical terms the attitude of the Whigs towards democracy was close to that felt by many Conservatives. These Liberals could justify the failure to support democratic rule in India by their commitment to good government which they saw India as incapable of providing for itself.

The second strand was Liberal imperialism which was related to what has been termed 'intellectual liberalism' and was not too far removed from the Whig tradition. In its Indian form it was developed by some members of the Indian Advisory Council. This argued against the extension of the power of government to the ignorant. This approach also had something in common with the technocratic version of utilitarianism except that it assumed the automatic superiority of English civilisation and of those who were its bearers.

The third strand was Gladstonian liberalism. This was associated with Gladstone who spoke in favour of self-determination as a key Liberal principle. Gladstone supported the free trade views of Cobden and Bright and, at least when it came to rhetoric, was opposed to imperialism. Gladstone also remained wedded to a very limited role for the state and viewed the maintenance of the rule of law as the core state function. He claimed that Britain secured no economic advantage from its possession of India and that it had no interest in that country except to promote its well-being. He also argued that Britain had a duty to promote education in India in order to create the conditions for self-government.

He complained about Conservative policies which resulted in further expansion in the region and in military involvement in Afghanistan. However, when the Liberal Party returned to power in 1880 it retained *de facto* British control of Afghanistan through the device of a puppet ruler. When Britain occupied Egypt in 1882 Gladstone required the Indian government to pay part of the cost of this operation on the grounds that securing the Suez Canal route to India was of benefit to India. In effect, this meant that Indian taxpayers were being required to pay for the expansion of British imperialism as a means of maintaining, at least in the short term, British control of India. The contradictions within Gladstonian liberalism were also apparent in the stance taken towards the annexation of Upper Burma in 1886 during the period in office of a Conservative government. Gladstone justified his support for this on the grounds that without it India would have been subject to danger and insecurity (Moore, pp 29-30 and p.49).

The question of India played a role in the splits which took place in the Liberal Party in the late nineteenth and early twentieth century. The main issue on which the British Liberal Party split concerned 'home rule' in Ireland. In theory Liberalism implied rights of national self determination and was opposed to imperialism. In practice, however, the situation was more complex since the Liberal Party, like the Conservative Party, played a major role in representing the interests of the traditional landowning class due to the aristocratic Whigs who played a major role in the party and amongst whom support for imperialism was strong. In practice, the leadership of the Liberal Party often found itself in the position of being obliged to support imperialism. This contradiction between principle and practice, or between rhetoric and reality, was most clearly demonstrated in the career of Gladstone. After the retirement of Gladstone in 1894 Liberal policy became even more under the control of Liberal imperialists. When the Conservatives were re-elected in 1895, some Liberal imperialists took office under a Conservative Prime Minister.

The Conservative Party

The traditional conservative ideology of the landowning upper class in Britain had strong links with the old colonial system. The combination of military conquest and the acquisition of wealth through plunder and the forcible exploitation of colonial labour had a long history. However, conservatism began to modernise itself as it came to terms with the new demands made on traditional rulers by the emergence of urban living and industrial capitalism. The Conservative Party itself made important moves towards accommodating the new interests represented by the industrial bourgeoisie by the mid-nineteenth century. This was most clearly demonstrated in the abolition of the Corn Laws in 1845. As a result it was possible for cheap imports of wheat to come into Britain thus keeping down the working class cost of living. This benefited manufacturers since it reduced pressure for higher wages although it had an adverse impact on the landowning class because of lower returns to farmers. It represented a partial move away from an exclusive pursuit of the interests of this class. Further rapid changes took place in the Party as a result of the growing move towards democratisation and the appearance of a mass electorate.

Paternalistic aristocratic rule was a facet of the British approach to governing India which was consistent with traditional conservative values. The English tradition of the squiremagistracy combined executive and judicial functions in a paternalist model. In India this sometimes involved a combination of Tory evangelical paternalism combined with authoritarian Benthamism. This approach became especially attractive as a governing strategy after the 'Mutiny'. In Oudh, the area most affected by the mutiny, the policy was to restore the authority of the traditional landowning class. The talukdars were given title to their land and some were given powers of magistracy. Where no feudal class existed the British helped to create one since this class was seen as a bulwark of order (Gopal pp.6-7). Many Conservatives viewed rule by the an aristocratically led state bureaucracy in India as constituting a form of enlightened despotism. They saw a close parallel between the position of the working classes in nineteenth century Britain, who were excluded from any say in power, and native Indians who should be kept in a similarly powerless position.

The 'Mutiny' had helped to place imperialism at the top of the British political agenda. The constant portrayal of Indians as unchristian and uncivilised played a part in establishing a public opinion favourable to imperial conquest. British control of India played a central part in the invention of imperialist ideology by the Conservative leader Disraeli. Imperialist ideology became associated with the Conservative Party which was, at this time, seeking a means of mobilising mass electoral support as the right to vote was extended following the 1867 Reform Act. In 1876 Disraeli secured an Act which proclaimed Queen Victoria as the Empress of India. By enhancing the position of the monarchy in this way, the position of the upper class was also reinforced since the monarchy was itself the pinnacle and the symbol of this class. Imperialism and the cult of the monarchy thus played a central role in the invention of modern Conservatism in which traditional institutions, imperialism and nationalism were combined with a paternalistic concern for the poor in the conditions of mass democracy.

In the late nineteenth century military considerations began to play a key part in the ruling class debates about the retention of India. Imperialist competition meant that any British withdrawal might well be followed by attempts by other countries take the country over. Many imperialists viewed India as an essential link in the empire which was based on the white settler colonies, some smaller possessions, and India, which was by far the largest possession. Some imperialists also wanted to promote India itself as a great power in the East. The imperial role of the army also played an important part in the growth of popular national sentiment which itself further strengthened the conservative and militarised element in British imperialism. The Jingoism which was developed in the popular press in the last quarter of the nineteenth century integrated a number of ideological themes into a coherent 'national' ideology. These included racism and a general contempt for foreigners, the glorification of military power under aristocratic leadership, nationalism, and a reinforcement of the cult of military heroism.

British control of India contributed to the maintenance of the position of the traditional British upper class. It gave its members practice in government. It also provided an important outlet for the younger sons of propertied families who had to seek their own fortune because the family property would not be passed on to them. India also played a role for the upper class in developing and maintaining an aristocratic lifestyle. India played a part in cementing the sense of identity which the English rulers developed for themselves. The British upper class identified with some features of Indian society. Brahmins could be seen as a cultivated and classically educated elite corresponding to the English governing class. The English landed class could see itself a superior caste, as a hereditary ruling group distinguished by its culture, its social exclusivity, and it's 'breeding'.

The army also played a role in the establishment of this sense of identity. In Britain it was a key pillar of aristocratic influence and conservative opinion. Army officers made up a very influential section within the landed class and they played a major political role in the nineteenth century (Spiers). Even by the end of the century they made up around 10% of all MPs. In most units of the Army commissions promotions could be purchased, which further guaranteed the exclusiveness of the officer corps. The pay of officers was low and generally their extravagant lifestyle reflected a traditional feudal emphasis on leisure activities linked to warfare including horsemanship, hunting and shooting, that they were expected to pursue.

The Conservative approach to India was exemplified by Curzon. He was a modernising Conservative aristocrat who became Viceroy in 1895. He established a new Department of Commerce and Industry and increased expenditure on public works. This was done in ways which were primarily designed to reinforce British rule. Indigenous economic development was largely subordinated to the quest for the maintenance of effective British political control. Britain concentrated its expenditure on economic infrastructure on building railways rather than on agricultural projects such as irrigation. The railways could be used to expand trade under British control as well as having a strategic importance for the maintenance of political domination. Development in India was also adversely affected by the system of taxation which was employed to raise the revenues used to pay for the armed forces and for railway investment. Taxation generally was levied on agriculture and agricultural activities.

Curzon also undertook the partition of Bengal which encouraged communal conflict between Hindus and the Muslims. One element of the conflict between these two groups was a common Muslim belief that their interests would be better served under British rule than if government was in the hands of the Hindu majority. British officials did little to discourage these antagonisms and in some respects sought to exploit them in order to weaken and deflect nationalist opposition to British rule. The priority given to political control over economic development was symbolised by the removal of the capital from commercial Calcutta to Delhi, an ancient seat of Moghul imperial power.

The Legacy of the Contradictions of British Rule

The development of political discourse

One effect of the British presence in India was to establish a new vocabulary for political debate. The Benthamite strand of British political language was secular, rational, and directed towards the pursuit of defined ends. Indian political language came to incorporate this element of British political thought, although it retained a strong attachment to ultimate values and language which placed an emphasis on spiritual rather than material considerations.

Towards the end of the nineteenth century as nationalist sentiment began to develop in India along with the growth of the stratum of educated Indians, Britain made considerable efforts to mould the character of Indian nationalism in a moderate direction. Acceptable nationalist sentiment in India reflected back the concerns of Gladstonian Liberalism in relation to the government of India. A liberal political rhetoric, which was substantially derived from Gladstonian Liberalism, exercised something close to hegemony over the political and social thought developed within the moderate nationalist movement in India and ultimately incorporated as part of the ethos of Congress.

There was also a place for conservative ideas and interests. This strong conservative element was retained in Indian political culture and administrative practice through the special privileges guaranteed for the princes and for the position of the Indian landowning class which was given a degree of constitutional protection of its rights to hold on to its land. This conservative element also played a major role through its incorporation in the ethos of the armed forces. Just as in Britain, these played an important role in the maintenance of conservative ideology. Conservative ideas also contributed to the encouragement of the pursuit of great power status.

During the course of the nineteenth century British aspirations for India shifted from a belief in wholesale reform leading to indigenous development to the Conservative policy of maintaining control and keeping order. This was partly rationalised by Liberal imperialists employing those elements of Benthamite thought which stressed the role of expertise and technocracy. Towards the end of the century a nationalist movement began to develop amongst the urban middle classes of India. However, they were no longer able to find many allies amongst their English middle class counterparts in India itself. These now belonged to an Anglo-Indian social elite which had succumbed to the desire to establish itself as a form of expatriate aristocracy.

A key part in enabling many Liberals to support imperialism in India was played by the dual legacy of Benthamism. The political rhetoric derived from the democratic version of Benthamism enabled supporters of the Gladstonian Liberalism to maintain a belief in India's progress towards democracy. The technocratic strand in Benthamism allowed the Liberal imperialists, and those Gladstonian Liberals who reluctantly conceded the necessity for temporary British control, to support the continued denial of political freedom to India.

Contradiction and coherence in British rule

In Victorian Britain there was a contradiction at the heart of British economic policy. While economic policy was ostensibly based on free trade, governments pursued policies which increased the numbers and importance of British overseas possessions. The reasons for this were related to the balance between the traditional ruling class and the new classes which emerged with industrial capitalism. The strategic direction of state policy was kept largely in the hands of the traditional landed class and City interests through the Treasury, the Bank of England, leadership of the armed forces, the judiciary, the Foreign Office and the Diplomatic Service. The mainly conservative landed interest had considerable control over the process of colonial expansion. This was not primarily motivated to ensure the expansion of capital accumulation although this was often a factor. Just as important were beliefs in the British superiority and in the imperial ideal.

The industrial bourgeoisie never achieved political domination in Britain (Ingham). It partly fused with the landed class so that their extremes remained distinct but the border between them disappeared. The social and cultural integration of new class was organised around the concept of the 'gentleman'. This was done in the public schools in which the old and the new sections of the capitalist class were educated.

The followers of Bentham believed that they could transform and civilise society. However, the hopes held by the Benthamites were never fully realised in Britain or in India. The failure of the reform movements to press home their assault on all the strongholds of aristocratic influence was part of a political compromise in which essential issues directly involving business, such as the Corn Laws were resolved in favour of industrial capital, while other important perquisites of the landed class were left undisturbed. The changes that took place in the state apparatus gave the bourgeoisie guarantees of the conditions necessary for domestic capital accumulation without giving them complete control of the entire machinery of the state. In general the new middle classes only dominated newly formed parts of the apparatus such as the Poor Law and the public health administration.

In foreign policy the reformers, and after them the Liberal Party at the time of Gladstone, never fully pursued the vision of a 'rational' British state in a 'liberal world order'. The principles of free trade pointed to a world of independent capitalist states engaged in peaceful economic competition. However, British Liberalism was never able to extricate itself from imperialism.

In both England and in India the failure of the middle class and of the reform movements to tackle the position of the aristocracy was a source of subsequent weakness. The social divisions which this sustained and the continued institutional guarantees for aristocratic groups gave them a prolonged role in the exercise of political power in both countries and subsequently blocked efforts at reform and the modernisation of the state.

A large part of the secret of the puzzling and incoherent legacy of British rule in India lies in the unreconciled contradictions of British policy which were determined by the complex character of ideological and class relations in Victorian England. Conservatives, Liberals and Benthamites eventually struck an implicit compromise around a paternalistic and autocratic reforming bureaucratic administration. This was allowed to exist alongside traditional institutions and patterns of rule in many parts of India in which the influence of the landowning class was perpetuated. The legacy itself is therefore a complex mixutre of rational elements derived from a Benthamite concern to institute its version of enlightenment principles, of the rhetoric of Gladstonian liberalism, and of support for conservative institutions and principles designed to sustain traditional values and the maintenance of a hierarchical order.

There are parallels between the contradictory impact of this legacy in India and the contradictory character of many aspects of the British state, the key features of which were established in the Victorian period. These parallel features include:

— a rhetorical attachment to equality along with a respect for hierarchy;
— a democratic constitution but with special privileges (until recently in India) for hereditary rulers;
— a belief in modernity but with special guarantees for the maintenance of traditional institutions;

— a belief in the peaceful co-existence of a liberal family of nations along with an attachment to the idea of great power status.

Both Britain and India today still reflect the failure of any one side in the Victorian struggle between Gladstonian liberalism, Benthamism and the traditional conservative order, to prevail decisively over the others.

References

Basham, AL ed. (1975) *A Cultural History of India,* OUP, Oxford.

Bolt, C (1971) *Victorian Attitudes to Race,* OUP, Oxford.

Brown, JM (1994) *Modern India,* 2nd ed., OUP, Oxford.

Cain, P and Hopkins, AG (1993) *British Imperialism 1688-1914,* Longman.

Cain, P and Hopkins AG (1993) *British Imperialism 1914-1990,* Longman.

Chester N (1981) *The English administrative System 1780-1870* Clarendon Press, London.

Corrigan, P (1980) *Capitalism, State Formation and Marxist Theory,* Quarter Books, London.

Edwardes, M (1969) *Bound to Exile: the Victorians in India,* Sidgwic & Jackson.

Gowan, P New Left Review.

Greenberger, AJ (1969) *The British Image of India,* Routledge.

Griffiths, P (1952) *The British Impact on India,* MacDonald, London.

Hobsbawm, E (1969) *Industry and Empire, Penguin,* Harmondsworth.

Hume, LJ (1981) *Bentham and Bureaucracy,* CUP, Cambridge.

Hutchins, FG (1967) T*he Illusion of Permanence: British Imperialism in India*, Princeton U.P.

Ingham, G. (1984) *Capitalism Divided: The City and Industry in British Social Development,* Macmillan, London.

Khilnani, S (1997) *The Idea of India*, Hamish Hamilton, London.

Kiernan, VG (1969) *The Lords of Human Kind: European Attitudes to the Outside World in the Imperial Age,* Weidenfeld & Nicolson, London.

Lawson, P. (1993) *The East India Company,* Longman.

Metcalf, TR (1964) *The Aftermath of Revolt: India 1857-1870,* Cape, London.

Moore, RJ (1966) *Liberalism and Indian Politics,* Edward Arnold, London.

Phillips, CH (1940) *The East India Company.*

Porter, B (1984) *The Lion's Share*, Longman, London.

Scull, A (1984) *Decarceration,* Prentice Hall, New Jersey.

Spear, P (1965) *The History of India,* Volume 2, Penguin, Harmondsworth.

Spiers, EM (1980) *The Army and Society 1815-1914,* Longman, London.

Stokes, E (1959) *The English Utilitarians and India*, Oxford U.P.

Wiener, MJ (1985) *English Culture and the Decline of the Industrial Spirit 1850-1980,* Penguin, Harmondsworth

Wilkinson, R (1964) *The Prefects,* OUP, Oxford

Woodruff, P (1953, 1954) *The Men who Ruled India, 2 vols,* Cape, London

2

Europe's Development and South Asia's Underdeveloped: Globalisation and the Role of State

HARTMUT ELSENHANS

Europe's development and South Asia's underdevelopment.

Europe and South Asia share a long history. The freedom movement in South Asia has viewed the poverty and underdevelopment of the Subcontinent as the result of European imperialism which allowed backward Europe to overtake an originally more technically advanced South Asia. Europe had built its Industrial Revolution on the drain of resources from India through exploitation and on the prosperous markets it conquered on the Subcontinent and which it slowly destroyed by deindustrialising India.

This paper does not wholly disapprove of this perspective. It integrates the empirical facts underlying the argument of Europe's development creating South Asia's underdevelopment into a more complex perspective. This perspective does not only concentrate on resource flows and uneven specialisation, but adds the conditioning of technical progress by internal social structures in both economies. It argues that the same mechanism which allowed Europe to use South Asia in support of its own Industrial Revolution can nowadays be turned into support for a rapid catching up of South Asia if globalisation of international economic relations is intelligently complemented by state interventionism in South Asia and if the industrially leading countries (ILCs) play their role of locomotives with expanding internal markets at least for a longer transition period.

The paper integrates two sets of arguments for the discussion of the two-way relation between South Asia and Europe. The first set concerns the lessons which can be drawn from the historical experience of Europe's development and South Asia's underdevelopment for today's challenges of overcoming underdevelopment in South Asia. Focusing only on the drain of resources from India and on the destruction of Indian industries through European, especially British, competition, the internal conditions for Europe's Industrial Revolution are overlooked. Europe, because of its poverty, was able to develop a pattern of specialisation which favoured productivity increases in wage goods, especially food production. Because of this, it also increased marginal productivity in the wage goods production of its own labour, thus helping to alleviate and ultimately eliminate poverty. By concentrating on mass markets, technical progress was promoted which reduced the costs of production and allowed mass consumption, first of basic necessities, then of newly invented and even old luxuries, which became accessible for the great majority of its population. In order to benefit in a similar way from rising export opportunities even in manufacturing, South Asia would also have to develop its internal market by empowering the poor. The safest means of empowering the poor consists in raising the marginal product of the poor. If this marginal product is high, labour becomes scarce, so that real wages can rise, with the result of a rapidly expanding internal mass market which triggers off additional investment, especially by means of locally produced technology.

The second set of arguments is based on the opportunities constituted for both areas by the intensification of international economic interactions, i.e., globalisation. The increasing competitiveness of Third World production sites is not the result of low real wages but of new possibilities of transforming comparative advantage into cost effectiveness by means of devaluation.[1] There are two important implications for export-oriented industrialisation in Third World economies.[2] ILCs are not able to block the export drive of the new competitors through wage depression, as this will just result in new changes in the exchange rates in favour of the ILCs. Catching-up economies are not competitive because of the low product wages of their workers in their export sectors, but because of their capacity to provide from their local economies basic wage goods for additional workers in the export sectors. If ILCs opt for wage repression, they contribute to underconsumptionist tendencies by a low expansion of their own economies and their imports.[3] As long as Third World countries continue to concentrate only on export promotion without caring for the spill-over of export multipliers into their overall level of economic activity, they limit their productivity growth to a few sectors and the transfer of capitalist structures is decisively limited. The overcoming of poverty does not hamper their cost effectiveness, as their costs of labour in international currency do not depend on real wages in national currency but on exchange rates.[4]

Globalisation implies hitherto unknown possibilities for improving productivity in sectors where there is sufficient demand, in the case of export-oriented industrialisation, through access to the world market. The ILCs lose their technical monopolies which had previously sheltered their labour from competition. They are no longer primarily interested in cheap products but in increasing the imports of the until now low-cost countries. Only if mass incomes in these low-cost countries increase, is there a hope of limits to devaluation, as overall productivity growth will lead to large balance-of-trade surpluses in the case of too low exchange rates. If the internal-market-oriented sectors do not experience productivity growth, high productivity growth in the export sectors will be accompanied by very low exchange rates (which are determined by the low productivity in the import-competing sectors), so that cost competitiveness in large but limited sectors increases. As – particularly in the case of South Asia – the export sectors will never be sufficient for creating full employment, the best use for export-oriented industrialisation in South Asia is high multiplier effects, which increase if complementary measures in the internal social structure contribute to a limiting of the supply of average-skilled labour.

In contrast to the colonial division of labour where the exploited nations were competitive only in products with low income elasticities such as raw materials, the new competitiveness of low-cost countries in income and price elastic products creates on the part of the ILCs an interest in the internal social set-up of the underdeveloped countries: if they are indefinitely capable of undercutting the ILCs through devaluation, they threaten employment levels in the ILCs, as the exchange rates are determined by the still high productivity in the technically leading branches of the ILCs and low marginal productivity in the industrially backward countries (IBCs). The exchange rates may be so high that average-skilled labour in the ILCs may receive lower real wages than in the underdeveloped countries because of lower prices for non-tradables in the underdeveloped countries.

The debate about labour standards is a misguided one, as the limits to devaluation do not depend on labour costs in the export sectors but on marginal productivity in the import-competing and potentially new export sectors, which have not yet experienced productivity growth and have not yet achieved international competitiveness. But this debate shows that there is an interest of the ILCs in limiting the race for devaluation which the underdeveloped countries can pursue if they are producing enough wage goods for additional export workers.

In the globalising world, the relations between India and Europe are particularly important with respect to the organisation of this new objective convergence of interests. Neither of the two regions is in a particularly advantageous position for benefiting from the opportunities created by globalisation. Both regions are threatened by the prospect of becoming peripheral with respect to the other growth poles of the world economy. Japan and the United States have access to a virtual gold mine of cheap labour on the Pacific rim, especially Eastern Asia. Latin America constitutes another source of cheap labour for the U.S. economy close to its market. The backyard of European neo-colonialism, the southern shore of the Mediterranean and sub-Saharan Africa, will not become the basis of a division of labour between Europe and its near-periphery comparable to the one organised by the United States with Latin America and the countries of the Pacific rim and by Japan with the countries of the Pacific rim. This is not because of people in the countries of the southern shore of the Mediterranean and in sub-Saharan Africa not being poor. The essential reason is that the small agricultural surpluses of these countries do not allow them to devalue their currencies to levels comparable to East Asia or Latin America. They have poor workers which in international currency are expensive, because a considerable portion of their wage goods has to be imported.[5]

India suffers from locational disadvantages in comparison to the countries of the Pacific rim with respect to Japan and the United States. It is geographically the closest region to Europe which can proceed to devaluation-driven export-led growth. Europe can succeed in creating a periphery comparable to the East Asian mainland for Japan or Latin America for the United States only through an intensification of its economic relations with South Asia.

As long as the drain and deindustrialisation-based explanation of India's underdevelopment through European colonialism persists in its undifferentiated form, India will be reluctant to engage in such a preferential arrangement, and miss growth opportunities. As long as Western Europe continues to accept that wage depression is a means for dealing with globalisation, it will not be an attractive partner. India may come to the conclusion that more unequal exchange is necessary in order to achieve rapid growth,[6] if by these means the overcoming of marginality allows the transition to a truly (welfare) capitalist system. This implies that Europe does not artificially limit the expansion of its internal market. Both fear exploitation, India because the devaluation of the rupee limits export earnings in relation to at least temporarily essential imports of technology. Europe has to fear exploitation of India because this exploitation translates into cheap supplies of more and more industrial products on the world market which outcompete average-skilled European labour.

Whether both partners can accept this new perspective depends on a new interpretation of the economic relations between India and Europe, in which the parallel operation of a drain and conquest of markets is shown to be historically limited. When technical monopolies in income elastic products are lost, the "exploited" nation with deteriorating terms of trade gains in economic dynamism, whereas the exploiting economy, i.e., the economy with improving terms of trade, is temporarily rich but threatened by falling behind. In order to present such a theoretical perspective, world system analysis has to be applied – not, however, on the basis of a fundamentally Marxist economic paradigm, but on the basis of a Keynesian one.

The argument I will develop is at variance with Andre Gunder Frank's "Development of Underdevelopment" but agrees with Frank and Wallerstein's underlying concern.[7]

The two points of agreement are the following:

(1) The world system is characterised by a considerable windfall for

those countries, economies, regions or nations who happen to be first in the transition to capitalism.

(2) The continuing existence of limits to the transfer of the capitalist mechanism of growth at the global level, especially in lagging-behind economies, implies serious challenges for a peaceful market-regulated world economy which would allow all economies to develop potentially existing productive forces.[8]

The points of disagreement are constituted by a radically different view of the fundamentals of capitalist growth. My points, which I do not develop further in this contribution, are the following.

(1) Capitalist growth is not investment-driven but demand-driven.[9] Surplus transfer and hence exploitation are of minor importance for the "development of underdevelopment." This view is based on two arguments: profit depends (in the usual stylised capitalist two-class economy, with workers spending their total incomes on consumption and capitalists spending their revenues on investment, i.e., accumulation) on expanding demand for machine-produced goods, which trigger off net investment.[10] Capitalists cannot create this demand through higher luxury spending (by themselves, by other dependent classes or even by the state) without abolishing competition, hence capitalism.[11] Likewise, they cannot create this demand through increasing investment spending, as any investment increases productive potential (and reduces unit costs) in relation to incomes paid for consumption (the Bortkiewicz criterion).[12] Capitalism, therefore, cannot exist without rising mass incomes.

(2) Due to specific requirements for the functioning of capitalism, leading countries develop tendencies to allow the development of lagging ones to some degree – which is, however, too limited in order to create the conditions for self-sustained growth in these lagging-behind economies. The integration of lagging-behind economies into the capitalist world system does not lead automatically to full employment, which would empower labour and hence create Sen's "entitlement"[13] or Hirschman's "voice."[14] Without shifting the balance of social power in favour of the weaker

sections of society, increasing amounts of surplus in the hands of "elites" in not yet capitalist, i.e., welfarist economies contribute to disempowerment of labour through rent, at least as long as there are no important countervailing mass movements.

I apply within the theoretical perspective of world system analysis a fundamentally Keynesian approach which is characterised by a labourist orientation. This labourist orientation can be made clear in my interpretation of the absence of a theory of state failure in Keynes' work.[15] In contrast to North American economic modernisation theory, which looked into the state's capacity to contribute to productivity growth, Keynes' proposal of state-spending during economic crisis only aims at empowering labour in the case of unemployment and hence absence of the wage drift. After the restoring of labour's bargaining power in the wake of full employment, the capitalist mechanism of entrepreneurs competing in discovering innovations will resume with labour incomes rising according to the growth of total factor productivity. State-spending is, directly, inefficient with respect to productivity growth, but creates the conditions for capitalism's capacity to resume growth because of the empowerment of labour. If the economy is not flexible, flexibility being the case of an advanced capitalist one, the creation of purchasing power has to be effected in a way which does not overstretch the existing capabilities of the productive apparatus to adjust.[16] These capabilities are more limited the more the economy concerned has lost its capacity to innovate in the wake of unequal specialisation.

The approach presented here consists of:

— A model of transition to capitalism which insists on some preconditions normally not discussed in the literature and which can be summarised as the marginality-cum-rent situation which any process of non-capitalist stratification should normally lead to. There is no issue to this marginality-cum-rent situation at the economic level.[17]

— A model of capitalist growth where investment is a function of increases in mass demand.[18] This model is consistent with critical approaches to mainstream and Marxist theory which are appropriated and disfigured by the new growth theory.[19]

— A theoretical perspective of overcoming underdevelopment which is based on the eclectic combination of various measures which may contribute to empowering labour.[20]

— A theory of rent and its implications for political dynamics which concentrates on the emergence of mechanisms by which rent-appropriating classes may overcome their tendency to waste in settings where there are economic and political checks to their spontaneous tendencies.

In order to conform to the topical interests of the conference, I have selected for this contribution four sets of mechanisms from my theoretical approach:

— the marginality-cum-rent model;

— the importance of being first and the privileges connected to it;

— the possible contributions of non-market subsystems for the transition from the marginality-cum-rent situation to a capitalist situation;

— the roles the state can play with respect to the new opportunities created by the process of decreasing transborder transaction costs, called globalisation.

The Marginality-cum-Rent Model

The textbook view of capitalism is based on the assumption that employment is dependent on wages being sufficiently low to allow a surplus for the capitalist employer from any worker he engages. He earns this surplus as a profit. This assumption is contradicted by empirical reality. At low levels of average and marginal productivity there may be a sufficiently important number of workers who, despite their most dedicated efforts, cannot produce more than their inevitable costs of reproduction, defined as the costs of a worker's subsistence and the costs of maintaining a family large enough to guarantee demographic reproduction of the workforce.

The possibility of workers producing less than these costs of reproduction depends on three conditions: there has to be a branch of production with decreasing returns; this branch of production has to be important for overall levels of employment, because its decreasing returns to scale would otherwise be compensated by adjustments in relative prices of products; the major inputs of this branch are also its outputs.

As long as the environmental consequences of industrial production do not have to be paid by private enterprises, any industrial technology can be reproduced. In this case, there are no long-term technological causes for decreasing returns to scale in manufacturing. Decreasing returns to scale only exist in primary production.

A primary production which is not dependent on its own output will maintain its capacity to pay average labour incomes and a profit corresponding to the average rate of profit if decreasing returns to scale can be compensated by increasing prices for output, which will only marginally affect this production line's prices of inputs. I give as an example rising costs of oil production since the late 1960s, at least outside the Middle East.

The implied change in the terms of trade between the products of the branch with decreasing returns and the rest of the economy requires that losses in productivity can be compensated by rises in productivity in the rest of the economy, which is the more easy the less the share of the branch with decreasing returns in the total economy.

Suppose now that agricultural activities are characterised by decreasing returns to scale. This is a realistic assumption for economies with low levels of technological development and high demographic growth. There will be a surplus of resources and labour surplus. More and more labour asks for employment on fertile soils; less and less productive soils have to be put into use. Both tendencies push down marginal productivity, as discussed in the latifundio-minifundio paradox[21] and the labour-surplus models of the Indian debate of the 1960's.[22] With agricultural production Y_{agr} being a function of labour L, $Y_{agr} = f(L)$, and $1>f'>0$ and $f''<0$, and subsistence wages so that the costs of reproduction of agricultural labour $C_L = aL$, then demographic growth will lead to a level where $f'(Y_{agr}) = a$. Beyond that level, which I call threshold of marginality,[23] any additional worker in agriculture produces less than his costs of reproduction. I call this excess labour marginal because it cannot be employed by any surplus-maximising landlord.

There is therefore a maximum of total employment which is constituted by the sum of

— surplus-producing labour in agriculture,

— labour in industrial production which provides necessities for itself and the surplus-producing labour in agriculture,

— labour producing luxuries for the surplus appropriating class (SAC).

At this level there is a surplus which is appropriated as rent, i.e., whose appropriation does not depend on technical efficiency but on power. In the simplified version of the model presented here, this surplus is equivalent to the consumption of food and luxuries of the SAC.

The total of this gainfully employed labour may be less than available able-bodied average skilled labour. In this case, there is no possibility of real wage increases, and hence no possibility of expanding markets for simple machine-produced products. Thus, there is no interest in capacity-increasing net investment, on the basis of which surplus in the form of profit earned by capitalists on competitive markets can emerge.

The condition for the existence of labour surplus is demographic growth being unchecked by famine. The condition can be fulfilled because of the behaviour of labour and the SAC. For labour, the demand for its services is of a lottery type. There are more labourers who can render the necessary services for surplus production on the available land than required for maximising surplus. Who will be chosen by the land owners depends on many factors, all of them non-economic. In any case, only obedient labour will be chosen. Labour will increase the probability of its employment by offering non-economic services (such as political support) and will engage in patron-client dependence relations. The chances of being chosen increase with the number of members of a solidarity group, like a family. There is no reason for checking demographic growth. The chance of being protected from the consequences of marginality through redistributive mechanisms implemented by a powerful lord increases if no member of such a group challenges the existing power relation without being sanctioned by the solidarity group.[24]

This cheap solution of maintaining the existing order creates an interest on the part of the SAC to engage in arrangements with employed labour that allow this labour to feed more family members than the nuclear family. The SAC therefore has an interest in social pacts,[25] through which demographic pressure as well as marginality are maintained. According to the model, this interest increases because the SAC appropriates surplus on the basis of political means, hence power. Any member of the SAC can increase his standing over his rivals in the SAC by the number of clients he controls. As long as perfect competition does not yield higher returns than power, the members of the SAC will limit competition and use resources for maintaining political power. They struggle for influence, resources and prestige. One element of this strategy is the creation of an acceptable number of obedient clients. Demographic growth beyond the threshold of marginality does not need any explanation beyond these two interests of the SAC and labour.

Technical progress in the production of luxuries does not raise the level of marginality. Rather, more or better luxuries are produced for the SAC. It may lead to more luxury production employment if more or better luxuries intensify the struggle over the surplus with the result that previous members of the SAC are excluded from it. In this case, food available for labour employed in luxury production increases. But the basic mechanism of conflict resolution within such a class – i.e., an increase of the rate of exploitation in order to increase the size of resources to be appropriated – makes this solution improbable, as shown in the theory of the dynastic cycle.[26]

Technical progress in the production of non-food necessities lowers the cost of agricultural labour. The threshold of marginality rises. It cannot rise, however, beyond the level where additional labour produces less than the share of food in its costs of reproduction. This shows, however, that a cheapening of industrial mass consumption goods, as occurred during demographic growth in Western Europe in the wake of the great plague (16th and 17th centuries),[27] may counteract marginality. A thriving and dynamic informal sector in today's industrially backward countries (IBCs) may do the same.[18] An increase in productivity in agriculture may raise the volume of surplus of already employed labour and therefore increase luxury consumption. This may be sufficient to create full employment and lead to the Prussian way of transition to capitalism. In this case, industrial capital may be promoted if the SAC seeks technical progress in its consumption too, for example, in order to maintain its military power against the SAC of another country. Such an outcome depends on the patterns of consumption of SACs, which normally will consider the repression of labour protest as their main task.

Agricultural progress, however, may also increase marginal product. In this case labour may become scarce. As labour scarcity hits the weaker parts of the SAC first, this class may defend its access to income by trying to improve productivity through investment. Such members of the SAC may join emerging capitalists from other walks of life and fight against the greater monopoly of the richer parts of the non-capitalist SAC. Labour will become even more scarce. The tendencies to rising mass consumption, and with it capitalist investment, as well as to declining centralisation of the SAC will be enhanced.

Agricultural progress which increases marginal product is the only set-up which triggers off quasi-automatically the transition to capitalism, because it is accompanied by an increasing independence of the weaker parts of the SAC from the centralisation of the surplus, increasing bargaining power of labour and the transformation of the weaker parts of the SAC into capitalists. This transformation is greatly supported by a rising demand for machine-produced products which makes investment in technological innovation profitable and ultimately mandatory for all members of the SAC, when the capitalist sector has achieved technological superiority. It will be accompanied by political struggles against the political bases of the old pattern of rent appropriation which are usually labelled bourgeois revolutions. The model allows us to understand that these movements do not necessarily draw their members only from the capitalist entrepreneurial class, but from all walks of society which are opposed to rent appropriation. It is bourgeois because it is against rent, not because its recruitment is based on a bourgeois social standing.

The model implies two types of technical progress, both of them demand-dependent. Technical progress in luxuries aims at producing a higher quality product and consists of the skills of craftsmen transmitted from generation to generation and acquired through training. Technical progress in necessities consumed by the masses aims, at any level of consumption, at the reduction of unit costs of production of average quality standardised products, which are produced in large series and therefore allow the employment of machines, which are, subsequently, improved. Production skills are easily accessible for a large majority of workers with average intellectual qualities, as technical progress is incorporated in machinery. Standardised production allows for the broad implementation of machinery, non-standardised products do not (with the exception of the production of raw material inputs and their transport). The decisive capacity of innovation is to be found in the skills of engineers, and is transmitted through intellectual training where cumulative effects can be realised.[28]

The Privilege of being First

For the more advanced and even leading pre-capitalist economy there is no particular advantage to being first in the transition to capitalism. The relatively backward pre-capitalist economy has less rent than the more advanced one. Because it has less rent, it also has less marginality, because it cannot finance extensive social pacts. If, initially, marginal product is equally high in a rich and a poor pre-capitalist economy, the SAC of the rich economy will drive marginal product down, because it is able to favour demographic growth and is interested in doing so.[29] It is the very poverty of the backward economy which protects it from the blockage to the transition to capitalism constituted by the wealth and the sophistication of the performing pre-capitalist economies. The poor economy may be backward not only in luxury products but also in mass consumption industrial products. But it has its comparative advantage in mass consumption products and regular famines keep marginals from impacting on the labour markets. If its marginal productivity is high enough to allow the transition to capitalism with scarcity of labour, it ultimately will overtake the more advanced pre-capitalist economy in luxuries.

Let us assume two marginality-ridden economies engaging in trade. One of them is characterised by a low volume of agricultural surplus i.e., rent, the other one by a high volume of agricultural surplus. There are two cases to be distinguished: a case where food is tradable and a case where food is not tradable. If food is tradable, the opening up of the marginality-ridden economy which is backward in luxury products will lead to this economy selling off its agricultural surplus against luxuries from the more advanced pre-capitalist economy. If food is not externally tradable, the backward economy cannot buy the luxuries of the advanced ones with food, but has to find some other mechanism. It is realistic to assume that food and other bulky products are initially not tradables, at least not on long distance traffic routes. At a later stage, this restriction on trading food and other bulky products may be removed, as industrial development in at least one of the two economies brings long-distance transport costs down via the application of industrial technology to sea-going vessels and eventually land transport (railways). For the purpose of our model, we stylise this difference as two stages. In an early stage, food is not tradable, whereas in a later stage it is. This distinction is obviously relevant, as the possibility of engaging rent in its original physical form (food) has a bearing on the pattern of exports of the poorer economy.

The poor economy, by definition, has a low surplus of agriculture. It is this small volume of rent which precludes the emergence of a powerful and rich SAC. Due to the low volume of surplus in agriculture, its progress in luxuries is limited. The amount of stones which were moved and carved in the construction of South Asian monuments as well as the speed of execution of these monuments in comparison to the centuries required for comparatively smaller (as measured in stone volume) European cathedrals can be quoted here as an example for Europe's inferiority in surplus production.

Such a poor economy is inevitably characterised by a low difference between average and marginal productivity in agriculture. Otherwise, there would be a large surplus in relation to population to be controlled. There may be some high yielding areas, but there is a large sector of agriculture where product is almost at the level of marginal product and which then requires for its exploitation a numerous SAC in order to appropriate this surplus. Food consumption out of the rent of the SAC with its repressive apparatus is too high to support numerous luxury workers. But it is also possible that throughout the agricultural areas yields and product per worker vary little. In both cases, the possibilities of creating networks of patronage in favour of the marginals are financially limited. The surplus population is regularly decimated by famines. The bargaining power of the surviving peasantry is relatively large. Such an economy is not capable of supporting rapid economic growth based on rent.

This type of economy is a stylised description of pre-17th century

Europe. Europe may have not been able to create a sufficient surplus for a rich and sophisticated ruling class. Europe's agriculture did not depend on irrigation. Average productivity seems to have been so close to marginal productivity that productivity divergences were not even dealt with in the theoretical discussion about the consequences of internal colonisation, the clearance of until then forest-covered hilly land around the old established settlements (since the 12th century[30]). Surplus was then limited, whereas possibilities of exit through emigration were important. Braudel has mentioned the improvement of the bargaining power of the peasantry (and, as a result of this, of labour).[31] The rich economy is characterised by a high agricultural surplus from which a rich SAC with powerful military instruments can prosper. If we assume that population growth goes unchecked until marginal product reaches the cost of reproduction, such empires are probably characterised by large populations. The SAC is able to create dense networks of patronage, and to maintain at its service large populations fed out of the rent. Through the refinement of its tastes it promotes the quality of luxuries in the economy. The bargaining power of its peasantry is low due to the efficiency of the military establishment and the availability of a large marginal population. It must be assumed that productivity in agriculture outside the realm of its control is limited. The low productivity areas will either not be under its control or will be attached to the empire in a loose manner for strategic reasons, not for economic ones. The North African distinction between bilad al-maghzen and bilad as-siba, the area subject to fiscal administration of the king and the area of suzerainty of the king over self-governing tribes can be quoted here.[32] There are certainly similar arrangements in the old Indian states, which probably left traces in the geographical distribution of the populations today called tribal.

The possibilities of exchange between the advanced luxury-producing and the poor pre-capitalist economies depend on whether or not food is tradable. If food is tradable, the less performing economy in luxuries will sell the surplus of its agriculture and shed its luxury workers. If food is not tradable, the two economies will specialise according to comparative advantage in non-food goods. It is sufficient that food is not tradable between the two regions, although it may be tradable within each region (which was the case for the maritime provinces of Europe from Lisbon to the Baltic states beginning at the end of the 16th century).

Neither economy can produce more tradables for export than it can "finance" from the surplus of its local agriculture. If food cannot be traded, both economies follow vent for surplus strategies.[33] The poorer economy can sell its industrial products only if it achieves very low prices, i.e., if it targets the rather limited market of dependent labour in the richer economy. This will be difficult if transport costs are high. The poor economy will simply not sell anything. The SAC of the poor economy can acquire the luxuries of the richer one only with great difficulties. It may dispose of some raw materials such as tin or copper. It may be blessed with mineral riches and pay with species, so that the richer economy becomes a net species importer. It may acquire species through war-like activities, such as plunder and pirating. It may even sell part of its own or neighbouring populations as slaves, as Europe already did until the end of the Middle Ages before the Atlantic slave trade. It will have difficulties, however, in catching up in luxuries with the richer economy unless it does not achieve industrial transformation.

The poor economy will remain inferior, and perhaps periodically engage in war and plunder when the rich economy is characterised by the troubles of a downturn in the dynastic cycle.

The rich economy can well accept this behaviour from the poor, as it is rather self-contained. It has no use for foreign expansion, and only tries to control its foreign trade in order to maximise earnings. If it expands beyond its frontiers, the main economic reason is the enlargement of its tax-base.

The poor economy, however, has a major advantage in transforming to a capitalist one as described above. Famine periodically eliminates its marginal population, as its SAC simply does not have a large enough surplus at its disposal in the form of rent, which in that case can and – in order to avoid social unrest – has to be used for sustaining the hungry ones. Even the slightest entitlement of the marginal population to such a surplus in a rich economy is stronger than the strongest political entitlement to a non-existing surplus in a poor one. The volume of marginal population in the poor economy is therefore limited, whereas the bargaining power of the non-marginal peasantry is relatively large, as there is a small surplus of labour. There are historically accidental circumstances which have reinforced this mechanism in medieval Europe, especially certain technical innovations which allowed the cultivation of until then uncultivated land in the northern and eastern territories of Europe.

Due to its bargaining power, the non-marginal peasantry becomes a market for industrial products manufactured by the marginals as largely described in the theory of protoindustrialisation.[34] The orientation of industrial production to mass demand for low quality products favours technical progress which aims at cost reduction and not at product excellence. The reduction of the costs of non-agricultural necessities leads, in the model, to a decline in marginality, as the threshold of marginality rises due to lower costs of agricultural labour. Under conditions of low levels of marginality, this may lead to an overcoming of marginality. Suppose that this leads to capitalist development, because the economy experiences agricultural progress parallel to demographic growth or opens up new areas for cultivation. The poor economy now engages in a pattern of development characterised by cumulative technical progress in necessities production based on tendential full employment (or appropriate measures to deal with marginality because of the bargaining power of labour) and productivity-oriented wage increases. These wage increases may be initially low because of the necessity of increasing agricultural production at high costs, so that such real wage increases are statistically difficult to prove. Industrial productivity increases rapidly, but average productivity does not.

If the poor economy engages in this pattern of development, it strengthens its comparative advantage in non-luxury industrial products, which, however, already existed before due to its low productivity in luxuries. Both the rich and the poor economy develop parallel and only partially contradictory interests in the modalities in which their trade should be carried out. The price elasticities of luxuries and industrial wage goods can be assumed to be different, low-quality industrial goods having a high price elasticity in both societies even if both types of society are characterised by increasing rates of exploitation. The demand for luxuries can be considered as being not price elastic, but as elastic to the rate of exploitation/surplus appropriation also in the poorer economy. However, in order to buy more luxuries, the necessities-producing economy has to feed more workers; the luxury-exporting one, on the other hand, is less under this pressure, and can pursue its interest in raising the rate of exploitation more efficiently, which further limits the possibility of the poor economy to sell its shoddy industrial products.

The poor economy needs for its exports its own unqualified non-rural labour (and may even engage its rural labour in non-rural employment) as well as access to the markets of the rich economy. The SAC of the rich economy is satisfied in the case of export monopoly and high rates of exploitation of its peasantry.

Both SACs struggle over monopoly in the luxury trade. The SAC of the poor economy can gain from control over this monopoly, too, as it gets its luxury imports at lower prices. With respect to monopoly in the luxury trade, the two SACs have parallel but antagonistic interests. They contend with each other for control of the monopoly in luxuries and are equally interested in necessities being sold more cheaply in the rich economy: lower costs of necessities reduce the cost of labour in the rich economy which allows increasing tax pressure in the rich economy. The poor economy increases its export earnings through larger sales of its shoddy products.

If both economies have equal productivity in warfare and necessities, the poor economy will gain comparative advantage in both of these because of its low productivity in luxuries. This comparative advantage is strengthened if machinery can be utilised to increase the productivity in necessities production and the performance of military equipments.

The interest of the poor economy in selling necessities and in warfare unleashes contradictory tendencies in its political system. It will favour the strengthening of its military establishment, especially with respect to its capacity to strike outside its own territory (and less so with respect to its capacity to police its own labour), as well as the strengthening of its exporters of necessities, who are not necessarily interested in monopoly but only in the safety of trade routes.

The rich economy, however, aims only at maintaining its monopoly in the sales of luxuries, including its control over its luxury producers, who have to be prevented from selling at cheap prices to interlopers or free-riders in its inland trade.

The economy specialising on necessities has an interest in closing its own market and in destroying or taking over the monopoly-creating structures of its trading partner, but can accept competition for its own exports. The economy specialised in luxuries must maintain the monopoly-creating structures for its own trade, but is less concerned with preserving its own internal market. The earning capacity of both economies' exports depends on the forms of access to each other's markets. If the luxury-specialised economy can impose restrictions on the volume of exports on its own territory, and therefore manipulate the sale price of its exports in terms of the imports from the other one, it improves its terms of trade and its earning power. If the luxury-importing economy restricts its exports, it will not improve its earning capacity, does not increase its employment, and faces decreasing volumes of imports of luxuries.

The luxury-exporting economy will favour monopoly for its exports and accept free trade for its imports. The economy with comparative advantage for industrial necessities will tend to impose a free-trade strategy for its exports – and try to take over the monopoly for its imports, which may even lead to politically destroying the monopoly capacity of the luxury-exporting one, first through unilateral control of trade routes, then through occupation of the area of production of the luxuries.

Poor Europe could sell only in the case of access to markets where its products achieved low prices but were in demand at these low prices. Rich Asia could sell without forcing the access to markets,[35] but its exporters, whether European long-distance monopolistic trade companies or their Asian (Muslim) predecessors, had an interest in maintaining monopoly (and not in free markets). The model explains why the transition to capitalism occurred not in the technically superior, most developed tributary modes of production which were built around the Asian fluvial plains (India, China, but also Egypt), but in a rather less developed area.

Although both economies have similar interests in controlling trade routes, the precise objectives to be achieved by them are quite different. The interests of the luxury-importing economy, i.e., monopoly directed against the luxury-exporting economy, is not seriously hurt by interlopers. The latter merely threaten the capacity of the monopoly-enforcing agency to finance its outlays from its monopoly profit. The interloper is, at the macroeconomic level, acceptable for the SAC of the luxury-importing economies, as shown by the controversies over the monopoly of the English East Indian Company which was established at the end of the 17th century. The luxury-importing economy does not have to achieve closure of its society as long as it is able to earn income through its exports of necessities. It engages in these exports precisely because its SAC wants to buy luxuries from outside. Closure of the economy in the necessity-exporting countries only has to be pursued if luxury imports grow very rapidly in favour of less wealthy classes. The poorer economy may have become so wealthy that the demand for imported luxuries becomes price elastic, as was the case in England at the end of the 17th century. At that time, England was able to impose customs duties efficiently due to its naval superiority.

The luxury-exporting economy, however, has to fear the interloper, as the rent appropriated by the interloper is inevitably lost for the income of its SAC. The earnings of the luxury-exporting economies consist of a rent and the costs of production, which are basically labour costs, as we assume that there are no net investments in luxury production. The earnings of the competitive necessities-exporting economy are labour and profit required for net investment. The necessities-exporting economy can try to buy lower strata of the SAC in the society of the luxury-exporting economy by expanding its sales through accepting intermediary profits. In addition, it can bribe the lower strata of the SAC in the luxury-exporting society by sharing the rent earned in luxury exports without incurring losses, for example, by enabling corrupt elements of the SAC in the luxury-exporting economies to circumvent the local monopoly-creating structures. The necessities-importing economy will favour the strategy of cheapened imports from the necessities-exporting economy, and cannot accept the interloper in its own ranks for its luxury exports.

The free-rider in the luxury trade threatens the rent of the SAC in the luxury-exporting country. The free-rider in the necessities trade contributes to the growth of volume in the necessities-exporting economy.

Technical growth in necessities production, which mainly occurs in the economy which specialises in necessities, has implications for comparative advantage in luxury production.

Technical progress in process innovation is also the basis of future product innovation, and process innovation is dependent ultimately on large series being produced. As an illustration one can quote aeroplane or missile production, which cannot be understood without referring to the technical breakthroughs achieved in automobile production and related mechanical engineering, or, as well, the serious spurt of steam engine production on the basis of the mechanisation of some parts of the textile production in the late 18th century.

The assumption of technical progress having spill-overs even into the productivity in luxuries allows us to consider luxuries as being at least divided into two large segments: a segment of products which are craft-dependent and where artistic skills determine the quality of the product, so that there are no significant spill-overs into technological capacities in process innovation; and the segment of products which depend on technological innovation in process technologies. This second segment contributes to increasing efficiency in mass production (democratisation of consumption of new goods)[36] and the discovery of new products which are initially luxuries. Specialisation on industrial wage goods is the basis of the future acquisition of comparative advantage in such types of luxuries. We may add that among the luxuries which are most dependent on this type of innovation are military goods, due to the importance of mechanical engineering in mass production technologies and in military equipment as well.

Long-term superiority in luxury production is therefore dependent on ever-increasing technical progress which may allow mass consumption to rise if food production increases. A rising mass consumption creates incentives for reducing labour costs through process innovation as well as for capturing new outlets through product innovation. New products ultimately enhance the performance of the originally poor economy in new luxury products, which on its own market may become mass consumption products, but which in the originally richer economy are still luxuries. The originally richer economy becomes a lagging-behind economy. In the long term, the economy with comparative advantage in necessities will also acquire comparative advantage in new luxuries and eventually comparative advantage in necessities.

In principle, the originally richer luxury-exporting economy will now be forced into the situation experienced by the originally poor economy, but under conditions of a high level of marginality.[37] But as far as it can maintain its pre-capitalist political structures, it can survive in relative isolation by preserving its own market and relying on its home production, which the exporter of necessities will try to overcome. The various efforts to open the Chinese market between the end of the 18th and the middle of the 19th century can be quoted as examples of this set-up.

We drop now the assumption that food is not tradable. The possibility of trading food over long distances is supposed to be the result of improved transport technology. There are two possible cases: the marginality-cum-rent-ridden economy has comparative advantage in food production because of the relative decline in demand for its own luxuries and the low level of its industrial necessities production. In this case, it sheds its luxury workers and sells the surplus of agriculture against imports of better luxuries. If, however, comparative advantage in agriculture cannot be translated into agricultural exports – because of marginality and hence inelasticity of supply, comparative advantage lying with industrial necessities, the world market being unable to absorb additional food exports, or the SAC of the now lagging-behind economy deliberately blocking such exports – the old luxury-exporting economy has to proceed to the same mechanisms as the previously poor economy, starting, however, from a low level of development in cost-reducing technologies.

We start with the first alternative, because the second one is the basis of the possibility of catching up after temporarily falling behind in the contemporary process of globalisation. Suppose that the formerly poor economy is able to supply better luxuries or military equipment than local labour fed from the surplus of the local agriculture of the formerly richer economy. In this type of marginality-ridden economy, employment decreases as luxury-producing workers are shed off and the agricultural surplus they had once consumed is exported, especially if the supply elasticity of agriculture is low because of decreasing marginal output. The decline of industrial capabilities in the wake of the disappearance of the luxury-producing sector will seriously hamper any future industrial development, as the luxury producing sector can be supposed to be the technically most advanced one among the different segments of industrial-craft production. The shedding off of the luxury workers also leads to the contraction of internal demand for the already lagging behind industrial-necessities-producing sector.

As the process of increasing competitiveness in the production of luxuries and necessities in the originally poor country had depended on technical development in machinery production with spin-offs for military technology, the originally poor economy can strengthen its demand for free access to the market of the luxury-producing economy and for the dismantlement of its monopoly-creating structures, and, moreover, can increase unilaterally the degree of closure of its home market. It further benefits from demand-driven technical development and enjoys increases in technological superiority. The luxury-producing economy will experience declining terms of trade because of the dismantlement of its monopoly-creating structures, possibly even because of the dismantlement of its pre-capitalist state structures (or their being overtaken by staff from the rival economy). It does not increase its technical capacities and reduces its employment level.

An initial comparative advantage in necessities allows the economy which is less performing in luxury production to develop it necessities sector. If technical development in the necessities sector is the basis for discovering new products which are initially luxuries, it will undersell the originally superior luxury producer also in luxuries. If at this later stage the export of food becomes possible, the economy which was initially superior in luxury production sells its food surpluses and sheds its luxury workers.

Europe was hence poor and unable to produce luxuries. Asia was superior. Europe could buy Asian products only when it was able to sell specie, slave labour or low-quality goods whose production could be mechanised, or by waging wars. Because of its poverty, England acquired an initially, perhaps slight comparative advantage in mass consumption goods (despite even absolute backwardness in some textiles), and could succeed in the less difficult task of imposing free trade in India's imports on the basis of superior naval power with the concomitant result of easing its own problems of marginality. India, on the other hand, had to accept closure of the English market for its textiles at the beginning of the 18th century, and subsequently specialisation on some luxuries and agricultural cash crops which did not compensate the effect of shedding off labour in basic industrial goods and agriculture. Shedding of labour in basic industrial goods was the result of the famous de-industrialisation of India.[38] Shedding of labour in agriculture was the result of an increasing pressure to maximise the surplus available for the "Indian" SAC, possibly the British raj.[39] Both developments aggravated the already existing tendencies to stagnation because of de-industrialisation, first in mass consumption industrial products, then even in luxuries, and finally through the squeeze of agriculture, where the mechanism implied in the "social contract" in favour of some marginal labour could no longer be upheld.

In this process, the unequal distribution of incentives for growth between the initially poor and initially rich economy is decisive. The poor economy does not overtake the rich one because its accumulation of capital is financed from the surplus – rent – appropriated in the rich one. The struggle over rent is secondary. The decisive mechanism consists in the poor country having a chance to reduce marginality, which is already lower than in the rich one, and to specialise in products which promote that type of technical progress which, despite its orientation to necessities, ultimately provides superiority also in new luxuries.[40]

Although this process does not imply a transfer of resources from the falling behind economy to the getting ahead one, such a transfer will ultimately occur. The luxury-producing economy will not avoid unequal specialisation even in the case of improving terms of trade, whereas the necessities-exporting economy may have an even greater export drive if it is unable to destroy the monopoly-creating structures of the luxury-exporting economy.

The contribution of its success in destroying these monopoly structures to the growth of the necessities-exporting, originally poorer economy does not consist primarily in a cheapening of its imports – which may, however, render less burdensome the claims of its SAC on its local factors of production, as this SAC continues to consume luxuries of the originally richer economy.[41] The decisive result will be the prevention of the SAC of the old luxury-exporting economy from closing and restructuring its economy after it has lost comparative advantage in a large segment of luxuries due to the introduction of new luxuries.

Being "poor" is a favourable condition for the transition to mass-consumption-based capitalist growth, provided that marginal productivity in agriculture grows. The European inability to acquire Indian luxuries by means other than developing its own technology in necessities production and, derived from this, the military sector ultimately destroyed India's capacity to use its own state power – as its state power was confiscated by the British raj – for restructuring its own economy when the consequences of unequal specialisation were felt.

Being first allows supporting the process of transition to capitalism, although being first is not the primary reason for getting ahead. Vice-versa, being late creates obstacles to the overcoming of marginality, but dealing with marginality is not primarily a problem of foreign trade strategy.

Instruments for Dealing with Marginality or the Necessarily Eclectic Character of Overcoming Underdevelopment

The problem of dealing with marginality has two aspects, a technical one and a political one. Both are shaped by the simultaneous existence of surplus of resources and surplus of labour. The technical problem consists in how to channel the surplus of resources into overcoming marginality by creating additional, ultimately profitable employment, whereas the political problem consists in the lack of commitment of the SAC to do so.

The technical problem can be described by examining the various strategies discussed in development theory.[42] The channelling of rent into overcoming marginality implies market failure. If a capitalist system performs and reaches full employment, the scarcity of labour reduces the surplus of resources to the amount necessary for capacity-creating, technically efficient and therefore economically profitable investment.[43] Market failure can be corrected only by mechanisms which draw on non-market subsystems of the social structure. The surplus circulating in these other subsystems is by definition not controlled by competition, so that the problem of waste is pervasive as in any other case of rent/tax.[44] The design of interventions based on non-market subsystems of the society has to take into account this danger, and to create as far as possible automatisms which exclude rent appropriation in favour of particular interests which are not growth-inducing.

State-sponsored import-substituting industrialisation and devaluation-driven export-led industrialisation may be considered as two extreme, opposite examples of such a mobilisation of rent. In the framework of state-sponsored import-substituting industrialisation, a centralised state which replaced the rent-based oligarchies in the wake of the world economic depression of the 1930s,[45] or which – even with some already engaged programs in late colonialism[46]– replaced the colonial powers in the wake of decolonisation, tried to maximise rent through export taxes and an increasingly higher internal tax pressure. This "development state" of what I have called state-class-dominated bureaucratic development societies[47] was able to raise the share of investment in total GNP. Because of multiple and competing (e.g., profitability vs. employment creation) economic aims, the process of allocation of the investible resources took the form of political negotiations between segments of these state classes who pursued the aims of power, prestige and resources. Within the framework of power games, the link between the perception of reality and the reality itself by necessity had to become weaker.[48] The results of such processes were not necessarily investment projects which allowed labour absorption and an increase in mass consumption or contributed to an overcoming of marginality, so that the persistence of rent could not be avoided. Resulting high capital output ratios and low capacity utilisation ratios led to the well-known savings gap. A rent-induced high foreign exchange rate allowed the reliance on imported technology, particularly in the case of raw material rich countries, and precluded the entry into the acquisition of technological competencies through the local production of initially less performing, "clumsy" technology. This further deepened dependency and contributed to the foreign exchange gap, especially after the success of the oil countries in raising their prices made other underdeveloped economies expect similar possibilities of improving their terms of trade which they continued to cherish in the period of internationally low interest rates (piling up debts in the hope for future recovery through the implementation of a New International Economic Order, and considering banks being unable to recover sovereign risks).

The strategy of export-led growth which resource-poor and debt-ridden countries had to apply, often under the pressure of the international financial institutions, ultimately differed from import-substituting industrialisation only with respect to how the rent (which in their case was much lower) was used. Export-oriented industrialisation is based on devaluation in order to make local labour internationally competitive. These economies have comparative advantage in their export sectors, but often lag in physical productivity behind the industrially leading countries (ILCs). In order to transform comparative advantage into cost effectiveness, the international price of local factors of production has to be lowered through devaluation. Devaluation is possible if local factors of production, especially labour (because it is not internationally mobile), can be "reproduced" from a local surplus, i.e., the surplus of local agriculture.[49] An economy which until now has not been able to achieve competitiveness on the world market can transform comparative advantage into competitiveness

— if international food prices decrease,
— if its absolute levels of productivity in industrial products increase, or
— if it is able to devaluate to levels where export workers do not earn their costs of reproduction and this on the basis of a higher agricultural surplus.

These three conditions apply to the case of an originally luxury-exporting country which cannot transform comparative advantage in agriculture into agricultural exports, as mentioned above.

A low-wage economy is characterised by a high direct share of food in the consumption of labour and hence additional export-sector workers (roughly 50-60%), and a high indirect share of food in the rest of their consumption, which consists of industrial products and services supplied actually or (in the case of devaluation) potentially by the small-scale sector, which is often called the informal one.

An economy which produces enough food for all its labour can accept any rate of devaluation, even with marginal export earning becoming negative,[50] if its priority is to transform its social structure through full employment, mass consumption, and the implied reduction of import dependent luxury consumption. The Green Revolution has provided such agricultural surpluses at least to the rice-growing agricultures of East and Southeast Asia, whose internal labour prices are completely disconnected from their levels of real wages.[51]

The rent from agriculture is supplied in its physical form (food) to additional export workers (and workers employed on the basis of multiplier effects from export production). In its financial form, it goes partly to the additional workers (wages) and the importing countries (improving terms of trade). The only condition for the success of such a strategy is a sufficiently high agricultural surplus and regulations which preclude exports.[52] The strategy of dumping agricultural surpluses of the ILCs on the world market, the effects of the Green Revolution in the industrially leading countries[53] (with the terms of trade for food deteriorating against low-productivity-growth industrial products, where catching-up economies have by definition comparative advantage) and the efforts to improve productivity in industry in the logging behind economics (even through previous import-substituting industrialisation, but also through export promotion and foreign direct investment) have the same result: more food can be bought for additional export workers so that comparative advantage can be transformed into cost effectiveness and competitiveness on the world market.

The experiences of the successful exporters of manufactured goods in East and Southeast Asia show that an export drive can be successful in transforming the labour markets if it is complemented by economic and social reforms which reduce marginality. Agrarian reforms present a major economic and administrative advantage[54]. Suppose that land is distributed in an egalitarian manner. Marginal labour, i.e. labour time the use of which adds less to total production than its share in total work time of a labourer (under the assumption that total labour time just leads to a level of production sufficient for subsistence - including his family's subsistence) is internalised within the farm in case of such a redistribution. The farmer will reach an already high level of production by working some hours per day, but this level of production is not sufficient for providing the basic necessities to him and his family. As the requirements for these necessities do not increase in line with hours worked, the farmer will also provide additional labour time in order to survive with his family. Such an agriculture presents advantages for the development of industry. Besides the often praised effect of equalling out income distribution, some farmers will achieve through the investment of additional labour time higher levels of productivity, and also surpluses, which they will sell on the market for buying non-food items. Less efficient farmers will prefer non-agricultural by-employment in small-scale enterprises which will provide these items[55]. They will accept for their labour time wages which equal their marginal product in agriculture, which they forego by working outside agriculture. Wages will be low and obviously subsidised by the rent which previously went to a surplus-maximising landlord. Landless labourers can be employed by industry if the daily wage rate there corresponds to the daily subsistence needs and not only to the marginal product a farmer produces in his least productive hours. This will make industrial products cheaper and relatively inexpensive in relation to agricultural products. This effect may promote small-scale mass-market-oriented industries.

The redistribution of land, however, seems possible only in exceptional political situations. All the countries which have succeeded in this task are today candidates for an effective transition to capitalism (Taiwan, South Korea, Mainland China, Vietnam), although often after painful transitions or under exceptional circumstances.

Redistribution of income is an administratively difficult task in which most state administrations have failed. One version is the English Poor Laws, where parishes taxed the rich independently of the levels of employment they provided, and subsidised marginal labour which then could be employed at wage rates which did not cover the costs of subsistence.[56] NGOs may claim to pursue investment aims when raising productivity but their programs very often do not differ from inefficient state programs as the niches of profitable production are already occupied by the informal sector. They sustain activities whose income-generating capacity does not allow for covering the costs of reproduction of marginal labour.[57] They are therefore an instrument of channelling a rent to the marginal ones, which may be exposed to more outside checks than subsidies from state budgets. Nevertheless, NGOs rarely escape the dangers of clientelism and bureaucratic behaviour[58] after the first generation of idealistic promoters are forced to hand over control to a staff which is recruited from middle strata of society and whose outlook it will share. Recent developments point to the growing disappointment of the target groups.[59]

If neither the redistribution of land nor the redistribution of income through bureaucracies or NGOs is possible, and if the process of channelling resources into efficient investment fails, there may be a solution of despair. I have suggested the creation of an artificial resource industry for Bangladesh:[60] donors would stop providing aid and would apply a scheme based on well identifiable stones, which they would scatter over remote areas. They would fix an exchange rate which covers the cost of subsistence of an ordinary gatherer including the transaction costs between the area of collection and the exchange office. The poor, but not the above-subsistence farmers, would go to collect these stones and exchange them at rates which cover their subsistence, because each of them has to reproduce his labour power hence cover the labour value expended. Under the conditions of this model, the poor gatherers would buy simple goods for which demand increases, so that small-scale entrepreneurs perceive marketing opportunities, order appropriate technology, etc., in the wake of which the role of technical co-operation agencies can be reduced to suppliers of appropriate technology which compete on markets. In contrast to increased exports, the solution implies no threat to employment in the West, and relies, with the exception of the operation of the exchange office, entirely on market mechanisms.

Any such measure is characterised by diminishing returns in relation to financial and administrative efforts, already mentioned in the case of import-substituting industrialisation (the mild versions of which were so successful that there is a serious argument about a revised form of it based on mass markets).[61] Export-led growth faces the problem of the absorptive capacities of the markets in the ILCs. Redistributive measures even if effected through NGOs lead to patronage, clientelism and "assistentionalist" attitudes of target groups, the latter being difficult to define, leaving discretionary power to lower ranks in the (public, private or voluntary) agencies charged with their implementation. Radical agrarian reforms have been implemented only through the political clout of anti-capitalist forces, which create fear in all walks of society about respect of property rights in future, especially when marketing organisations (marketing boards or monopolies) were introduced following reform which took away incentives for peasants to increase production.

Dealing with marginality implies on a technical level the combination of eclectic measures in order to create synergies.

This, in turn, implies that objectives are not clear cut. The design is not of a simple character, and leads to a large scope of interpretation. The larger the scopes of interpretation in rent-determined negotiation processes, the less the possibilities of rationalising the rent-based struggles of segments of state-classes with a view to implement the overcoming of marginality against self-privileging. In the theory of the simultaneously progressive and wasteful character of state-classes, I have insisted on the necessity of complementing inevitable state interventionism by recurring to the market mechanism wherever possible.[62]

A successful fight against marginality is therefore dependent on limited and, hence, at least potentially accountable state interventionism, eclectic but administratively low-cost non-market measures, and the use of market mechanisms wherever applicable.

New Opportunities through Globalisation

The role of the state in an era of globalisation can be determined from the discussion of the conditions for dealing successfully with marginality. Globalisation does not require less state interventionism, but, rather, a more intelligent interventionism than that which has been practised in most IBCs until now. The shift, even in the Washington Institutions, in the controversy over Third World state interventionism from its extent to its quality is proof of this.

Any strategy of successfully catching up with ILCs through IBCs requires an appropriately low foreign exchange rate. From the discussion of export-led growth, it follows that this requirement can only be fulfilled in the case of a sufficiently high agricultural surplus. This condition is less narrow than the condition of marginal product in agriculture being higher than the costs of reproduction of labour. To this extent, transition to (self-sustained and welfarist) capitalism in the globalised economy is easier than it was for the front-runners of the industrial revolution. A rise in agricultural earnings for a mass of agricultural producers through agrarian reform is, however, a powerful tool for accelerating the process of agricultural growth, as it limits the amount of necessary investment (as labour replacing investment is undertaken only in the case of high opportunity earnings of this – family – labour outside of their farms, hence only after general productivity growth is already underway).

A strategy of devaluation should not aim at rates of devaluation where the last available worker not yet employed gets a job in export production. The new competitiveness of production sites of the IBCs is initially limited to those branches where there is not only comparative advantage but where the perspective of achieving relatively low lags in productivity with respect to the ILCs are bright.[63] Real productivity growth achieved through export-orientation concerns, at least initially, only a small number of production lines, often characterised by low price and income elasticities.

Industrial policies of support for internationally not yet competitive products are relatively easy to define for an IBC because they are characterised by known technologies.[64] They can be launched without an exhaustive state interventionism, which would be addressed to particular enterprises, such as licensing, special credit on a case per case basis, etc.[65] Ultimately, such programs are financed out of a rent, as shown by Singapore's taxing of highly competitive but technically less demanding exports for the financing of programs of skill upgrading.[66] South Korea, when facing a low price elasticity of its textile exports, banned the import of textile machinery.[67] Its highly competitive textile producers had to turn to local suppliers of machinery. They were initially only able to get less efficient machinery, but due to a low price elasticity of their exports the additional cost could be charged to the export prices (and, in the case of indefinite capacities to devalue, this would not have even implied higher international prices). This is a case of quasi-automatic channelling of rent without any state intervention other than a change in the import regulations. The second-tier newly industrialising countries of Southeast Asia are even more dependent on the support of rents for their export drives.[68]

The chances for broadening productivity growth through a spill-over of new skills from the export sector to internal-market-oriented branches is greatly enhanced if small and medium-scale enterprises (SMEs) are dynamised. There are few indications that SMEs can really benefit from programs of direct support which make them dependent on the promotional agencies. Promoted SMEs tend to transform such agencies into their own captives by using their alleged "sickness" for channelling their own financial resources into other economic and often socially less desirable activities such as real estate, bribes, etc.

SMEs or the informal sector become dynamic if there is a market which can emerge in predominantly still agrarian economies from surpluses of small farmers.[69] SMEs will not face credit problems if two conditions are fulfilled: outlets where their product can be sold profitably and a supply of appropriate investment goods at accessible prices. As this type of goods may not be available from imports at least reasonable prices due to the orientation of most of the world's investment goods industries to high technology, a policy of technology promotion in basic machinery will allow launching the SME sector to increase the local supply of industrial wage goods and at the same time limiting the rate of dependency on imports for employment creation.[70]

Differences between Asian tiger economies demonstrate the importance of the quality of state interventionism in a way already observed in Europe. France had been the leading nation in the 18th century, but fell back in industrial development, first behind Britain and then also Germany.[71] Both countries tried to catch up with the leading industrial nations. Both were successful, but to different degrees. Their rate of overall productivity growth differed and the branches where they acquired comparative advantage were not the same.

France was able to develop state-led high technology industries such as aircraft and computers (the latter at least for some time) and oil production. Germany was more efficient in machinery production, and was able to enlarge her lead after the Second World War to an extent that France lost the capacity to realise expansionary economic policies in the case of state-promoted increases in the rate of investment due to her dependence on machinery imports.[72] Germany's innovation system had been based on the promotion of general skills, France's innovation system had been based on promoting state-owned or state-supported enterprises.[73]

The Asian crisis of 1997 reveals a similar difference between South Korea and Taiwan which was predicted a decade earlier.[74] State-led growth of the Chaebols relied largely on imported technology, so that investment and hence the business cycle became completely dependent on the ups and downs of foreign demand (despite an important share of the domestic market in industrial production). Taiwan developed, with less enterprise-oriented state intervention, a local machinery industry in a rather "chaotic" manner, so that even industrial norms had for a long time not been introduced.[75] But this industry constitutes the basis for Taiwan's capacity to cope with problems of faltering external demand through employment-creating adjustment. Korea had to accept increasing dependency and further indebtedness.

The example of Taiwan shows how the new opportunities provided by globalisation can best be used. The process of upgrading the technology mix of its exports was characterised by an initially much lower sophistication of technology imported and a greater reliance on local technology. This was accompanied by a pattern of specialisation where low-cost mass consumption goods of an initially low technology level were more important than in the export mix of South Korea. Taiwan was therefore, able to use the combined local and external markets for creating technological efficiency, both markets being supplied to a higher degree than in the case of South Korea by products manufactured with locally produced equipment.

Certain characteristics of the actual globalisation process favour the Taiwanese strategy. Western analyses focus on the implications of the globalisation process for the possibilities of sheltering their labour from low-cost competition through increasing the share of so-called high technology products in their export mixes. The new competitiveness of Third World production sites, however, is not the result of real wage differences but of differences in international labour costs, which are determined by exchange rates. High international labour costs in the ILCs indicate a high exchange rate, which can only be the result of high levels of competitiveness in products with high productivity advances in the ILCs in relation to the IBCs. It is not very probable that the entry into new technologies will provide ILCs with productivity advances similar to those which persist in the old high technology branches, where the catching-up IBCs will not achieve comparative advantage because of the effects of disembodied technological progress and even avoid doing so, because they may not be the growth branches of the future.[76]

The low-cost economies enter world competition with low as well as high technology products provided that their productivity lags are less great than in the old high technology branches. The sustainability of this catching up depends on the capacity to devalue, hence to be efficient in the production of wage goods and technology.

Efficiently using the opportunities of globalisation implies the same conditions as the overcoming of marginality, i.e., the creation of a broad innovation system through generalised technological improvement, also in the internal-market-oriented branches, and hence a rise in marginal productivity in all sectors, including agriculture.

Such an interpretation requires a complete revision of the (pre-1998) Frank and Wallerstein models of unequal distribution of opportunities created through the emergence of a world system. It is not the unequal distribution of potentially investible surplus which explains the simultaneous "development of development and development of underdevelopment." Internal structures have an impact on the position in the international division of labour. The mechanism is, however, not based on the capacity to attract investible resources as claimed by Prebisch and, in a more nuanced manner, by Singer.[77] On the contrary, internal structures are the principal mechanism by which the orientation of the use of surplus – which is available in most economies (even the ones characterised by marginal product being lower than the costs of reproduction) – is determined. It may be channelled into cost efficient and therefore profitable investment to an extent where other forms of surplus appropriation (rent) are clearly put under political control of capital and labour, but will not be chanelled so just because it is available.

If societies of different types interact – in our case societies where this process of orienting the productive potential to mass consumption has got started and societies where this process could not get under way – even initial technological backwardness will provide the mass-consumption-oriented society with opportunities to draw advantage from foreign trade for its technical advance.

In the Indo-European relationship, this process was embedded in the more visible process of a struggle over financial resources. This struggle, however, was in itself not conducive to unequal development. Whether the nabobs built their palaces in India or in England had no effect for the Industrial Revolution in Britain. Their spending on political power in Britain even contributed to weaken the power of labour there. Popular movements were consequently directed against them as part of the monopolies.

The poorer nation had an advantage in military technology due to the importance of metallurgy and mechanics in mass-oriented manufacturing. There is a superficial parallel here to the military superiority of more egalitarian nomadic societies over highly stratified sedentary societies, which over many centuries led to the permanent invasions of highly developed tributary modes of production by nomads (the Arabs of the 7th century, the Mongols of the 13th century, and even the Mughal take-over of India). The parallelism stops here, because the nomads could not transform their greater military power into comparative advantage in technology promoting low-quality manufacturing, as did the poor societies of late medieval Europe.

The struggle over the surplus, the so-called drain of India, is the way the privileged strata in both settings imagined their conflicting interests. The real issue, however, was that the English ruling class could not impose lower mass incomes in Britain, whereas it could impose near subsistence or even lower mass incomes in India, either by co-operating with the Indian ruling class or by depriving it of resources, thus forcing this class to increase the rate of exploitation. It has to be admitted that in this struggle the English ruling class had to respect the mass interests in its home society in order to be able to impose itself in

India, although it was also able to draw on resources in India for that purpose.

Globalisation with the possibility of transforming comparative advantage in old labour-intensive production as well as in high technology production lines into new cost competitiveness shifts such opportunities at the economic (not the military) level to the until now disadvantaged IBCs. The East and Southeast Asian tigers have shown that development on the basis of unequal exchange and perhaps even declining terms of trade is possible, provided that the type of specialisation favours learning in skills and technologies. The successful ones among the newly industrialising countries demonstrate that learning and skill promotion can be greatly enhanced if the export drive is combined with increasing local mass markets. Like in the European case, it is the internal structure which explains why Taiwan and even South Korea have succeeded where the Philippines have failed (at least until now). Exploiting the new opportunities provided by globalisation depends on the state's capacity to integrate the export sector into the transformation of its own economy and society to (welfare) capitalism. This requires additional efforts, as the export sector by itself is not large enough to effect this transformation alone (with the exception of the city-states such as Hong Kong or Singapore). Such internal efforts ultimately consist in the taming of rent, which inevitably continues to exist or even emerges in the case of marginality-ridden and/or devaluation-driven export-led economies. The taming of rent is always dependent on political power and hence on power relations between social groups.

One problem of my analysis with the (pre-1998) Frank-Wallerstein formulation of the mechanisms which determine the behaviour of the world system consists in the utopian character of their alternative. They admit social movements as being progressive only if they are anti-systematic. By definition, such movements cannot develop a piecemeal strategy as presented here. Such a strategy, however, is essential for overcoming marginality through taming the rent, especially as market competition is a very powerful instrument for limiting rents provided that the macroeconomic and macropolitical framework is "favourable."

The problem of my analysis with the Washington Consensus consists precisely in the political character of this framework. Market regulation and hence deregulation are not sufficient for taming the rent.

The Washington Consensus does not take into account the at least initially low bargaining power of labour as long as there is marginality.

The theoretical thrust of my contribution is obviously to demonstrate that market mechanisms can be used for overcoming marginality provided that they are complemented by judicious forms of non-market measures.

Potential political and social bases for such strategies can be seen in the new social movements which are labelled as the third wave of democratisation or the emerging local civil societies in the IBCs. With the historical failure of really existing socialism to promote the growth of productive forces, these movements avoid an ideological commitment to precise economic doctrines. One of their social bases are middle strata which can no longer be co-opted into the economically and politically declining state-classes because of resource scarcity.[78] They are anti-statist because the state appears as a rapacious fisk, but not clearly committed to the Washington Consensus. They are in favour of property rights, and can use both elements in their attempt to capture the poor by valorising traditional values; e.g., religion.

But the same strata are also the basis of recruitment for NGOs and other voluntary agencies which are committed to the economic improvement of the poor by rather direct assistance. They are for something "new", but their project lacks precision. Parts of their middle class social basis even support the rejection of the importance of economics, under the pretext of the necessity to return to authenticity. The other basis for these new movements are the poor and marginalised ones. They no longer trust in great designs or movements which they cannot control. They have been promised improvements for too long, which have only ended up in repression or corruption. Thus, their social practice is of a piecemeal and local character.

They will be able to adhere to larger perspectives only if this piecemeal and local character of their social praxis becomes a constituent part of such a greater design. The fundamentally complex character of the theoretical argument, parts of which have been developed in this paper, might hopefully contribute to the discussion of a complex perspective against simplistic statist or free market orthodoxies.

Will the new social movements which claim to establish democracy and autonomous civil societies despite persisting economic dominance of rent be able to keep ahead of the economic bases in place, and develop a complex perspective of overcoming marginality where eclectic piecemeal reforms combine with synergetic effects? This can only come about as the result of an intellectual struggle over such perspectives.[79]

The outcome of this struggle is, however, influenced by the possibilities of rapidly increasing employment in the technically backward underdeveloped economies also through exports. It is admitted that the export drive will not suffice for creating full employment in economies like India and China or even Bangladesh. It can, however, decisively contribute to triggering off multiplier effects, as was the case for Germany and Japan following World War II. In order to provide such incentives for growth for the catching-up economies of today's South, the ILCs should enlarge their markets through real wage increases, and keep them open.

Whenever marginality is decisively reduced in the catching-up economies and labour becomes scarce, labour engages in struggles over distribution.[80] The social structure becomes less and less determined by vertical ties of patronage, which are the political result of the predominance of rent (much less of cultural heritage).[81] Instead, entrepreneurs and labour can develop their independence on the basis of outlets and booming investment. Entrepreneurs earn profits on the basis of demand-determined net investment spending. Labour achieves independence from rentiers because of its scarcity.

If Europe is interested in engaging in preferential relations with India, it should not align with the Washington Consensus in trying to impose export-orientation with deregulation, but should admit the necessity of more export-orientation and of state-led measures for social reform and technical improvement in South Asia. Otherwise, it will import the rent structures of the South and maintain them in the underdeveloped world.[82]

References

1. Tzannatos, P. Zafiris: *International Competitiveness in East Asian Manufacturing: Unit Labor Cost Analysis for Selected Countries* (Washington: World Bank, 1997).
2. Elsenhans, Hartmut: "Globalization or Dutch Disease: Its Political and Social Consequences", in: Singer, Sir Hans W.; Hatti,

Neelambar; Tandon, Rameshwar (eds.): *New World Order Series, Volume 16: Technology Diffusion in Third World Contents* (New Delhi: D.K.Publishers, 1999); 458. Elsenhans, Hartmut: "Globalisation: Myths and Real Challenges", *Journal of the Third World Spectrum*, 4, 2 (Autumn 1997); pp. 1-22.

3. Elsenhans, Hartmut: "Social Consequences of the NIEO. Structural Change in the Periphery as Precondition for Continual Reforms in the Centre", in: Jahn, Egbert; Sakamoto, Yoshikazu (eds.): *Elements of World Instability: Armaments, Communication, Food, International Division of Labour* (Frankfort on the Main; New York: Campus, 1981); p. 86-95. Elsenhans, Hartmut: "Absorbing Global Surplus Labor", *Annals of the American Academy of Political and Social Science*, 492 (July 1987); pp. 124-135.
4. On the importance of exchange rates for the cost of labour: Golub, Stephen S.: "Comparative Advantage, Exchange Rates, and Sectoral Trade Balances of Major Industrial Countries", *IMF Staff Papers*, 41, 2 (June 1994); p. 307. Klein, Michael W.; Rosengreen, Eric: "The Real Exchange Rate and Foreign Direct Investment in the United States. Relative Wealth vs. Relative Wage Effects", *Journal of International Economics*, 36, 3/4 (May 1994); p. 379. Givens, W. L.: "Economic Cocaine. America's Exchange Rate Addiction", *Foreign Affairs*, 74, 17 (July/August 1995); pp. 17-22. Papadakis, Maria: "Did (or Does) the United States Have a Competivity Crisis", *Journal of Policy Analysis and Management*, 13, 1 (Winter 1994); pp. 1-20. Bortho, Andrea: "Was Japanese Growth Export-Led", *Oxford Economic Papers*, 48, 3 (July 1996); p. 426. Flassbeck, Heiner: "Standort Deutschland in Gefahr", *Vorwärts*, 11 (1995); p. 18-19. Mundorf, Hans: "Die realen Nettolöhne sind nicht zu hoch", *Handelsblatt* (29. August 1995); p. 2. Neuthinger, Egon: "Germany's Enduring Current Account Surplus", *Intereconomics*, 24, 3 (May/June 1989); pp. 138-148. Hence exchange rates do not necessarily correspond to purchasing power parity: Chen, Haichun; Gordon, M.J.; Yan, Zhiming: "The Real Income and Consumption of an Urban Chinese Family", *Journal of Development Studies*, 31, 1 (October 1994); pp. 201-213. Yotopoulos, Pan A.; Lin, Jenu-Yih: "Purchasing Power Parities for Taiwan: The Basic Data for 1985 and International Comparisons", *Journal of Economic Development*, 18, 1 (June 1993); p. 11.

Guillaumont-Jeanneney, Sylviane; Hua, Ping: "Politique du change et développement des exportations manufacturées en Chine", *Revue économique*, 47, 3 (May 1996); pp. 851-860. Shinohara, Miyohei: "Trends and Dynamics of East and Southeast Asian Economies", *Asian Development Review*, 3, 1 (1985); p. 59. Park, Chong-Min: *The Nature and Sources of Political Discontent in Democratizing Korea* (Seoul: International Political Science Association, August 1997); p. 16. Lafay, Gèrard: "Les origines internationales du chômage européen", *Revue d'Economie Politique*, 106, 6 (November/December 1996); pp. 948; 963. Narrasiguin, Philippe: "Croissance tirèe par les exportations et politique de change: Le cas de l'île Maurice", *Revue d'Economie Politique*, 105, 2 (March/April 1995); p. 325.

5. Elsenhans, Hartmut: "Option export-led et structures rentières dans les pays du sud de la Méditerranée", Sid Ahmed, Abdelkader (ed.): *Économies du Maghreb: L'impératif de Barcelone* (Paris: CNRS Editions, 1998); pp. 280-282. Elsenhans, Hartmut: "Globalisation and the European Integration Process", *International Studies,* Vol. 36, No 3, (New Delhi), (July - Sept. 1999) pp. 217-52.
6. Cf. for a critique of Emmanuel's unequal exchange theory and its implications for growth: Suh, Suk Tai: "The Theory of Unequal Exchange and the Developing Countries", Kim, Kyong Dong (ed.): *Dependency Issues in Korean Development. Comparative Perspectives* (Seoul: Seoul National University Press, 1987); p. 111.
7. Frank, André Gunder: "The Development of Underdevelopment", *Monthly Review*, 18, 4 (September 1966); pp. 17-31. Wallerstein, Immanuel Maurice: *The Capitalist World Economy* (Cambridge: Cambridge University Press, 1979); pp. 69-70.
8. This point will not be developed here, cf. Elsenhans, Hartmut: "Discourse on Economic Globalization vs. Problems of Marginality", *Journal of the Third World Spectrum*, 5, 1 (Spring 1998); pp. 1-22.
9. Elsenhans, Hartmut: "Égalité et développement. L'experience européenne et le monde sous-développé d'aujourd'hui", *Cultures et développement*, 15, 2 (1983); pp. 187-216. Elsenhans, Hartmut: "Rising Mass Incomes as a Condition of Capitalist Growth:Implications for the World Economy", *International Organization*, 37, 1 (Winter 1983); pp. 1-38. Elsenhans, Hartmut:

"Grundlagen der Entwicklung der kapitalistischen Weltwirtschaft", in: Senghaas, Dieter (ed.): *Kapitalistische Weltökonomie. Kontroversen über ihren Ursprung und ihre Entwicklungsdynamik* (Frankfort on the Main: Suhrkamp, 1979); pp. 101-148. Elsenhans, Hartmut: "Foundation of Development of the Capitalist World Economy", Elsenhans, Hartmut: *Equality and Development* (Dhaka: Center for Social Studies, 1992); pp. 21-79.

10. Kregel, Jan A.: *Rate of Profit, Distribution and Growth. Two Views* (London: Macmillan, 1971); pp. 145-147. Robinson, Joan Violet: *Collected Economic Papers* (Oxford: Basil Blackwell, 1951); p. 174.
11. Luxemburg, Rosa: *Die Akkumulation des Kapitals. Ein Beitrag zur ákonomischen Erklórung des Imperialismus* (Berlin: Vereinigung internationaler Verlagsanstalten, 1923); pp. 97-107.
12. Bortkiewicz, L. von: "Wertrechnung und Preisrechnung im Marxschen System, 3. Teil", *Archiv für Sozialwissenschaft und Sozialpolitik,* 25, 2 (1907); pp. 451-466. Rediscovery: Okishio, Nobou: "Technical Changes and the Rate of Profit", *Kobe University Economic Review,* 7 (1961); pp. 85-90. Further references: Elsenhans, Hartmut: "A Welfare Capitalist World System or the Feudalisation of the Global System", Babu Ramesh (ed.): *Changing Global Political/Ideological Context and Afro-Asia. Strategies for Development* (New Delhi: South Asian Publishers, 1996); pp. 60-104.
13. Sen, Amartya Kumar: *Poverty and Famines. An Essay on Entitlement and Deprivation* (Oxford: Clarendon, 1981); esp. p. 162.
14. Hirschman, Albert O.: *Exit, Voice, and Loyalty. Responses to Decline in Firms, Organization, and States* (Cambridge, Mass.; London: Harvard University Press, 1970); pp. 3-19.
15. Elsenhans, Hartmut: "The Relevance of the Principles of Keynesian Economics for the Transition to Capitalism in Today's Underdeveloped World", Davidson, Paul; Kregel, Jan A.(eds.): *Improving the Global Economy. Keynesianism and the Growth in Output and Employment* (Cheltenham: Edward Elgarm 1997); p. 285.
16. This is the often voiced criticism against the applicability of Keynesian economics to typical Third World situations. Cf. Vakil,

C.N.; Brahmananda, P.R.: *Planning for an Expanding Economy: Accumulation, Employment and Technical Progress in Underdeveloped Countries* (Bombay: Vera, 1956); p.219. Ardant, Gabriel: "Financial Policy and Economic Infrastructure of Modern States and Nations", Tilly, Charles (ed.): *The Formation of National States in Western Europe* (Princeton, N.J.: Princeton University Press, 1975); p.239. Raup, Philip M.: "Land Reform and Agricultural Development", Southworth, Herman M.; Johanston, Bruce F.(eds.): *Agricultural Development and Economic Growth* (Ithaca, N.Y.: Cornell University Press, 1967); p.275.

17. Elsenhans, Hartmut: "Rent, State and the Market: The Political Economy of the Transition to Self-sustained Capitalism", Pakistan Development Review, 33, 4 (December 1994); pp.393-405. Elsenhans, Hartmut: "Úberwindung von Marginalitát als Gegenstand der Armutsbekámpfung", Schafer, Hans Bernd (ed.): *Bevólkerungsdynamik und Grundbedúrfnisse in Entwicklungsländern. Schriften des Vereins fur Socialpolitik, Bd. 241* (Berlin: Duncker & Humblot, 1995); pp. 194-204; Elsenhans, Hartmut: "Die Rente und der Úbergang zum Kapitalismus. Grundfragen der politischen Ókonomie von Unterentwicklung", in: *Journal fur Entwicklungspolitik,* 8, 2 (1992); pp. 111-134. Elsenhans, Hartmut: "Rent and the Transition to Capitalism", *Asien-Afrika-Lateinamerika,* 25,6(1997); pp. 653-667.

18. Elsenhans, Hartmut: "Egalitarisme social comme condition du développement économique", *Cahiers du CREAD,* 7(1987); pp. 91-128. Elsenhans, Hartmut: "Overcoming Underdevelopment Through Mass Production for Mass Consumption: Evolution of A New Development Concept", in: Elsenhans, Hartmut: *Equality and Development* (Dhaka: Center for Social Studies, 1992); pp. 80-129. Elsenhans, Hartmut: "Overcoming Underdevelopment. A Research Paradigm", *Journal of Peace Research,* 12, 4 (December 1975); pp. 293-313. Elsenhans, Hartmut: "State and the Market in Economic Development, in: Weiland, Heribert; Braham, Matthew (eds.): *Towards a New South African Economy: Comparative Perspectives* (Freiburg: Arnold-Bergstraesser Institut, 1992); pp. 3-34. Elsenhans, Harmut: "Growth and Income Distribution: Theory and Experience", in: Kurth, Helmut (ed.):

Economic Growth and Income Distribution (Quezon City, Philippines: Moed Press, 1989); pp. 14-54.

19. Crafts, Nicholas: "The First Industrial Revolution. A Guided for Economists", *American Econimic Review,* 86, 2 (May 1996); pp. 192-206. Elsenhans, Hartmut: *Est-ce que la théorie de la croissance endogéne implique vraiment un changement radical de la théorie du développement et du commerce international* (Sfax: Groupes de Recherches Interdisciplinaire sur la Méditerranée, May 1998); Elsenhans, Hartmut: *Political Economy or Economic Politics? The Prospects of Civil Society in an Era of Globalization, Indian Journal of Public Administration* 46, 4 (October-December 2000), fourthcoming
20. Elsenhans, Hartmut: "Eklektizismus zur Erreichung von Koharenz. Die Theorie der Rente und ihre Implikationen fur das Zusammenwirken ókonomischen, politischen und sozialen Engineering in der Entwicklungspolitik", in: Kappel, Robert (ed.): *Weltwirtschaft und Armut* (Hamburg: Deutsches Úbersee-Institut, 1997); pp. 19-28. Elsenhans, art. cit. fn 15, pp. 294-297. Elsenhans, Hartmut: "Empowering the Poor for Succeeding in Liberalisation", in: *Indian Journal of Public Administration,* 42, 2 (July/September 1996); pp. 302-308. Elsenhans, Hartmut: "Myth of Globalisation and Necessity of Development Politics", *International Studies,* 33, 3 (1996); pp. 255-272.
21. Feder, Ernest: "The Latifundia Puzzle of Professor Schultz; Comment", *Journal of Farm Economics*, 49, 2 (May 1967); pp. 507-511. Sternberg, Marvin J.: "Agrarian Reform and Employment, with Special Reference to Latin America", *International Labour Review*, 95, 1/2 (January/February 1967); p. 12.
22. Dandekar, V.M.: "Economic Theory and Agrarian Reform", *Oxford Economic Papers*, 14, 1 (February 1962); pp. 69-80. Sen, Amartya Kumar: "Peasants and Dualism with or without Surplus Labour", *Journal of Political Economy*, 74, 5 (October 1966); pp. 427-450.
23. Elsenhans 1994, art. cit. fn. 17, p. 395. Elsenhans 1995, art. cit. fn. 17, p. 195.
24. Elsenhans, Hartmut : "Die Rolle internationaler Entwicklungszusammenarbeit unter veränderten wirtschaftlichen

und gesellschaftsstrukturellen Rahmenbedingungen", in: Barsch, Dietrich; Karrasch, Heinz (eds.): *Die Dritte Welt im Rahmen weltpolitischer und weltwirtschaftlicher Neuordnung* (Stuttgart: Franz Steiner, 1995); pp. 141-145.

25. Schäfer, Hans-Bernd: *Landwirtschaftliche Akkumulationslasten und industrielle Entwicklung: Analyse und Beschreibung entwicklungspolitischer Optionen in dualistischen Wirtschaften* (Berlin; Heidelberg; New York: Springer Verlag, 1983); pp. 23-30.

26. Ibn Khaldûn, Abd-al-Rahman: *Discours sur l'Histoire universelle. Al-Muqaddima. Traduction nouvelle, préface et notes par Vincent Monteil* (Paris: Sindbad, 1967); pp. 570-571, pp. 599-606. Reischauer, Edwin O.; Fairbank, John K.: *East Asia. The Great Tradition* (Boston, Mass.: Houghton Mifflin, 1960); p. 117. Wakeman, Frederic: "Rebellion and Revolution: The Study of Popular Movements in Chinese History", *Journal of Asian Studies*, 36, 2 (February 1977); pp. 204 ff. Skinner, G. William: "Chinese Peasants and the Closed Community: An Open and Shut Case", *Comparative Studies in Society and History*, 13, 3 (July 1971); p. 273. Usher, Dan: "The Dynastic Cycle and the Stationary State", *American Economic Review*, 79, 4 (December 1989); p. 1044.

27. Achilles, Walter: "Die Auswirkungen der Getreidepreissteigerungen gegen Ende des 18.Jh. auf das Realeinkommen von Erzeuger und Verbraucher", in: Bog, Ingomar et al. (ed.): *Wirtschaftliche und soziale Strukturen im säkularen Wandel. Festschrift für Wilhelm Abel zum 70. Geburtstag* (Hanover: M. & H. Schaper, 1974); p. 124. Saalfeld, Diedrich: "Ländliche Bevölkerung und Landwirtschaft Deutschlands am Vorabend der Französischen Revolution", *Zeitschrift für Agrargeschichte und Agrarsoziologie*, 37, 2 (1989); pp. 117-123. Saalfeld, Diedrich: "Die Wandlungen der Preis- und Lohnstruktur während des 16. Jahrhunderts in Deutschland", in: Fischer, Wolfram (ed.): *Beiträge zu Wirtschaftswachstum und Wirtschaftsstruktur im 16. und 19. Jahrhundert* (Berlin: Duncker & Humblot, 1971); pp. 10 f. Tucker, Rufus S.: "Real Wages of Artisans in London, 1729-1935", *Journal of the American Statistical Association*, 31, 1 (1936); p. 81. Rioux, Jean-Pierre: *La révolution industrielle 1780-1880* (Paris: Seuil, 1971); p. 144. Bog, Igomar: "Das Konsumzentrum

London und seine Versorgung", in: Abel, Wilhelm; Borchardt, Knut; Kellenbenz, Hermann (eds.): *Wirtschaft, Geschichte und Wirtschaftsgeschichte* (Stuttgart: Gustav Fischer, 1966); p. 144.

28. Tokman, Victor E.: "Una exploración sobre la naturaleza de las interrelaciones entre los sectores informal y formal", in: Klein, Emilio;Tokman, Victor E. (eds.): *El subempleo en América Latina* (Buenos Aires: El Cid, 1979); p. 203-242. Mettelin, Pierre: "Petite production marchande et activités informelles urbaines en Afrique noire", in: *Cultures et développement*, 17, 1 (1985); p. 3-27. Sethuraman, S. V.: "The Role of the Urban Informal Sector", in: Sethuraman, S.V. (ed.): *The Urban Informal Sector in Developing Countries. Employment, Poverty and Environment* (Geneva: International Labour Office, 1981); p. 33. Lewin, A.C.: "The Dialectics of Dominance: Petty Production and Peripheral Capitalism", in: Bromley, Ray (ed.): *Planning for Small Enterprises in Third World Cities* (Oxford et al.: Pergamon Press, 1985); p. 109. Schmitz, Hubert: "Growth Constraints on Small-Scale Manufacturing in Developing Countries. A Critical Review", *World Development*, 10, 6 (June 1982); p. 432.
29. Frank's observation that Europe experienced less demographic growth than Asia does not address the explanatory variable but the result of different pre-capitalist economic and social structures. He is still caught in his idea about surplus being important for growth. Frank, André Gunder: *ReOrient. Global Economy in the Asian Age* (Berkeley et al.: University of California Press, 1998); p. 109.
30. As an example cf. Barg, M.A.: "Die Arbeitsproduktivität im England des 11. bis 13. Jahrhunderts", *Jahrbuch für Wirtschaftsgeschichte*, 2 (1974); p 178, who considers internal colonisation as a source for the increase in European medieval agriculture.
31. Braudel, Fernand: *La Méditerranée et le monde méditerranéen à l'époque de Philippe II* (Paris: Armand Colin, 1966); Vol 1, p. 67, insists on relatively free access to land in the Northern and Central parts of Medieval Europe as compared to Southern Europe.
32. Laroui, Abdallah: *Histoire du Maghreb. Un essai de synthèse* (Paris: Maspéro, 1970); pp. 225; 241. Lacoste, Yves: *Ibn Khaldoun. Naissance de l'histoire passée du tiers monde* (Paris: Maspéro, 1973); 267 p. Vielle, Paul: "The State of the Periphery

and Its Heritage", *Economy and Society*, 17, 1 (February 1988); p. 52-89. Lacoste, Yves: "De l'Antiquité à la colonisation: une histoire movementée", in: Lacoste, Camille/Lacoste, Yves (eds.): *L'Etat du Maghreb* (Paris: La Découverte, 1991); p. 46.

33. Myint, Hla: *Economic Theory and the Underdeveloped Countries* (London: Oxford University Press, 1971); pp. 130 ff.

34. Eley, Geoff: "The Social History of Industrialization: 'Proto-Industry' and the Origins of Capitalism", *Economy and Society*, 13, 4 (November 1984); pp. 519-539. Kriedte, Peter; Medick, Hans; Schlumbohm, Jürgen: "Proto-Industrialization on Test with the Guild of Historians: Response to Some Critics", *Economy and Society*, 15, 2 (May 1986); pp. 254-272. Kriedte, Peter; Medick, Hans; Schlumbohm, Jürgen: *Industrialisierung vor der Industrialisierung. Gewerbliche Warenproduktion auf dem Land in der Formationsperiode des Kapitalismus* (Göttingen: Vandenhoeck & Ruprecht, 1977). Kriedte, Peter: *Spätfeudalismus und Handelskapital. Grundlinien der europäischen Wirtschaftsgeschichte vom 16. bis zum Ausgang des 18. Jahrhunderts* (Göttingen: Vandenhoeck & Ruprecht, 1980). Jeannin, Pierre: "La protoindustrialisation: Développement ou impasse", *Annales E.S.C.*, 35, 1 (January/February 1980); pp. 52-65. Coleman, D.C.: "Proto-Industrialization. A Concept Too Many", *Economic History Review*, 36, 3 (August 1983); pp. 435-448. Mendels, Franklin F.: "Agriculture and Peasant Industry in Eighteenth-Century Flanders", in: Parker, William N.; Jones, Eric L. (eds.): *European Peasants and Their Markets. Essays in Agrarian Economic History* (Princeton, N.J.: Princeton University Press, 1975); pp. 179-204.

35. On Indian textile production and trade cf. the recent contribution of Hall, Kenneth R.: "The Textile Industry in Southeast Asia 1400-1800", *Journal of the Economic and Social History of the Orient*, 39, 2 (May 1996); pp. 87-135.

36. Heckscher, Eli F.: "The Aspects of Economic History", in: *Essays in Honour of Gustav Cassel* (London: Allen & Unwin, 1933); p. 729. Weatherhill, Lorna: *Consumer Behaviour and Material Culture in Britain, 1660-1760* (London; New York: Routledge, 1988); pp. 169-171. Nef, John U.: *Cultural Foundations of Industrial Civilization* (Cambridge: Cambridge University Press,

1958); p. 131. Brady, Dorothy: "Relative Prices in the Nineteenth Century", *Journal of Economic History*, 24, 2 (June 1964); p. 177. Williamson, Harold F.: "Mass Production, Mass Consumption, and American Industrial Development", in: Braudel, Fernand; Postan, Moisei M.; Söderlund, E. (eds.): *Première Conférence Internationale d'Histoire Economique* (Paris; The Hague: Mouton, 1960); p. 144. Bolino, August C.: "British and American Horology: A Comment on Hoke", *Journal of Economic History*, 48, 3 (September 1988); p. 667. Cochran, Thomas C.: *Business in American Life. A History* (New York: Mac Graw-Hill, 1972); p. 14.

37. This is formalised in a model by Patnaik, Prabhat; Ghosh, Jayati: "De-Industrialisation without an Import Surplus: A Theoretical Note in the Context of a Stylised Colonial Economy", *Economic and Political Weekly*, 26, 11/12 (March 1991); pp. 649-654.

38. Dutt, Amitava Krishna: "The Origins of Uneven Development: The Indian Subcontinent", *American Economic Review*, 82, 2 (May 1992); p. 145. Bagchi, Amiya Kumar: "De-industrialization in India in the Nineteenth Century: Some Theoretical Implications", *Journal of Development Studies*, 12, 2 (January 1976); pp. 135-164. Wolcott, Susan: "British Myopia and the Collapse of Indian Textile Demand", *Journal of Economic History*, 51, 2 (June 1991); pp. 367-384. Krishnamurty, J.: "Deindustrialization in Gangetic Bihar During the 19th Century: Another Look at Evidence", *Indian Economic and Social History Review*, 22, 4 (October 1985); pp. 399-416. Harnetty, Peter: "'Deindustrialization' Revisited: The Handloom Weavers of the Central Provinces of India c. 1800-1947", *Modern Asian Studies*, 25, 3 (August 1991); pp. 455-510. Sarkar, Prabirjit: "Deindustrialization Through Colonial Trade", *Journal of Contemporary Asia*, 22, 3 (1992); pp. 297-302. Chattopadhyay, Raghabendra: "Deindustrialisation in India Reconsidered", *Economic and Political Weekly*, 10, 12 (22 March 1975); pp. 523-531.

39. Ghosh, Jayati: "The Determination of Land Rent in a Non-capitalist Agriculture: North India 1860-1930", *Modern Asian Studies*, 22, 2 (May 1988); p. 380. Chaudhuri, Binay Bushan: "Growth of Commercial Agriculture", *Indian Economic and Social History Review*, 7, 2 (June 1970); p. 214. Sen Gupta, Kalyan Kumar: *Pabna Disturbances and the Politics of Rent 1873-1885* (New Delhi:

People's Publishing House, 1974); p. 74. Migdal, Joel S.: *Peasants, Politics and Revolution: Pressures Toward Political and Social Change in the Third World* (Princeton, N.J.: Princeton University Press, 1974); p. 164. Cf. also Fei, Hsiao-tung: *Peasant Life in China. A Field Study of Country Life in the Yangtze Valley* (London: Routledge & Kegan Paul, 1939); p. 280.

40. Frank has now abandoned his original theoretical design: Asia lost because of "polarized income distributions, [...] constrained effective demand for mass consumer goods". He barely saves the old pardigm in claiming that, by his own model, Asia was superior, and explains the rising mass incomes in the West by slower demographic growth. Whether this is true is not examined in his book, because differences in demographic growth rates do not establish the scarcity of labour. Otherwise, sub-Saharan Africa would have been the winner. Frank, op. cit. fn. 30; p. 301. He does not even quote Emmanuel, Arghiri: *L'échange inégal. Essai sur les antagonismes dans les rapports économiques internationaux* (Paris: Maspéro, 1969); p. 304, whom he follows, nor the texts in fn. 3, where the argument had been developed eighteen years ago.

41. Davey, Brian: *The Economic Development of India* (Nottingham: Spokesman Books, 1975); p. 44.

42. Elsenhans 1997, art. cit. fn. 20, pp. 19-35. Elsenhans, Hartmut: "Kein Ende der großen Theorie", *Asien-Afrika-Lateinamerika*, 24, 2 (1996); pp. 126-134. Elsenhans 1996 Myth, art. cit. fn. 20 pp. 255-272.

43. Dandekar, V.M.: "Unemployment and Imbalances in the Economy. Leaflet of Forum of Free Enterprise", *Artha Vijanaa*, 14, 4 (December 1972); p. 22.

44. On the difficulties to distinguish rent and tax in precapitalist structures. Neale, Walter: "Reciprocity and Redistribution in the Indian Village: Sequel to Some Notable Discussions", in: Polanyi, Karl; et al. (eds.): *Trade and Market in the Early Empires* (New York: Free Press, 1965); p. 231. Cf. also Riggs, Fred W.: *Administration in Developing Countries. The Theory of Prismatic Society* (Boston, Mass.: Houghton Mifflin, 1964); p. 6.

45. Elsenhans, Hartmut: "The Great Depression of the 1930s and the Third World", *International Studies*, 28, 3 (1991); pp. 273-280. Elsenhans, Hartmut: "Decolonisation: From the Failure of the

Colonial Export Economies to the Decline of Westernised State Classes", *The Maghreb Review*, 19, 1/2 (1994); pp. 98-101.

46. Tyabji, Nasir: "State Aid to Industry: Madras 1921-1937", *Economic and Political Weekly*, 23, 31 (20 July 1988); pp. PE52-PE58. Chattopadhyay, Raghabendra: "An Early British Government Initiative in the Genesis of Indian Planning", *Economic and Political Weekly*, 22, 5 (31 January 1987); pp. PE19-PE30. Malmsten, Neal R.: "British Government Policy Toward Colonial Development, 1919-1939", *Journal of Modern History*, 49, 2 (1977); p. D1269. Smith, Tony: "Changing Configurations of Power in North-South Relations", *International Organization*, 31, 1 (Winter 1977); pp. 1-27. Elsenhans, Hartmut: *Frankreichs Algerienkrieg 1954-1962. Entkolonialisierungsversuch einer kapitalistischen Metropole. Zum Zusammenbruch der Kolonialreiche* (Munich: Carl Hanser, 1974); pp. 285-292. Tomlinson, B. R.: "The Contradiction of England: National Decline and the Loss of Empire", *Journal of Imperial and Commonwealth History*, 11, 1 (1982); p. 70. Gordon, David F.: *Decolonization and the State in Kenya* (Boulder, Colo.: Westview Press, 1986); p. 38. Onimode, Bade: *Imperialism and Underdevelopment in Nigeria* (London: ZED Books, 1982); pp. 116-118.

47. Cf. fn. 15. Cf. for later formulations: Elsenhans, Hartmut: "Staatsklassen", in: Schulz, Manfred (ed.): *Entwicklung, die Perspektive der Entwicklungssoziologie* (Cologne; Opladen: Westdeutscher Verlag, 1997); pp. 161-185. Elsenhans, Hartmut: "Third World Development State in Crisis and the Crisis of Mainstream Development Theory", *Journal of Social Studies*, 70 (October 1995); pp. 22-28. Elsenhans, Hartmut: "The Crisis of the Development State and the New International System", *Foreign Trade Review*, 29, 1 (April/June 1994); pp. 66-68. Elsenhans, Hartmut: "Die Krise des Staats in der Dritten Welt: Der Übergang zur Demokratie oder etwas 'anderes'. Festschrift für Wilfried Röhrich ", in: Schlüter-Knauer, Carsten; Krohn, Axel (eds.): *Die Demokratie überdenken* (Baden-Baden: Duncker & Humblot, 1997); pp. 325-344.

48. Elsenhans, Hartmut: "Dependencia, Underdevelopment and the Third World State", *Law and State*, 36 (1987); pp. 83-86.

Elsenhans, Hartmut: "Le problème de la libéralisation dans les pays à forte planification, illustré par les changements les plus récents en Algérie", in: Heintz, Peter (ed.): *Endogene Entwicklung: Wirklichkeit und Ideologie* (Diessenhofen, Schweiz: Rüegger, 1983); pp. 136-142.

49. Elsenhans, Hartmut: "Globalisation: Myths and Real Challenges", *Journal of the Third World Spectrum*, 4, 2 (Autumn 1997); pp. 1-4. Cf. also: Golub, art. cit. fn. 4; p. 302. Yotopoulos, art. cit. fn. 4; p. 11. Chen, art. cit. fn. 4; p. 211.

50. They only have to be higher than the costs of imported inputs. From this, the model can be enlarged by introducing the possibilities of substituting imported inputs. In this case, it can be shown that the possibilities of further devaluation depend on providing increasing shares of equipment from local production at any level of its local costs, concentrating imports on core parts of the technology used. Efficient rent appropriation and rent allocation becomes a condition for fulfilling the requirements of the Washington Consensus also with respect to investment goods production. Cf. Elsenhans Hartmut: *Rent and Technology Distortion: The Two Cul-de-Sac of State Correction and Market Orientations, Journal of Third World Studies,* 6, 1 (Automn 1999), pp. 414.

51. Tzannatos, *op. cit.* fn. 1; pp. 2-3. Chen, art. cit. fn. 4; p. 209. Guillaumont-Jeanneney, art. cit. fn. 4. Yotopoulos, art. cit. fn 4; p. 11.

52. The argument of Lewis insists on the limits for terms of trade deteriorations in the case of high agricultural productivity hence on a change to inward looking strategies in the case of devaluation. I insist on the possibility of improving economic flexibility based on the capacity to devalue. Lewis refers to average productivity. I refer to marginal productivity in order to raise average productivity. Cf., Lewis, William A.: *The Evolution of the International Economic Order* (Princeton, N.J.: Princeton University Press, 1978); pp. 16-19.

53. Luh, Yir-Hueih; Stefanou, Spiro E.: "Productivity Growth in U.S. Agriculture Under Dynamic Adjustment", *American Journal of Agricultural Economics*, 73, 4 (November 1991); pp. 1116-1123. Grigg, David B.: "The Agricultural Revolution in Western Europe", in: Bayliss-Smith, Tim P.; Wanmali, Sudhir (eds.): *Understanding Green Revolutions. Agrarian Change and Development Planning*

in South Asia (Cambridge: Cambridge University Press, 1984); pp. 12-14.

54. Elsenhans, Hartmut: "Agrarverfassung, Akkumulationsprozeß, Demokratisierung", in: Elsenhans, Hartmut (ed.): *Agrarreform in der Dritten Welt* (Frankfort on the Main/New York: Campus, 1979); pp.557-559. Janvry, Alain de: "The Role of Land Reform in Economic Development: Policies and Politics", *American Journal of Agricultural Economics*, 63, 2 (May 1981); pp.384-392. Ip, P.C./Stahl, C.W.: "Systems of Land Tenure. Allocative Efficiency and Economic Development", *American Journal of Agricultural Economics*, 60, 1 (February 1978); pp.23-25. Sternberg, Marvin J.: "Agrarian Reform and Employment: Potential and Problems", *International Labour Review*, 103, 5 (May 1971); p.476. Oshima, Harry T.: "A Strategy for Asian Development", *Economic Development and Cultural Change*, 10, 3 (April 1962); p.303.
55. The exchange rate for their labour in terms of food is determined by the efficiency of marginal work of the more efficient farmer and their own lower one. Suppose the marginal product of the more efficient farmer being y; the labour time required for it would allow him to produce x non-food items, whereas in the time devoted to this production the less efficient farmer could produce z food; $y > z$ holds, and, because the amount of food to be bought by the less efficient farmer is at least as much as he would produce on his farm, $y > x > z$ also holds in monetary terms. Because y is less than the wage rate to be paid for a labourer for this amount of time, wage costs decrease for industry. Elsenhans 1996 Welfare, art. cit; fn. 6; p. 96. Cf. also Dasgupta, Partha; Ray, Debraj: "Inequality as a Determinant of Malnutration and Unemployment", *Economic Journal*, 97, 385 (March 1987); pp. 177-180.
56. Elsenhans, Hartmut: "Englisches Poor Law und egalitäre Agrarreform in der Dritten Welt. Einige Aspekte der Theorie, daß Wachstum historisch die Erweiterung des Massenmarktes erforderte und heute die Erweiterung der Massenmarktes erfordert", *Verfassung und Recht in Übersee*, 13, 4 (1980); pp. 283-318. English translation: Elsenhans, Hartmut: "English Poor Law and Egalitarian Agrarian Reform in the Third World", in: Elsenhans, Hartmut: *Equality and Development* (Dhaka: Center for Social Studies, 1992); pp. 130-162.

57. Hashemi, Syed M.: *NGOs in Bangladesh: Development Alternative or Alternative Rhetoric* (Manchester: University of Manchester, 1990); pp. 66-68. Panda, Binaya Kumar: *Antipoverty Programmes and Political, Social and Economic Changes in Rural Orissa: A Study of the Bhuban Block of Dhenkanal District (1980-1990)* (Bhubaneshwar: Dissertation, 1997); pp. 356-58.
58. Cf. the contributions in Jain, Randhir B. (ed.): *NGOs in Development Perspective* (New Delhi: Friedrich-Ebert-Foundation, 1995). Fisher, Julie: "Is the Iron Law of Oligarchy Rusting Away in the Third World", in: *World Development*, 22, 2 (February 1994); pp. 129-143. Meyer, Carrie A.: "Opportunism and NG0s: Entrepreneurship and Green North-South Transfers", in: *World Development*, 23, 8 (August 1995); p. 1279. Kuhn, Berthold: *Participatory Development and Local Self-Government Reform in Rural India, Case Studies in Rajasthan* (New Delhi: Radiant, 1998); p. 258. Kothari, Rajni: "NGOs, the State and World Capitalism", *Economic and Political Weekly*, 21, 50 (13 December 1986); pp. 2177-2183. Bowden, Peter: "NGOs in Asia: Issues in Development", *Public Administration and Development*, 10, 2 (April/June 1990); pp. 141-152. Neubert, Dieter: *Entwicklungspolitische Hoffnungen und gesellschaftliche Wirklichkeit. Eine vergleichende Länderfallstudie von afrikanischen Nichtregierungsorganisationen in Kenia und Ruanda* (Frankfort on the Main; New York: Campus, 1997); pp. 401-425. Lewis, David J.: "Catalysts for Change? NGOs, Agricultural Technology and the State in Bangladesh", *Journal of Social Studies*, 65 (July 1994); pp. 63-100. Marcussen, Henrik Secher: "NGOs, the State and Civil Society", *Review of African Political Economy*, 24, 69 (1996); p. 420.
59. On Bangladesh, cf., Mushtaque, A.; Chowdhury, R.; Aminul Alam, M.: "Bangladesh: Politics, Development and Perspectives of the Poor", *Journal of Social Studies*, 80 (April 1998); pp. 20-21. Ebdon, Rosamund: "NGO Expansion and the Fight to Reach the Poor: Gender Implications of NGOs Scaling-Up in Bangladesh", *IDS Bulletin*, 26, 3 (July 1995); p. 49-56.
60. Elsenhans, Hartmut: "Problems Central to Economic Policy Deregulation in Bangladesh", *Internationales Asienforum*, 22, 3-4 (November 1991); pp.281-283.

61. Schmitz, Hubert: "Industrialisation Strategies in Less Developed Countries: Some Lessons of Historical Experience", in: Kaplinsky, Raphael; Schmitz, Hubert (eds.): *Third World Industrialisation in the 1980s* (London: Frank Cass, 1984); esp. p. 14.
62. Elsenhans, Hartmut: "Public Administration in Developing Countries: Specificities of the Notions of 'Public' and 'Administration' in Market Regulated Developing and Capitalistic Societies"; *Indian Journal of Public Administration*, 35, 1 (January/March 1989); pp. 22-25.
63. Dollar, David: "Convergence of South Korean Productivity on West German Levels 1966-1978", *World Development*, 19, 2/3 (February/March 1991); p. 268. Chen, Tain-Jy; Tang, De-Piao: "Offshore Assembly and Short-Run-Labor-Labor Substitution", *Weltwirtschaftliches Archiv*, 123, 1 (1987); pp. 140-148. Pilat, Dirk: "Comparative Productivity of Korean Manufacturing, 1967-1987", *Journal of Development Economics*, 46, 1 (February 1995); p. 140. Rasiah, Rajah: *The Export Manufacturing Experience of Indonesia, Malaysia and Thailand: Lessons for Africa. Discussion Paper 137* (Geneva: UNCTAD,June 1998); p. 52f..
64. Leff, Nathaniel H.: "Optimal Investment Choice for Developing Countries. Rational Theory and Rational Decision-Making", *Journal of Development Economics*, 18, 4 (August 1985); p. 347. Paqué, Karl Heinz: "Technologie, Wissen und Wirtschaftspolitik - Zur Rolle des Staates in Theorien des endogenen Wachstums", *Die Weltwirtschaft*, 3 (1995); p. 251. Elsenhans, Hartmut: "La transition à l'économie de marché à partir d'économies sous-développées", *Naqd - Revue d'études et de critique sociale*, 17, 3 (June/November 1992); p. 24.
65. Aoki, Masahiko; Murdock, Kevin; Okuno-Fujiwara, Masahiro: *Beyond the East Asian Miracle. Introducing the Market Enhancing View. CEPR Publication 442* (Stanford: CEPR, 1995). Teranishi, Juro: *Industrial Interests Versus Class Interests. Conflicts over Income Distributions in the Economic Development of Japan and Brazil* (Tokio: International Economic Association, 1996); p. 11.
66. Holtgrave, Wilfried: *Industrialisierung in Singapur. Chancen und Risiken industrieorientierter Spezialisierung* (Frankfort on the

Main; New York: Campus, 1987); pp. 59-81.

67. Mytelka, Lynn Krieger: "The Transfer of Technology: Myth or Reality?", in: Cosgrove, Carol; Jamar, J. (eds.): *The European Community's Development Policy: The Strategies Ahead* (Bruges: De Tempel, 1986); p. 258.
68. Jomo, Kwame Sundaram; Rock, Michael: *Economic Diversification and Primary Commodity Processing in the Second-Tier South-East Asian Newly Industrializing Countries. Discussion Paper 136* (Geneva: UNCTAD,June 1998); p. 12.
69. Mundle, Sudipto: "The Agrarian Barrier to Industrial Growth", *Journal of Development Studies*, 22, 1 (October 1985); p. 67. Dutt, Amitava Krishna: "Stagnation, Income Distribution and the Agrarian Constraint: A Note", *Cambridge Journal of Economics*, 15, 3 (September 1991); p. 348. Storm, Servaas: "On the Role of Agriculture in India's Longer-Term Development Strategy", *Cambridge Journal of Economics*, 19, 6 (December 1995); p. 773. Gray, Patricia; Singer, Hans W.: "Trade Policy and Growth of Developing Countries: Some New Data", *World Development*, 16, 3 (March 1988); pp. 395-403. Hwa, Erh-Cheng: "The Contribution of Agriculture to Economic Growth: Some Empirical Evidence", *World Development*, 16, 11 (November 1988); p. 1337. Grabowski, Richard: "Economic Development and the Traditional Sector: A Comparison of Japanese and African Experience", *Developing Economies*, 29, 1 (March 1991); p. 11. Mathur, Ashok: "The Interface of Agriculture and Industrial Growth in the Development Process: Some Facts of the Indian Experience", *Development and Change*, 21, 2 (April 1990); p. 276. Oshima, Harry T.: "'Labour-Force Explosion' and the Labour Intensive Sector in Asian Growth", *Economic Development and Cultural Change*, 19, 2 (January 1971); p. 170.
70. Elsenhans, Hartmut: *Marginalité, sous-développement et secteur informel. Document de Recherche du C.R.E.A. 97/01/C1-2* (Dakar: Centre de Recherches Economiques Appliquées C.R.E.A., January 1997); p. 35.
71. Crafts, Nicholas F.R.: "British Industrialization in an International Context", *Journal of Interdisciplinary History*, 19, 3 (Winter 1989); p. 427. O'Brien, Patrick Karl; Keyder, Çaglar: *Economic Growth in Britain and France 1780-1914. Two Paths to the Twentieth Century* (London: Allen & Unwin, 1978); p. 162.

72. Le Pors, Arnicet: "La contrainte extérieure - parlons en", *Economie et politique*, 302 (September 1979); p. 41. Lombard, Marc: "A Re-examination of the Reasons for the Failure of Keynesian Expansionary Politics in France, 1981-1983", *Cambridge Journal of Economics*, 19, 3 (April 1995); p. 371.
73. Shonfield, Andrew: *Modern Capitalism. The Changing Balance of Public and Private Power* (London: Oxford University Press, 1965). Franzmeyer, Fritz: *Industrielle Strukturprobleme und sektorale Strukturpolitik in der europäischen Gemeinschaft* (Berlin: Duncker & Humblot, 1979); pp. 101 f. Uterwedde, Hendrik: *Die Wirtschaftspolitik der Linken in Frankreich. Programme und Praxis 1974-1986* (Frankfort on the Main; New York: Campus, 1988); p. 29.
74. Yi, Guk-Yueng: *Staat und Kapitalakkumulation in ostasiatischen Ländern: Ein Vergleich zwischen Korea und Taiwan* (Saarbrücken: Breitenbach, 1988); pp. 97-104, pp. 137-144. Cf. also Fujita, Natsuki; James, William E.: "Export Oriented Growth of Output and Employment in Taiwan and Korea, 1973/74-1983/84", *Weltwirtschaftliches Archiv*, 126, 4 (1990); pp. 137-144.
75. Amsden, Alice H.: "The Division of Labour is Limited by the Type of the Market: The Case of the Taiwanese Machine Tool Industry", *World Development*, 5, 3 (March 1977); pp. 230 f. Amsden, Alice: "The Division of Labour is Limited by the Rate of Growth of the Market: the Taiwan Machine Tool Industry in the 1970s", *Cambridge Journal of Economics*, 9, 3 (September 1985); p. 282.
76. This is shown by the end of the hierarchies in the theory of the product cycle. Cf. Cantwell, John: "The Globalisation of Technology: What Remains of the Product Cycle Model", *Cambridge Journal of Economics*, 19, 1 (February 1995); p. 155-179. And, much earlier, Vernon, Raymond: "Storm Over the Multinationals: Problems and Prospects", *Foreign Affairs*, 55, 2 (January 1977); p. 257.
77. Prebisch, Raúl: "The Economic Development of Latin America and its Principal Problems", *Economic Bulletin for Latin America*, 7, 1 (February 1962); pp. 1-22. Singer, Hans W.: "U.S. Foreign Investment in Underdeveloped Areas. The Distribution of Gains between Investing and Borrowing Countries", *American Economic Review*, 40, 2 (May 1950); pp. 473-485, esp. p. 482.

78. Elsenhans, Hartmut: *Global Change and Implications for India* (New Delhi: Lancer Books, 1992); pp. 31-33.
79. Elsenhans, Hartmut: "Autonomy of Civil Society, Empowerment of Labour, and the Transition to Capitalism", in: Jain, Randhir B.; Khator, Renu (eds.): *Bureaucracy - Citizen Interface: Conflict and Consensus* (New Delhi: B.R. Publishing Corporation 1999); 15-60.
80. Kim, Eui-Young: *The Business Interest Association and The Political Economy of Development in South Korea* (Seoul: International Political Science Association,August 1997); pp. 2-7. Case, William: *Pseudodemocracy in South-East Asia: Uncovering State Leaders and the Business Connection* (Seoul: International Political Science Association,August 1997). Lew, Seok-Jin; Lee, Nae-Young: *Democratization and Changing Industrial Policy Making. A Case of the Southern Korean Automobile Industry* (Seoul: International Political Science Association,August 1997).
81. Manning, Chris: "Approaching the Turning Point? Labour Market Change under Indonesia's New Order", *Developing Economies*, 33, 1 (May 1995); pp. 55-58. Bai, Moo-Ki: "The Turning Point in the Korean Economy", *Developing Economies*, 20, 1 (March 1982); pp. 117-140. Minami, Ryoshin: "Economic Development of Japan: Factors, Consequences, Implications", *Journal of Economic Development*, 17, 2 (December 1992); p. 26. Irwan, Alexander: "Business Patronage, Class Struggle and the Manufacturing Sector in South Korea, Indonesia and Thailand", *Journal of Comparative Asia*, 19, 4 (1989); pp. 410-424.
82. Elsenhans, Hartmut: "New Tendencies in North-South Relations", *Pakistan Horizon*, 46, 3/4 (July/October 1993); pp. 37-56. Elsenhans, Hartmut: "The Logic of Profit and the Logic of Rent", *Voice of Peace and Integration*, 1, 1 (October 1992); pp. 4-48. Elsenhans, Hartmut: "State, Economy and Power and the Future of the International System", in: Friedrich Ebert Stiftung (ed.): *Europe-India: New Perspectives in Changing Power Structures in the International System* (New Delhi: Friedrich-Ebert-Stiftung, 1993); pp. 35-39.

3

European Political Co-operation and South Asia: From Indifference to an Institutionalised Dialogue

PURUSOTTAM BHATTACHARYA

The Treaty of Rome (signed on 25 March, 1957) which led to the establishment of the European Community (EC) on 1 January 1958 had essentially provided for a framework of economic and commercial co-operation among the member states as political issues had proved to be contentious. However, in spite of its conspicuous omission from the Rome Treaty formula the concept of political co-operation continued to be one of the corner stones which guided the philosophy of the European Community since its inception. The key element of this political co-operation was in the area of foreign policy and the objective was that the Community would increasingly speak with one voice in international affairs[1].

The need for co-ordination in the foreign policies of the member states was being increasingly felt in the late 1960s and the early 1970s in regard especially to events such as the East-West Détente, emergence of China and Japan as significant international actors and increasing volatility in regions such as the Middle East and Southern Africa. The process which crystallized under the rubric of the European Political Co-operation (EPC) in 1970 was to consist of foreign policy co-ordination among the member states of the Community conducted outside the framework of the treaties establishing the Community.

As the framework of the EPC became more well-knit and sophisticated over the next decade the Community focussed its attention on regions and issues of the world it considered to be matters of high priority. These included East-West relations, Middle-East, Southern Africa and Sub-Saharan-Africa[2]. Asia in general and South Asia in particular was accorded a lower priority in spite of the fact that nearly three-fifth of the humanity live in Asia, the largest of all the continents.

This paper proposes to analyse the place of India in the larger context of South Asia, in the EPC framework with an investigation into the EC's approach to Asia in general the areas of emphasis vis-à-vis India and South Asia within the limited focus the EC permitted itself, the institutionalisation of the political dialogue through the EC troika meetings with India and finally a look into the prospects for the future.

Approach to Asia in General and South Asia in Particular

It was through the evolution of its commercial and development policies in the 1960s and the 1970s that the EC's links with the outside world were primarily forged. The regions that received principal attention in this regard were, initially, the Francophone states of Africa and later, when the first of the home conventions was signed in 1975, the remaining developing states of Africa, the Caribbean and the Pacific (ACP)[3].

Asia, by contrast, was accorded a considerably lower priority by the EC and was placed at the periphery of EC developmental concerns which also influenced, at least in the early years, its political priorities. Several factors accounted for this. First, Asia of the 1950s and 1960s was viewed as an area of endemic poverty with a seemingly insurmountable problem of very high growth rates of population. Secondly, with the history of European colonialism fresh in their memory Asians seemed anxious to assert, rather forcefully, their independence from Europe. The only post-colonial institutional link between Europe and Asia was the British Commonwealth which was viewed by some continental Europeans with some suspicion as too Anglo-Saxon. The initial British refusal to join the Community further retarded EC relations with the newly independent nations of Asia, which were seen to be very much in the British "domain"[4]. Two different images of post-colonial Asia were perceived by the EC which it found troublesome. The first related to the immense existential odds that South Asia seemed to face as reflected in the racial and religious diversity, food deficiency and unchecked population growth in states such as India, Bangladesh, Nepal and to a lesser extent Pakistan. These were huge challenges well beyond the means of the Community to cope with. Besides, the Asia scenario clashed with the priorities the Community had already decided to accord to its focus on Africa.

The other image was concerned with the dimension of competition that was emerging between Europe and South-East Asia, particularly in the later 1960s. As one writer put it "vital economic and trade interest of the Community came to be seen as threatened by several of the countries of South-East Asia, which were following Japan's footsteps in producing and exporting an increasing variety of industrial commodities".[5]

Other obstacles to the development of co-operation between the Community and post-colonial Asia were also evident. Distance between Western Europe and mainland Asia, especially South and South-East Asia, seemed to be an impediment. Another hurdle seemed to be the exposure of the region to communist threat. The EC nations considered it prudent to leave the task of helping Asia face whatever threat it encountered to the United States.

Intra-EC tensions between the regionalist and the globalist views of EC development co-operation was one more hurdle to a deeper EC involvement in Asia. The predominance of the regionalists during the early years of the Community's policy-making ensured that the pre-eminent focus on Africa was retained. This phenomenon was reflected very clearly in the home conventions in which no Asian country was included[6].

EPC and South Asia: Areas of Emphasis

The background provided above is necessary to understand the approach of the EC to Asia as a whole and South Asia in particular. The region which comprised of the British Indian empire prior to 1947 – currently known as South Asia – has been seen in Western Europe in the post-second world war periods as essentially a British preserve. The decision of India, Pakistan and Sri Lanka (Ceylon at the time) to join the British Commonwealth was a major contributory factor in this regard. As mentioned earlier the initial British refusal to join in the creation of the EC was also an important factor in the region being neglected by the Community in the early years of its evolution.

As mentioned earlier, in the early 1970s when European political co-operation was in its formative stages the Community preferred to concentrate on issues and areas which were of major concern to it. These included the East-West Relations and the détente between the two super powers, the eruption of conflict in the Middle East especially the Arab-Israeli war of October 1973 and the world-wide oil crisis that followed it and the burgeoning conflict in Southern Africa especially in Angola, Rhodesia (now Zimbabwe) and South Africa.[7]

Therefore, the tentative nature of EC political co-operation and the compulsion to focus on issues and areas of higher priority precluded the development of a significant political relationship between the Community and South Asia. The entry of Britain in the Community in 1973 provided the opportunity for the first time for higher levels of co-operation between the EC and South Asia. The establishment of a framework of development co-operation between the European Community and the states of South Asia in the 1970s starting with the India-EC Commercial Co-operation Agreement (CCA) of 1973 provided the foundation for the emergence of a political relationship, albeit in a nascent form, in the 1980s.

In spite of the limited interest the Community has shown towards the major political issues in South Asia a careful examination would reveal that EC attention in the region has been primarily focussed on the three issues: (i) Kashmir and India-Pakistan relations; (ii) Democracy and Human Rights in the region, and (iii) Nuclear non-proliferation in South Asia.

Kashmir and India – Pakistan Relations

The issue of the accession of Jammu and Kashmir into the Indian union more than half a century ago continues to be one of the most serious unresolved political problems of South Asia today. It has devilled India's relations with Pakistan since 1947 having been the focus of three wars between the two states (in 1947, 1965 and 1971). As things stand there are very few signs of any movement in the direction of a settlement acceptable to all concerned.

The original member states of the EC and the Community itself have historically displayed considerable reticence regarding the Kashmir problem considered to be a British and American concern during the initial phase of international involvement on the issue in the 1940s and the 1950s; it is only in recent years that the Community has shown some interest in this regard. It should however be noted that even this show of limited interest in Kashmir is in the context of the emergence of full scale insurgency in the state since 1989 and the consequent lightened tensions between India and Pakistan both of whom are now nuclear weapon powers.

The position of the Community on Kashmir has been determined by two major considerations – the complexity of the issue and the EC's anxiety to be seen as even handed as possible so as not to alienate either India or Pakistan. Various statements and speeches made on behalf of the Community bear testimony to this cautious approach which has been the hallmark of the EC policy on Kashmir. For instance on 12 April 1990 the EPC statement recalled the good relations the member states had with both India and Pakistan, expressed their concern at the tension between the two countries and called on both parties to display restraint and moderation[8].

Ever since the re-emergence of Kashmir into the international limelight in the early 1990s the standard EC position has been that the issue is to be settled through a bilateral dialogue between India and Pakistan as provided for in the Simla agreement, signed by the two countries in 1978. However, the EC has not been able to stay clear of controversies altogether in this regard. For instance the handling of the insurgency situation by the Indian security forces in Kashmir has occasionally caused misgivings in Brussels, projected in statement issued by the Community. At the UN Human Right Commission session in March 1974 at Geneva a joint statement of the Community (known as European Union since 1 November 1993) deplored the "continuing violence and abuse of human right in Kashmir." It further observed that while terrorist violence must be firmly resisted the security forces in Kashmir, while doing so, "must show full respect for human rights and the rule of law"[9].

The community's concern about the situation in Kashmir was also conveyed during bilateral discussions between the two sides. In

April 1995 the EU side expressed an interest in knowing about the efforts undertaken by India to restore the political process in Kashmir[10]. EC envoys posted in New Delhi also visited the valley for an on the spot assessment a few years ago.

It may be reiterated that the concern showed by the Community in respect of Kashmir was primarily due to its potential as a flashpoint between India and Pakistan especially so in view of the nuclear situation prevailing in the sub-continent. This was highlighted in a telling manner very recently following the nuclear tests conducted by both India and Pakistan in May 1998 and the consequent escalation in tension between the two countries. As is invariably the case Kashmir becomes the focal point in any increase in tension between New Delhi and Islamabad and the present occasion has been no exception. The United States and the European Union lost no time in detecting a linkage between the nuclear tests by India and Pakistan and a possible conflict between the two countries over Kashmir. The two powers (the US and the EU) in a series of policy statements from different forums, have strongly urged the two countries to enter into a dialogue on Kashmiri and all other outstanding issues to defuse what they perceive as a dangerous situation[11]. Even though it has no plans to take a leading role in the resolution of the conflict in view of India's known stand of not accepting any third party mediation in the dispute the EU remains concerned about what it perceives as the potential of the Kashmir issue in triggering off a conflict between India and Pakistan.

Democracy and Human Rights

The principle of democracy and human right is an article of faith with the European Union enshrined in the Treaty of Rome and the subsequent agreements which expanded the EU's areas of activities. Apart from applying it as a precondition for would be members in Europe the principle has been invoked by the EU in its relations with all countries and regions in recent years. South Asia too has been no exception.

Till the later 1980s India and Sri Lanka were the only two democracies in the South Asian region. However, a steady process of democratization got underway following the death of president Ziaul-Haq in Pakistan in 1988 when the first democratic elections were held in that country since 1977. Bangladesh followed suit in 1990 after a popular uprising led to the ouster of General H.M Ershad. Even royalist Nepal felt the compulsion to fall in line with the king deciding to initiate wide ranging democratic reforms following a mass upsurge within the kingdom.

The Community warmly welcomed these developments. On 12 April 1990 the Community applauded the decision of the king of Nepal to remove the ban on political parties and to begin democratic reform[12]. The steps taken by the interim government in Bangladesh to prepare for free and fair parliamentary elections on 27 February 1991 were also welcomed by the Community and its member states. In a statement issued on 15 January 1991 they also appreciated the invitations extended to parliamentarians from the member states and MEPs (Members of European Parliament) to attend the elections as observers[13].

The deep commitment of the Community to the principles of democracy and human rights has been enshrined in all the agreements on development co-operation it has entered into with the countries in the region. Such a practice has at times even given rise to controversies and irritations. The co-operation agreement between India and the EC, initialling in late 1992, was not approved by the Indian Cabinet for a long time due to a misapprehension on the Indian side of a clause in Article one of the new treaty which stipulated "respect for human rights and democratic principles" as the basis for co-operation between the Community and India. This reference, after the initialling of the agreement, led the Government of India to infer that some kind of conditionality was being sought to be introduced and that a bad human rights record could lead to suspension of co-operation[14]. The agreement was signed on 20 December 1993 only after a clarification was offered from the EC side that no such intention existed.

The issue of human rights has been and continues to be an irritant in the relationship between the EU (and the West as a whole) and the countries in the South Asian region. These countries see the practice followed by the EC as an attempt to project, if not impose on them, the Community's own criteria of human rights and as an unwarranted interference in their domestic affairs. The member states of the European Union are not always aware of the sensitivities displayed by the South Asian countries in this regard and occasionally act in a ham handed manner. It should be noted, however, that in spite of its sensitive nature the issue of democracy and human rights is a part of the regular dialogue between the European Union and the South Asian countries.

Nuclear Non-Proliferation

The issue of nuclear non proliferation and disarmament presents one of the most formidable challenges facing the world today. It remains the most sensitive of all the political issues between the European Union and the South Asian states especially India and Pakistan.

Though they subscribed to the common objective of nuclear disarmament and eventually a nuclear weapons-free world the European Union and India sharply differ in their respective strategies with regard to the realisation of this goal. The European Union is committed to the promotion of the non-proliferation regime provided for in the Non-proliferation Treaty (NPT) of 1968 which came into force in 1970[15]. The EU and its member states – two of whom (Britain and France) belong to the nuclear club of five – consider the NPT framework as the most important instrument for furthering the cause of nuclear non-proliferation in the world[16].

The Indian perspective is different. From the very outset New Delhi had adopted the stand that the NPT was designed to prevent the non-nuclear states from developing nuclear technology even for peaceful economic purposes and hence was discriminatory. The very concept of nuclear power dictating terms in regard to who should have nuclear technology and what use it should be put to, is to India a gross violation of political traditions it has cherished and a major imperative of its foreign policy since independence — i.e. the legal and political equality of nations[17].

Thus it was on the ground of its discriminatory character that India has persistently refused to sign the NPT over the past three decades. A wide ranging domestic consensus on this issue exists and the policy followed by successive central governments was devoid of any partisanship in this respect. Caught in the vortex of South Asian regional politics – especially the strained relations between India and Pakistan as well as the unresolved border dispute between India and

China – the nuclear issue assumes a more troublesome dimension. The security calculations of India vis-à-vis China (with whom it has had a difficult relationship since the border war of 1962) and of Pakistan vis-à-vis India led to the emergence of a triangle in the region which made accession to the NTP, i.e. closing the nuclear option, problematic for New Delhi. Pakistan had already made its own accession to the NPT conditional on India doing the same.

The issue therefore primarily concerns the EU and India since the Pakistani stand is considered to be linked to the Indian position in refusing to sign the NPT and subsequently the CTBT (Comprehensive Test Ban Treaty)[18]. In view of this sharply diverging perspectives the issue has turned into a dialogue of the deaf between India and the EU with each side periodically reiterating its own position during bilateral meetings. For instance at the meeting between the EU Trioka and the Indian Minister for External Affairs, held in early 1995, the EU side told the Indian delegation of their continued commitment to the NPT regime and its indefinite extension. The Indian delegation, on the other hand, reiterated its own position that New Delhi wanted total non-proliferation, "but it must be based on multilaterally negotiated treaties, it must be non-discriminatory and universally verifiable[19].

The differences between India and the West (of which the EU is an integral part) have assumed crisis proportions in recent times following the nuclear tests conducted by India on 11 and 13 May 1998 closely followed by Pakistan on 28 and 30 May, 1998. The government led by the Bharatiya Janata Party (BJP) which assumed office in March 1998 following the general elections held in February 1998 decided to exercise the nuclear option, kept open by successive Indian Governments so far. The act triggered a crisis in India's relations with its two most important regional neighbours, Pakistan and China as well as with United States and the European Union. The Government of India interacted that the hostile regional security environment where India had to co-habit with two covert (Pakistan) and overt (China) nuclear weapon powers, having past records of belligerence towards New Delhi, had left it with no other choice. The unfair and discriminatory norms of the international non-proliferation regime which had contributed to the build up of a strong sense of domestic resentment acted, no doubt, as a powerful catalyst as well.

The international response was swift and strong. The United

States and Japan imposed economic sanctions on India. The European Union was more restrained in the sense that it did not impose any sanctions on India. However, it strongly condemned the Indian (and subsequently the Pakistan) action and emphatically disagreed with the Indian explanation relating to the causes of the provocation leading to this action. In a comprehensive response to the build up of tension in South Asia following the tests the 15 EU heads of Government in their final communiqué, issued on 16 June, 1998 after the three days EU summit in Wales, asked India and Pakistan to resume their negotiations with each other and with China. The communiqué said, "The EU is of the view that India and Pakistan should take early steps to reduce tension and instability in South Asia by resuming their bilateral dialogue with each other and with China, and seeking ways to build confidence between them". It also endorsed the tough stance taken earlier by the five permanent members of the UN Security Council at their meeting in Geneva and the G-8 group of industrial countries in Birmingham[20]. The summit also backed the G-8 move to set up a task force to promote non-proliferation in South Asia but said, "Further measures will only be considered if India and Pakistan fail to make progress on non-proliferation issues[21].

Thus it is clear that the EU views the Indian and Pakistani nuclear tests as a serious blow to the international non-proliferation regime which it promotes and defends. The EU is also greatly disturbed by what it perceives as a nuclear arms race in South Asia which is the inevitable consequence of the Indian and Pakistani actions. There is little doubt that the issue of nuclear non-proliferation will assume an even greater dimension in the EU's interaction with India and Pakistan in the foreseeable future. Whether the Indian and Pakistani moves will have any adverse long term repercussions on EU-South Asian relations is not clear at the moment[22].

Institutionalization of the Political Dialogue

As has already been noted it was only since the early to mid 1980s that the EC/EU started to take an interest in the political issues in South albeit in a limited way. The need to evolve a political dialogue with the region began to be felt as the community's development co-operation with South Asia, acquired a firmer foundation and the EC itself became a global political actor. Consequently a slow but gradual profess of institutionalization of the political dialogue between the EC/EU and the South Asian states got underway, a process which is still continuing.

The most notable arrangement that has been established so far is the annual meetings between India and the Troika of the European Union[23]. Such meetings were began since 1982. However the real breakthrough came in 1993 only with the signing of an updated partnership agreement between India and the EU along with a political declaration laying down guidelines for the Troika meetings. This has led to institutionalization of the Troika dialogue between India and the EU. The political declaration is worded broadly enough to allow a significant degree of political interaction between the two sides. For instance it states that the dialogue should "allow both sides to consider the position and interests of the other party in their respective decision-making process." This provision could be so interpreted as to theoretically allow India to ask that its views be considered in issues which are of interest to it[24]. The 1990s has thus witnessed an upswing in Indo-EU political relations which has to be viewed in the context that the EU is India's largest trade and investment partner. Recent years have been a fruitful period in relations between the two sides. Besides the visit to India in 1995 by Manuel Marin, the European Union Commissioner in charge of South Asia, the other notable developments have been meetings of the Indo-EU joint commission in Brussels and New Delhi, visits to India by several members of the European Parliament and by business and political delegations from individual EU member states. In fact constructive interest shown by the European Parliament in India's stance on important global developments has contributed to further enhancement of political relations[25].

The annual meeting of the EU Troika with India has proved to be a step towards the building up of the political relationship. The meeting held in March 1996 provided opportunity for a wide exchange of views not only on Kashmir and Indo-Pakistani relations but also on Yugoslavia, human rights, the West Asia peace process and the EU's relations with Russia[26].

In June 1996 the European Commission transmitted a document to the Council of Ministers proposing a more intensive political dialogue with New Delhi on issues including non-proliferation and disarmament which was deemed important in the context of India's refusal to sign the NPT and the CTBT. The need for a closer understanding with New Delhi was especially underscored on the proposed fissile material cut-off treaty, the NPT the CTBT, the Chemical Weapons Convention, the Biological Weapons Convention, transparency in arms control agreement and control of sensitive dual use goods and technologies.

In December 1996 the Council of Ministers endorsed the proposal of the Commission for an enhanced partnership with India. As part of plans to upgrade ties the Council proposed setting up of an India experts group to improve internal co-ordination between the Commission and the member states on co-operation with India[27]

Prospects for the future

South Asia has historically been at the bottom of the European Community/Union scale of priorities the reasons for which have already been discussed. However, as seen in the foregoing analysis, considerable advancement has taken place in the last few years from initial indifference to an institutionalized political dialogue between the EU and the largest of the South Asian states, India.

As noted earlier since the signing of its latest agreement with India in 1993 the EU has viewed its relationship with New Delhi in a more positive light and expressed its keen desire to upgrade these ties to that of a partnership between the two largest democratic entities in the world. The EU too is regarded in South Asia as one of the most important actors in international relations today along with the United States, China and Japan. South Asia is no longer as distant and irrelevant as it used to be from the EU perspective. The drive for economic liberalization which was set in motion in the economies of South Asia in the early 1990s turned the region into a window of opportunity for the EU and the rest of the industrialized world. Consequently EU trade and investment in the region have grown at a rapid pace providing the foundation for a stronger political relationship with South Asia.

However, in spite of these positive trends in recent years the prospect for the relationship developing to its full potential does not seem to be bright. There are a number of reasons for this.

First, the EU is preoccupied with its own programme of further integration in Europe which currently has two major elements. The first concerns the introduction of the single European currency - Euro – from 1 January 1999. This is the most ambitious venture undertaken by the EU to date and the future shape of European integration is largely dependant on the success or failure of the single currency project.

The second issue concerns the upcoming enlargement of the Union to incorporate the post-communist Central and Eastern European states. The successful integration of these countries with vastly divergent economic and political structures hitherto into the EU framework poses a grave challenge to the Union and its achievements thus far. Second, serious interest in South Asia is still confined to a handful of member states within the Union such as Germany, Britain and the Netherlands. A marked preference is noticeable among German and British leaders to deal with the South Asian states individually as part of their respective foreign policies rather than from within the EU common foreign policy framework. This is particularly so when it comes to issues such as nuclear non-proliferation and India-Pakistan relations. .

Third, in its new strategy for Asia laid out by the European Union in 1994, the EU has accorded a marked preference to East and South East Asia. The rationale of the strategy is to take account the growing strength of the Asian nations in the world economy and to strengthen the union's presence in Asia. Therefore, a proactive policy towards Asia was outlined highlighting the need to improve policy co-ordination at national and European levels and also to identify clear priorities in terms of countries and sectors.

The spectacular growth of the East and the South-East Asia economics in the 1980s and the 1990s seemed to mark them out as the obvious choice for forging the kind of partnership with Asia the EU had in mind. Consequently the two Asia-Europe summits held so far in this regard – the first at Bangkok in March, 1996 and the second in London in April, 1998 – included ten countries from East and South-East Asia and none from South Asia[28].

Fourth, the severe downturn in the fortunes of the East and South-East economies since July 1997 and the nuclear tests conducted by

India and Pakistan in May 1998 have further clouded the prospects for an enhanced partnership between the EU and South Asia as one looks ahead. The meltdown in the East and South-East Asian economies following the collapse of investor confidence there has created a great deal of uncertainty in EU-Asian relations. The EU would be expected to play an important role in bring in these economies back to health in its own interest as Asia (East, South-East and South Asia) continues to be the largest and potentially the most lucrative market in the new century.

As noted earlier the nuclear explosions in the South Asian sub-continent have generated new concerns about regional security. Though the precise ramifications of this development are not very clear at the moment there is little doubt that it would add to the wariness that has been the hallmark of EU approach towards South Asia for a long time.

It may not therefore be inappropriate to conclude that South Asia on the whole will continue to remain relatively peripheral to EU concerns in the near future. The achievement of recent years, however, would also continue to provide a firm foundation on which the relationship can be further strengthened if and when both sides are ready for it.

Notes and References

1. EC, office for official publications, *European Unification: The origins and growth of the European Community* (Luxembourg, 1986), p. 61.
2. For a more detailed analysis of the evolution of the institutional framework of EPC See Purusottam Bhattacharya, "Political Integration in Western Europe: A case study of European political co-operation", in Arun Kumar Banerji, ed. *Integration, Disintegration and World Order* (Calcutta, 1995). See also Purusottam Bhattacharya, "Foreign policy co-ordination in the European Community" *India Quarterly* (New Delhi), Jan.-March 1990.
3. For a brief account in this regard see Carol Cosgrove-Twitchett "The European Community and Regional Co-operation in the Third World", in Carol Cosgrove-Twitchett, ed, *European Co-operation Today*, (London, 1980). See also Kenneth J. Twitchett, *Europe and the World: The External Relations of the Common Market* (London, 1976); and Juliet Lodge, ed, *The European Community and the Challenge of the Future*, (London, 1989).

4. Enzo P. Grilli, *The European Community and the Developing Countries*, (Cambridge, 1993), p. 272.
5. *Ibid.*
6. *Ibid.* For details regarding the Lome Convention see Purusottam Bhattacharya, *Britain in the European Community: Implications for Domestic Politics and Foreign Policy* (Calcutta 1994), pp. 238-250.
7. For details see Bhattacharya, n. 2 & n. 6.
8. E.C. Commission, *XXIVth General Report on the Activities of the European Communities, 1990* (Brussels, Luxembourg, 1991), p. 349. An upsurge in insurgency in Kashmir in late 1989 led to an increase in tension between India and Pakistan at the time being referred to here.
9. *The Statesman* (Calcutta) 8 March, 1994.
10. *The Hindu* (Madras) 8 April 1995. In view of the full scale insurgency, actively aided and abetted by Pakistan from across the international line of control, Kashmir had been placed under a prolonged spell of central rule from 1989 to September 1996 when a popular government was installed following elections to the State Assembly.
11. In the final communiqué issued on 16 June 1998 after their three day summit in Cardiff, Wales, the 15 EU heads of Government called upon both India and Pakistan, in a reference to the Kashmir issue, to: "immediately resume their political dialogue to address constructively the issues which divide them." *The Statesman*, 18 June, 1998.
12. *EC Commission, XXIV the General Report on the Activities of the European Communities, 1990*, (Brussels & Luxembourg, 1991), p. 349.
13. E.C. Commission, *XXV the General Report on the Activities of the European Communities, 1991* (Brussels & Luxembourg, 1992) p. 351.
14. *Times of India* (New Delhi), 9 September, 1993.
15. For a compact analysis on the NPT see T.C. Bose, 'Twenty-Five years of NPT; What Next?", *Jadavpur Journal of International Relations* (Calcutta), Vol. I, 1995.
16. During the course of a scheduled meeting with India in early April 1995 the EU side made it clear that the unconditional and indefinite extension of the NPT, stated to be under consideration at the NPT Review Conference beginning on 17 April 1995, was one of the aims of the EU common foreign policy. See *The Hindu*, 8 April 1995.
17. Jyantanuja Bandyopadhyaya, *The Making of India's Foreign Policy* (New Delhi, 1979), p. 105.
18. India has refused to sign the CTBT also on the ground that the test ban regime provided for in it is highly discriminatory and favour the nuclear-have against the nuclear have-not states. For details see Kishor N. Bagchi, "The Proliferation Treaty and the Comprehensive Test-Ban Treaty: A Critical Perspective," in Arun Kumar Banerji, ed. *Non-Proliferation in a Changing World: India's Policy and Options* (Calcutta, 1997).

19. *The Hindu*, 9 April, 1995.
20. The G-8 summit at Birmingham, England, on 15-16 May 1998 had condemned the Indian nuclear tests though it failed to agree on any sanctions. It also urged India to sign the Comprehensive Test Ban Treaty (CTBT) and the Non-Proliferation Treaty (NPT). The five permanent members of the UN Security Council, meeting at Geneva on 4 June 1998 asked India and Pakistan to begin direct talk to reduce tension, refrain from deploying nuclear weapons and sign the CTBT unconditionally. For details see *The Hindu*, 17 May 1998 and *The Statesman*, 5 June, 1998.
21. *The Statesman*, 18 June, 1998.
22. The European investment community have been more circumspect in their reaction. According to this community – fund managers, financial analysts and business executives – the Litmus test of the Indian economy and Indian companies was related to their impressive credibility and profitability. As one of them put it, "Fund managers are greedy. They are not going to sell Indian stocks because of the nuclear tests." Another manager said, "we like India because we like Indian companies and cannot see how this will affect them." See Batuk Gathani, "Focus shifts to G-8 Summit", *The Hindu*, 15 May, 1998.
23. The Troika arrangement is a unique EU device whereby the current, preceding and succeeding presidencies of the Union operate collectively. For instance in a meeting between the Indian External Affairs Minister and the EU troika the Foreign Ministers from the current, preceding and succeeding Member states of the holding presidencies of the Union in that order and the responsible European Commissioner will be present.
24. Thomas Abraham, "The Indo-EU troika" *The Hindu*, 27 April, 1998 , See. Delegation of the European Commission, *The European Union and India: A Partner for Progress* (New Delhi, 1996). p-4.
25. *Ibid.*
26. *The Hindu*, 4 March, 1996.
27. The importance being attached to India was underscored by the fact that similar expert groups were also set up by the EU only for Japan and China. *The Hindu*, 12 Dec. 1996.
28. The South Asian states were excluded from the London summit in spite of the keenness of Mr. Manuel Marin, the EU commissioner in charge of South Asia, that India and Pakistan should be invited to the conference. *The Far Eastern Economic Review* (Hongkong), 11 July, 1996, pp. 27-28 For the EU Asian strategy see Delegation of the European Commission, n. 24, p.2

4

New Directions in the Development Policy of the European Union

PAUL SUTTON

The European Union (EU) is the world's biggest trader, accounting on average in recent years for around 20% of world imports and exports, and is the major market for many developing countries. Together with its fifteen member states, it is the largest provider of foreign assistance to the developing world. In recent years, it has been a major supplier of foreign direct investment, much of it directed to Asia. This economic presence has been matched by a growing and concerted programme to increase the EU's political presence in multilateral organisations and through bilateral arrangements with most of the world's countries. The EU is a signatory in its own right to many treaties and it now has more than 130 delegations in various countries and international organisations. The developing world is the host to the largest number of delegations, many of which are concerned with co-ordinating or implementing the EU's development assistance programmes.

This article outlines EU development policy. It begins by examining the basis of EU development policy and the pattern of what is frequently termed 'first generation' development policy. It then turns to examine the thinking behind proposals for change that emerged in the early 1990s and have led to the introduction of 'second generation' development agreements that have changed the orientation and character of the EU's relations with the developing world. Their application in the four major regions of the developing world are sketched out and briefly compared. The article concludes with the consideration of how the new development policy of the EU is likely to affect relations with South Asia.

The Architecture of EU Development Policy

The pattern of EU relations to the developing world has been characterised by a series of regional arrangements that have reflected past colonial ties, geopolitical concerns and the emergence of the EU as an economic and political actor with global interests. Most of these relationships are carried out in group-to-group arrangements where a complex mix of association and cooperation arrangements have established a 'pyramid of privilege' in which those at the top are provided with more favourable treatment than those lower down and at the base. These privileges include trade preferences and concessional financial and technical assistance. The pyramid is not a fixed structure since the position of any group of countries can shift with the revision of existing arrangements or the admission of new groups of countries. That is to say, a new group or existing group may be given greater concessions than those they already hold or are extended to others, leading to an erosion of the privileges of other groups and a shift in their relative standing. The position of the various groups in the pyramid before changes were introduced in the early 1990s was as follows.

The apex of pyramid was occupied, and had been for many years, by the then sixty-nine African, Caribbean and Pacific (ACP) countries signatory to the Lome Convention. These countries were all former colonies of EU states and the origins of their privileged relationship extended to the foundation of the European Economic Community in 1957 when they became Associates under Part IV of the Treaty of Rome, entitled to preferential trade and financial aid. The development of their relationship with the EC since then has been a long and complex affair that cannot be easily summarised, but has had at its core the belief by the EC and several EU states (notably France) that the position of Africa is special to the EU. This belief, comprehended by the geopolitical concept of 'Eurafrica', has focussed on a presumed complementarity of interests between Europe and Africa founded on interdependence and expressed in the Lome Conventions in the idea of 'partnership'.[1] Under the various Lome Conventions this has resulted in non-reciprocal trade preference which have grown to cover nearly all the goods exported by the ACP to the EU; an aid programme additional to that of the EU member states worth some 17.4 billion ECU in the fifteen year period 1975-1990; and an institutional framework for administering the conventions in which all signatories engage in regular and structured dialogue.

Next in rank in the pyramid of privileges were the southern Mediterranean countries. The idea of a specific set of agreements with a number of these countries was realised in the mind 1970s when individual (though identical) cooperation agreements were signed with the Maghreb (Algeria, Morocco, Tunisia) and Mashreq (Egypt, Jordan, Syria and Lebanon). These provided for duty-free access to the EC for a large number of manufactured and agricultural products, but significantly not all, and development assistance through financial protocols. As with the Lome Conventions, there were multi-annual aid programmes, but the volume of assistance was much less than under Lome and the developmental impact more diffuse, leading to dissatisfaction on the part of both the EC and the southern Mediterranean states. A 'renewed Mediterranean policy' was adopted in 1989 that provided for increased trade access and more assistance, reflecting an increased interest in the region by the EU following the accession of Greece, Spain and Portugal to the EU in the 1980s.

Further down still in the pyramid were the majority of Asian and Latin American countries (ALAs). In 1974, the EC announced it would be extending its development cooperation policy to some forty countries in these regions. They were to benefit from annual aid programmes directed toward the poorest and to rural development, as well as continued access to the EC market under the EC General System of Preferences (GSP) introduced in 1971. The least developed countries in both regions were targeted and were the major recipients of aid once the programme came fully on stream in the late 1970s. The EC also sought to strengthen or initiate dialogue with various regional organisations in South East Asia and in Latin America. By 1989 the various programmes had become established and the EC was looking for ways to strengthen its cooperation with both regions, but particularly with Latin America where it saw a new complementarity of interest.[2]

At the base of the pyramid were developing countries that had limited privileges. These included some of the newly industrialising countries of East Asia who benefited only from GSP and the oil rich Gulf states that maintained only a limited political dialogue with the EC. Finally, several developing countries, such as the communist states of Cuba and North Korea, South Africa under apartheid and Libya, had no formal agreements.

This pattern of relations has been described by Enzo Grilli as 'limping regionalism'. "The sequencing of the EC relations with different groups of developing countries, and often their development content, appears to have been haphazard, reactive and more dictated by events, sometimes fashions, than by plans, principles or even a broad strategy. The only recognisable constant in the maze of changing regional ties developed by the Community was the preservation of the relative primacy of the associated African (and subsequently Caribbean and Pacific) countries among those receiving concessions".[3] Clearly, the time had come for change. However, it was not the inadequacies of existing development policy that were to drive policy in new directions but developments internal to the EC which had major external effects.

The Development Impact of Closer European Union

The first of these was the completion of the Single European Market (SEM). This allowed for the free movement of goods, persons, services and capital within the EU as from January 1993. The move to a SEM was taken primarily for internal reasons and little thought was given to its effects outside, especially on the developing world. However, there were consequential effects in areas such as trade, the elimination of quotas, privileged access for goods and changes in trade in services. A study undertaken by Davenport and Page[4], that attempted to draw up a balance sheet for the developing world of the SEM, suggested a boost to developing world exports of some 5%. However, the positive picture overall needed to be qualified by recognition that for some countries gains would be cancelled out by losses, and that for a few there were serious long-term implications.

The other was the Treaty on European Union (the Maastricht Treaty), which was concluded in December 1991 and came into effect in November 1993. This marked the most important stage in the development of the EU since its initial founding in the Treaty of Rome. Important decisions were taken to deepen the processes of integration within the EU and to take an enhanced role in external relations. For the first time member states committed themselves to introducing a common foreign and security policy (CFSP) and set out specific objectives for development policy. The CFSP was the remain subject to intergovernmental cooperation that allowed individual member states to maintain almost exclusive determination of policy. However, EU development policy (as distinct from the development policies of individual member states) was to become a community policy in which decisions could be taken by qualified (weighted) majority voting rather than unanimity. This gave the Commission opportunities to seek to develop new policies within the general objectives of development policy. These were set out in Title XVII of the treaty as the sustainable economic and social development of the developing countries, and more particularly the most disadvantaged among them; the smooth and gradual integration of the developing countries into the world economy; the campaign against poverty in the developing countries; and the promotion of democracy, the rule of law and respect for human rights and fundamental freedoms.

The Commission's response, and the beginnings of the 'new direction' in development policy, was set out in a document released in May 1992 entitled Development Co-operation in the Run-Up to 2000 (usually referred to as Horizon 2000)[5]. In Horizon 2000 the Commission argued for a rethink of policy on several grounds. One was the radical changes that had taken place in international politics and the global economy in the late 1980s. The Commission argued that the end of the Cold War had led to a diminishing interest on the part of the major powers in the geostrategic potential of the developing world. At the same time, new forms of interdependence - population and environment issues, drugs and major endemic diseases such as AIDS - were replacing the traditional interdependence concerns focused on the security of supply of commodities. Another cause for a rethink was the failure of development policy to improve conditions in developing countries as a whole, and the less developed in particular, despite the large amount of resources mobilised to this end. While some of the blame was attributed to policies promoted by the developed countries, considerable emphasis is laid on the failures of government in the developing world to be politically accountable to their citizens. Finally, the Commission noted that the Maastricht Treaty had conferred upon it new powers in respect of development that allowed the Commission to take a co-ordinated and comprehensive approach to policy as a step toward devising a common development policy designed to enhance the EU's presence in international affairs.

The opportunities for change provided by this combination of circumstances are set out in Horizon 2000 as a statement of basic principles and objectives which should inform policy and a review of instruments to achieve desired ends. These were to be differentiated according to "the conditions, circumstances and needs of each developing country or group of developing countries"[6]. Horizon 2000 thus conclude with a list of priorities for the major developing regions as follows :

"*Sub-Saharan Africa* : economic restructuring, administrative overhaul and democratic reform should be a priority for Community aid. Such reforms, however, which are a long-term process, will call for a 'contract' of true partnership between Africa and the Community.

Mediterranean : here the major problems are political, environmental and social (emigration). Aid should be increased and refocused on family planning programmes, technical assistance for institutions with the aim of supporting reform, regional cooperation and economic cooperation.

Latin America : special importance will be accorded to a policy dialogue in all appropriate forums and to investment promotion and the private sector, without, however, neglecting the need for increased official development assistance for the poorest countries.

Asia : this continent presents widely contrasting situations. The overall objective should be to boost the Community's economic presence (exports and investment) in the most dynamic region of the world, while ensuring that the region's economic dynamism does not result in greater environmental damage. The means should be adapted to the areas and countries concerned. The least developed countries will continue to receive development aid of the traditional type"[7]

At the same time as Horizon 2000 was being prepared, a more in-depth study on The Future of North-South Relations was being undertaken by the Forward Studies Unit of the European Commission[8].

This unit, which reports directly to the Commission President, is tasked with monitoring European integration and identifying structural trends and long-term prospects that affect the EU. Its approach is therefore strategic in the wider sense that proposals from the various geographically focused directorates within the Commission are often not. In the event, the Unit proposed that a twin approach be adopted: a global strategy for the promotion of sustainable economic and social development and a geopolitical strategy for the EC and its member states.

The global strategy sought to harness the strengths of the EC as a 'soft power' i.e. its global economic interests. To this end it argued for a proactive policy by the EC in favour of the "better management of interdependence through a strengthening of multilateralism".[9] This meant the full participation of the EC with the world trade and financial institutions and the exercise of leadership in defining global priorities in areas such as peace and security, democracy, protection of human rights, demography, poverty, environment, migration, pandemics and drugs.

As far as the sustainable development of developing countries was concerned, it argued that the implementation of development cooperation policies should be left largely to member states and specialised domestic and multilateral agencies. This "would imply a progressive shift from geographically defined cooperation policies to horizontal and systemic policies and multilateral approaches" through what it termed 'development contracts'.[10] These were 'quasi-contractual long-term relations of partnership' between developed and developing countries that imposed commitments upon both recipients and donors. They included for developing countries respect for human rights, fundamental liberties, the rule of law, particularly political structures and social, economic, environmental and administrative reform programmes. In proposing such conditionalities the EC was accepting the development agenda as laid out by the World Bank and the major donor countries. This allowed it to more closely co-operative with others. At the same time, however, the shift to horizontal policies potentially diluted the distinctiveness of the EC regional programmes in developing countries in respect of the various instruments that had been used or any conditionalities that had been set. This especially applied to the Lome Convention where the report indicated there would need to be "a fundamental reorientation of the Lome scheme".[11]

The advocacy of a global approach also had implications for the geopolitical priorities of the EC. These were now seen to lie in the peace, stability and development of its neighbours. It was therefore proposed that policies toward the countries in Central, Eastern and South-Eastern Europe and Mediterranean region, as well as the countries of the former Soviet Union, Turkey and the Middle East be 'upgraded'. In respect of the Southern Mediterranean countries, it would mean "the creation of an economic cooperation zone progressively leading to a free trade area with the Community. Economic integration within each region through free trade areas (FTAs), customs' unions or cooperation agreements should be encouraged as steps towards integration into the economy of the Community. In terms of assistance policies, existing financial protocols should be gradually replaced by structural funds".[12] In other words, closer involvement than had hitherto been the case, involving the promotion of these regions and/or countries to the apex of the 'pyramid of privileges'. The ALA countries were to be subject to 'horizontal cooperation', sharing common cooperation instruments within the wider framework of development policy.

In retrospect, the approach of the Forward Studies Unit can be seen as signalling the beginning of a shift in favour of global policy and away from 'limping regionalism'. It did not yet advocate a full jettisoning of a regional approach. But it did indicate the lines of thinking around which fundamental revisions of existing regional agreements would take place. The Horizon 2000 proposals were more concrete, but pointed in the same general direction, signalling EU priorities in the regional agreements. It also sketched out the general principles that would inform the choice of development policies and instruments. The remainder of the 1990s were to see the elaboration of the new thinking in a new generation of association and development agreements.

The Lome Conventions

Some of the most far-reaching changes have been or will be introduced into the Lome Conventions. They began in a very small way with the introduction of limited conditionalities in Lome IV, were further developed and added to during the mid-term review and, at the time of writing, are yet to be concluded in current negotiations for a successor convention which formally began in September 1998. The changes introduced or proposed, have been so extensive that several years ago the prevailing view among those most associated with the Lome conventions was that a successor convention, to take effect from 2000, was unlikely. This is no longer the case, although what is clear is that the next convention will be radically different from previous conventions.

Lome IV was negotiated at the end of the 1980s. Its major innovations were the introduction of aid for structural adjustment, the admission of several new members, acknowledgement of human rights and decentralised co-operation, and the conclusion of a convention for a ten-year period (previously it had been only five years), subject to a mid-term review. Other changes were mainly incremental, seeking greater effectiveness of existing instruments and policies. This meant the majority of changes were informed as much by the past of previous conventions as by new development priorities, although such features as a structural adjustment facility and a chapter on decentralised co-operation indicated an awareness of a wider development debate on North-South co-operation. The radical changes in the international system that took place as the convention was being signed (notably the beginning of the end of the Cold War) were not anticipated and understandably not part of it.

The Mid-Term Review

The provision of a mid-term review allowed such changes in the international system to be included. The review was more wide-ranging and deeper than anticipated by the ACP, constituting in essence another set of negotiations, involving the amendment, deletion or addition of 71 articles (out of 369 in the existing convention) as well as changes and an addition to the protocols[13]. The details are too numerous to give, although the broad headings are indicative of new thinking and new priorities, most of which were proposed by the Commission. They may be grouped into four sections.[14]

Political and Institutional Issues : On the proposal of the Commission, a new article was added recognising the application of democratic principles and the consolidation of the rule of law as 'essential elements'. This allowed for a country to be suspended if it violated such elements. Other features were an enhanced political dialogue, to include foreign policy and security issues; support for administrative and institutional reform; a greater role for parliamentarians in the twice-yearly meetings of the ACP-EU Joint Assembly; and a provision recognising the importance of the development of the market economy and the private sector in ACP states.

Trade : A review of trade was proposed by the ACP. The emphasis shifted from trade preferences to trade promotion. This recognised the importance of developing trade competitiveness with the objective of ensuring the smooth and progressive integration of the ACP countries into the world economy. Other measures included easing the few remaining limitations on total non-reciprocal access to the EU market; revising the rules of origin to enable some sourcing for production from geographically proximate non-ACP developing countries; some minor beneficial changes for the ACP to the banana and the beef and veal protocols; and the conclusion of a new protocol on the sustainable management of tropical forests.

Financial and Technical Co-operation : The single largest issue was the amount to be given for the five-year European Development Fund (EDF) aid programme. Several EU member states, notably Britain and Germany, were opposed to any increase. The French, supported by the Commission, sought a figure that would be at least equivalent to the existing EDF brought up-to-date in real terms. The failure to agree a figure saw the negotiations extended beyond their deadline, with the final figure only being agreed by heads of state and government of the EU at the Cannes Summit in June 1995. This delivered an overall increase, but not as large as might have been anticipated given the contribution of three new member states (Austria, Finland and Sweden) to the EDF. Another controversial issue was the delivery of aid in two tranches. The first tranches would amount to 70% of the overall sum allocated to an ACP country over the five-year period. The remaining 30% would only be disbursed if a review could show that good use had been made of the first tranches in accordance with a programme agreed between the EU and the ACP state. Such close oversight had not been a feature of previous conventions. Other measures included a dialogue on aid programming which would include the EU development priorities as set out in the Maastricht Treaty as well as those determined by the ACP state; increased support for structural adjustment in ACP countries; support for the private sector through funding chanelled through the European Investment Bank; and the future provision cf all aid on grant basis to limit ACP debt.

Thematic and Sectoral Aspects : Under this heading a number of measures were agreed to improve support for industrial development; expedite implementation of decentralised co-operation; and improve the operation of Stabex.

The EU saw the outcome of the mid-term review in positive terms. It had enhanced "the political dimension of ACP-EC relations through an enlargement of the political dialogue and also, and above all, through the designation of human rights, democratic principles and the rule of law as an 'essential element' "; improved "the effectiveness of cooperation thanks to more consistent instrument and the institution of a more flexible and performance-oriented approach to programming, which is the driving force behind financial assistance"; and redirected "the economic component of cooperation towards the private sector and efforts to make ACP products more competitive (which in itself is indicative of the new approach to trade lying at the heart of ACP-EC cooperation".[15] The ACP were not so content. Their objectives had been limited "in the sense of not seeking to radically the areas and instruments of the Convention, but to sharpen them and to make them more effective, and in some cases more appropriate".[16] This was not the case and the ACP were obliged to accept far reaching reforms which, in the words of its Deputy Secretary General, challenged "the concept of partnership" and indirectly raised the issue of "a return to colonialism".[17] Non-governmental development organisations (NGDOs) in the EU were also critical of the outcomes and the direction the convention was taking. In particular, they and others were concerned that the EU might now abandon Lome, seeking instead new and radically different arrangements negotiated separately with regional groupings or even individual countries.

The Green Paper and the Negotiating Mandates

In late 1996, the EU issued its Green Paper on the future of EU-ACP relations[18]. This set in motion an unprecedented and intense structured dialogue involving non-governmental organisations, states and the Commission at national, regional and international level. The result has been the most systematic general discussion of the value of Lome conventions since their inception. In the course of the debate, which is impossible to summarise given the amount of material generated, the argument has swung from the anticipated end of the convention to its expected continuation through at least the first decade of the coming century.

The Green Paper was in two parts. The first contained the reasons for change. These set out familiar themes addressed in Horizon 2000 and The Future of North-South Relations. There was also a review of the successes and failures of the various conventions that repeated criticisms and changes introduced at the mid-term review. Much was therefore familiar. What were different were the proposals in the second part for a new partnership signalling a radical change in direction.

Some of the most controversial were the proposal on trade. The EU outlined four options, but in practice there were two: (a) to negotiate preferential and reciprocal trade agreements with individual countries or with groups of countries (regional differentiation); or (b) to abandon existing provisions and harmonise trade policies under the GSP, in which less developed countries would receive special benefits (differentiation according to levels of development). Both options entailed ending the uniform treatment of ACP countries that had been a feature of previous conventions. This would disadvantage some ACP countries unless they negotiated free trade agreements between the EU and ACP regions (or states), eventually involving reciprocal access to ACP markets. The EU also confirmed that all trade agreements would need to be WTO compatible.

The Green Paper proposed further reform of the aid programme. In particular, it argued for significant role for the private sector and NGDOs in the delivery of aid. The private sector is seen to the best agent to promote economic growth, with the role of the state being primarily that of facilitator. It also argued for a greater focus of aid on poverty reduction and for a fresh look at the financial instruments to simplify them. New management arrangements giving an enhanced role to the Commission were also suggested. The net effect of these proposals would be to reduce the role of the ACP state. Hitherto, the state had played an almost exclusive role in the delivery and the determination of aid priorities, it would now do so in co-management with others.

This meant a greater emphasis on dialogue than had previously been the case. The Commission proposed this should advance issues of good governance, democracy, human rights and the rule of law. It would encourage ACP countries to promote institutional reform and develop policies fulfilling the objectives of the EU's development policy as set out in the Maastricht Treaty. In other words, the link between the EU's foreign policy and its development policy should be explicitly acknowledged. The idea of a 'neutral' development policy (i.e. one addressed exclusively to the development needs and priorities of ACP states), which was a feature of the earlier conventions, was here finally laid to rest.

Lastly, the Green Paper raised the issue of geographic coverage. It posed the question of whether the ACP group was still an appropriate partner for the EU given the diversity of situations within the ACP group. It made no explicit recommendation, although it was clear that it thought the ACP should be divided into a least three regions corresponding to Africa, the Caribbean and the Pacific. The rationale being that it would be easier to negotiate specific trade agreements with separate regions, tailor aid programmes to take their needs into account, and identify common interests in a regional setting. The distinctive identity of the ACP as one of the largest group of developing countries was thus under threat.

The debate on the Green Paper underlined the contentious nature of many of these proposals. The ACP response was contained in outline in The Libreville Declaration issued at the end of a summit meeting of ACP heads of state and government[19]. While this subscribed to some of the arguments in the Green Paper, the ACP highlighted the many positive elements of the existing convention and affirmed the unity and solidarity of the ACP group. These were taken forward and further elaborated in its negotiating mandate that was presented at the end of September 1998. The emphasis was on preserving and improving the convention. For its part, the EU modified some of its earlier proposals and its mandate sought to retain some features of the current convention as well as to press for fundamental change. The EU and the ACP therefore shared some common ground, but there were also potential major differences between them, particularly over trade and the idea canvassed by the EU the general principles and frameworks should be reached first, with detailed implementing proposals to follow later. The ACP saw this as potentially divisive and proposed instead "a frank political discussion of an overarching kind as to the nature and scope of negotiations before us" with the proviso that "nothing is agreed until everything is agreed".[20] The history of previous negotiations has seen the EU mostly gain what it wants. The circumstances of the present negotiations ensure that once again it is the stronger partner. The outcome of negotiations is therefore likely to be closer to the EU mandate that it is to that of the ACP. In the process, the Lome Convention will not be jettisoned, but it is likely to be overhauled to admit new principles to govern development co-operation: the differentiation of richer and poorer countries; the concentration of aid on the poorest; the graduation of the richer and more successful ACP countries from the aid programme; the promotion of the private sector and to a lesser extent of the NGOs; and the eventual integration of the ACP, including the poorest and most vulnerable, into the global economy.

The Mediterranean

The New Mediterranean Policy, which came into force in the early 1990s, was both a reinforcement of existing development efforts and a departure from them. As before, the main features were trade concessions and development assistance, but unlike before these were to be more focussed. This was particularly the case with development assistance, which was increased substantially. Although the amounts available to individual countries through the five-year financial protocols was increased to 2075 million ECU, an almost equal amount of new funds was committed to horizontal co-operation. This was to be between non-government actors in the Mediterranean and the EU and was directed at supporting regional cooperation, with particular priorities for decentralised cooperation, environmental protection and conservation, demographic issues and private investment. The intent here was to encourage economic reform and closer identification of interests, particularly but not only among the various sub-regions of the Maghreb and Mashreq.

The new pattern of development with the Mediterranean was set out in the Barcelona Declaration agreed in November 1995 between the EU and eleven Mediterranean countries and the Palestinian governing authority. The EU was the driving force behind the Declaration and the proposals for a Euro-Mediterranean Partnership. In a series of papers in the early 1990s the Commission developed a coherent approach to the Mediterranean. At the core of its interests were security and social stability. As the key document defining the new policy put it: "The Mediterranean basin constitutes an area of strategic importance for the Community. The peace and stability of the region are the highest priority to Europe". Accordingly "The Union's policy should be directed towards support for establishing a zone of stability and security and creating the conditions for lasting and sustainable rapid economic development in the Mediterranean countries. With a clear commitment to economic reform, the countries concerned could achieve higher levels of employment and reduce the prosperity gap with the Community. This could best be facilitated by the progressive creation of a Euro-Mediterranean Economic Area, comprising as its main features progressive establishment of free trade and economic integration, accompanied by adequate support from the Union for the economic and social adjustments which this process will entail, as well as closer cooperation in the political and security fields".[21] In short, development was to serve political and security goals.[22] In the Barcelona Declaration three areas of partnership were defined.[23]

Political and Security Partnership : This seeks to establish a common area of peace, stability and security. Among the measures agreed are commitments to human rights, democracy, the peaceful settlement of disputes, the fight against racism, drugs and organised crime, and the promotion of regional security through adherence to various international and regional non-proliferation regimes in the nuclear, chemical and biological areas.

Economic and Financial Partnership : This was the centrepiece of the Declaration. Agreement was reached to establish a free-trade area by 2010 through the negotiation of new Euro-Mediterranean Agreements. It envisages the progressive elimination of tariff and non-tarrif barriers on manufactured products and a progressive liberalisation of trade in agricultural products and services. It is to be supported by economic cooperation and concerted action in a number of areas, including the promotion of investment, environmental protection, improving the position of women, modernising and restructuring agriculture, and developing the infrastructure. Substantial additional financial assistance amounting to 4685 billion ECU was also to be provided for the period 1995-1999.

Partnership in Social, Cultural and Human Affairs : Support is to be given to developing human resources, promoting understanding between cultures, and facilitating exchanges between civil societies. There is also an acknowledgement of the importance of migration and a commitment to strengthen cooperation to reduce migratory pressures and illegal immigration.

The Declaration has the ambition of creating a new Euro-Mediterranean region. It is very much the product of a European vision for the region that has been described as "paternalistic, full of contradictions and offering little hope of resolving the social, economic and political problems of the region"[24]. Only time will tell if this is a valid criticism. In the meantime, several new Agreements with Mediterranean countries have been signed and others are being negotiated. Typically they include statements on respect for democratic principles and human rights, provision for political dialogue, agreement on the free circulation of goods, sections on economic, financial, social and cultural cooperation, and institutional arrangements. There is also an ongoing regional dialogue involving regular meetings of foreign ministers and numerous meetings at lower levels to discuss themes of common interest. These cover the three areas identified in the Declaration with particular attention being given to the political and economic dimensions. The EU is therefore actively determining the agenda. In the course of doing so it is exercising a stronger presence in the Mediterranean that it has shown for many years and profoundly influencing the future development of the region.

Latin America

Writing in the early 1990s about the previous twenty years of policy of Latin America, Enzo Grilli claimed: "Latin America lies at the outer limits of the Community's development reach. Relative to that of sub-Saharan Africa and the Mediterranean, the position occupied by Latin America in the scale of development cooperation priorities pursued by the Community has not changed much since the 1950s. The region has remained a marginal concern of the Community, notwithstanding the attempts made at different times to expand the geographical reach of EC development cooperation".[25]

Such a statement applies no more. The 1990s have seen a steady intensification of relations between the EU and Latin America. The basis of the new dynamism was laid in the late 1980s when the Commission began to differentiate its Latin American development priorities from the ALA programme under which it and Asia had been collectively considered. An annual dialogue was launched in 1990 with the South American countries plus Mexico (the Rio Group), supplementing an earlier annual dialogue with Central America established in 1984, and in 1994 the European Council approved a Basic Document on the Relations of the European Union with Latin America and the Caribbean. This proposed, within the framework of the CFSP, "to undertake common efforts with Latin America and the Caribbean to bring about a new partnership of the two regions aimed at safeguarding peace, ensuring universal respect for human rights, increasing balanced economic exchanges, fostering sustained development, combatting poverty and environmental degradation, and activating cultural and scientific bonds".[26] The CFSP dimension is important as it signals the subordination of development interests to wider foreign policy interests, particularly mutual interest that can come from increased trade and investment and wider political dialogue.

The substance of such interests were fully developed in a Commission paper released in October 1995 that set out the proposed basis for partnership to the year 2000[27]. It is founded on two premises. The first is that Latin America is an emerging regional economy in which it and the EU have complementary interests. For Latin America this will come from opportunities for "diversifying its outlets and sources of supply, technologies and capital" and the prospect of securing "the cooperation of partners able to provide constructive assistance" and for the EU "in consolidating and improving its trading and technological position in a region of strong growth potential".[28] The Commission therefore proposed that further efforts be directed toward developing trade links (the EU was the main export market for Brazil, Chile, Panama and Peru and the main non-Latin American export market for Argentina, Bolivia, Paraguay and Uruguay in the early 1990s) and investment opportunities (in the 1980s the EU provided marginally more foreign direct investment to the region than the USA). A case is also made to improve the competitiveness of Latin America through European support for macroeconomic reform, regional integration, the development of the private sector and the promotion of co-operation in the fields of industry, the information society, and science and technology.

The second premise is that Latin America is asserting itself in the international community, providing the EU, through a structured political dialogue with the region, with an opportunity to be "a driving force for Latin America's increasing involvement in the running of international affairs"[29]. This involves formal bi-regional political dialogues with the Rio Group and with Central America where a variety of social, environmental and political issues are raised. These include questions of peace and democratic consolidation as well as measures to combat drugs, organised crime and money laundering. More generally, dialogues have served to heighten awareness of each other in both the EU and Latin America, the culmination of which will be the first ever summit meeting between the heads of state of the EU and Latin America in June 1999.

The interest of the EU have thus shifted and widened as compared to the 1980s. Then, the political problems of conflict in Central America were foremost, now trade and co-operation agreements with the potential economic giants of Latin America such as Mercosur (including Argentina, Brazil and Chile) and Mexico command more attention. Framework co-operation agreements have been signed with Mercosur in 1995 and Mexico in 1997. Agreements have also been concluded with Chile (1997) and with the Andean Community (including Colombia, Peru and Venezuela) in 1993. One particularly interesting aspect of these agreements is the "future developments" clause that allows both sides to expand and set up their co-operation. On this basis, the EU and Mercosur have entered into discussions on trade liberalisation leading to an eventual free trade area between the two regions.

The aid dimension of the EU relationship with the region has also been significant. The Commission is a major donor and along with the member states the EU was the largest single source of official development assistance to Latin America in the early 1990s. In the period of 1990-94, 925 million ECU was allocated directly to the region and a further 905 million ECU indirectly through indirect measures in food aid programmes, humanitarian aid, NGDO actions etc, the overall total being double the amount for the previous five years.[30] The major beneficiaries have been the poorest countries among which have been Peru, Nicaragua, El Salvador, Guatemala and Bolivia. Assistance has also been given to developing the private sector (Al-invest), improving energy use (ALURE), urban development (URB-AL) and co-operation in higher education (ALFA).

In the period 1996-2000 the Commission proposed further increases in funding and a concentration on three priorities in conjunction with three issues of mutual interest. The priorities are institutional support and consolidation of the democratic process (all the framework co-operation agreements contain references to the maintenance of democracy as an essential element for receiving assistance); combating marginality, poverty and social exclusion (which should be the main priority and receive the greatest amount of assistance); and supporting economic reforms and improving international competitiveness. Although these will require allocations for individual countries, the Commission further proposes that implementation should take account of various horizontal programmes which it considers are areas of mutual interest. These include support for regional co-operation and integration; education and training; and management of North-South interdependence (the environment, energy and drugs). It also urges greater co-ordination between member states and the Commission in identifying priorities and providing aid, noting the fact that as the EU is the largest donor this "gives Europe a considerable edge in quantitative terms", implying an ability to set the agenda and exert leverage in this area.[31]

Asia

As with Latin America, so with Asia there has been a new interest by the EU. Instead of Europe and Asia "growing apart from one another"[32] which was the case prior to the early 1990s, the EU and various countries and regional organisations in Asia have embarked on a programme to define a new set of closer relations. The key document outlining the new approach from the EU was published in 1994 as Towards a New Asia Strategy.[33]

In this document the Commission are frank about previous neglect arguing that the "European Union needs to accord Asia a higher priority"[34] and that it should do so as a matter of urgency. The central thrust of argument is toward greater economic engagement: "Europe's interests in Asia are (i) to benefit from the economic opportunities and to respond to the economic challenges in the region which contains the world's fastest growing countries, and which could represent a quarter and a third of the world economy by the year 2000; (ii) to integrate into the open, market-based world trading system those Asian countries such as China, India or Vietnam which are moving from state controls to market-oriented economies; and (iii) to assist in the enormous problem of poverty alleviation".[35] Supplementing it are proposals for more regular and intense political dialogue on a broad range of subjects, including democracy and human rights; and a concern with security issues, particularly "in the area of arms control and non-proliferation, regional disputes (Korea, Spratly, Kashmir) and the security of sea lanes".[36] The sum effect of such engagement will be an enhanced European presence that will more effectively compete with the USA and Japan. The broad perspective within which the new relations with Asia are to develop is therefore one in which there are foreign policy concerns, even though it is acknowledged that the instruments available to the Commission to pursue its objectives are essentially economic.

On their part, many Asian countries have welcomed the new interest of the EU. The East Asian and ASEAN countries have set in motion the so-called ASEM process that was inaugurated with a summit meeting in Bangkok between the heads of state or government in the EU and ten Asian countries in 1996. A second summit meeting was held in London in April 1998. The agendas of the ASEM summits are focussed on economic and political concerns[37]. Among the former are concerns with trade and investment. A trade facilitation action plan (TFAP) and an investment promotion action plan (IPAP) have been adopted and an Asia-Europe Business Forum established to bring ASEM leaders and senior business representatives into direct dialogue. Political dialogue has concentrated on broad issues including reform of the UN, the WTO and various regional and security issues. There has also been approval of programmes to foster social, cultural and scientific co-operation. The ASEM process is still in its infancy and so it is early to make a judgement. But overall the process now seems firmly established, not least through the agreement to continue bi-annual summit meetings, plus the many new initiatives launched that give it a foundation and a sense of purpose.

Although the EU has identified an overall Asian strategy and encouraged a collective approach via the ASEM process, it continues to recognise significant differences within Asia that calls for flexibility in dealing with the three major sub-regions of East Asia, South-East Asia and South Asia and the individual countries within them. The political dialogues and various framework trade and/or cooperation agreements established with ASEAN (1980) and individual countries (China, Macao, Mongolia, India, Pakistan, Sri Lanka, Nepal, Vietnam, Bangladesh, Cambodia and Laos) remain important. The most recent agreements cover a number of areas including trade, rural development, poverty alleviation, protection of the environment and political dialogue. The absence of an effective regional organisation in South Asia is of potential significance since it means relations between the EU and the countries of this region will be essentially bilateral, in which the balance of advantage in negotiations on economic and development matters will inevitably lie with the much stronger EU.

Development Policy towards Asia

An important innovation in the new engagement with Asia (and to a lesser extent Latin America) has been the distinction within the EU between economic co-operation and development aid. Economic co-operation "is aimed at improving the business and regulatory environment in partner countries in order to stimulate two way trade and investments with the direct participation of the private sector to the benefit of both the Union and the partner country".[38] It is primarily directed toward the newly emerging markets of the ASEM countries but also includes India and Pakistan. Among the measures the EU has proposed have been clarification of regulations on intellectual property rights; mutual recognition agreements on standards, testing and certification; providing policy expertise and policy advice to the ex-state trading countries of Asia; promoting business co-operation between European companies and their Asian counterparts; establishing better links between with European business associations and chambers of commerce; developing technological links, including establishing European technology centres in the region; and supporting investment with financial incentives, such as through the European Community Investment Partners (ECIP) scheme (which provides finance to initiate and develop local/EU join venture private investments.[39] The emphasis in all this is very much on the private sector as the 'motor of development' with the role of the EU and member governments as facilitators. It therefore reflects the new development agenda adopted by the Commission.

At the same time, the Commission makes it clear that it will continue to offer more familiar forms of development assistance to the less developed countries. This applies to ASEAN and South Asia. Between 1986-1995 the EU committed 3871 million ECU to its Asian programmes, of which 2161 million ECU was allocated to South Asia, 961 million ECU to South-East Asia and 280 million ECU to East Asia.[40] Such assistance has been widely distributed across sectors with the largest shares going to agriculture, food aid, humanitarian aid, development and social infrastructure and services. This accords with the increasing practice of concentrating development assistance on the poorest. Those countries identified as having major poverty problems and therefore likely recipients of aid are China, Mongolia, Cambodia, Laos, Vietnam, India, Bangladesh, Bhutan and Nepal (and Afghanistan and Burma when political conditions permit).[41]

The EU and India

Relations between the EU and India date back to 1962. There have been three cooperation agreements, the most recent entering into force in 1994. Over the years the relationship has been the subject of several in-depth studies and cannot be easily summarised in a few short paragraphs. However, the general view from the Indian perspective is that the relationship could and should have been closer, for which India as well as the EU is to blame.[42] While from the European side the relationship has been described as one of 'asymmetrical interdependence' in which the EU's importance for India has been growing while India's importance to the EU has been diminishing.[43]

The latest cooperation agreement and accompanying statement on political dialogue are designed to remedy this in part, although there are many sensitivities to overcome, not least over the issue of the recent nuclear test, which the EU condemned, and the EU's assertiveness in demanding economic change in India.

The current co-operation agreement is a typical third generation agreement. It includes respect for human rights as an essential element; development and diversification of trade and investment in the mutual interest of both partners; encouragement of understanding and strengthening of ties between the two regions in respect of technical, economic and cultural matters; building up India's economic capability to interact more effectively with the EU; promotion of exchanges and communication between business communities; acceleration of India's development to support new Indian policies in key areas fostering sustainable social progress and poverty alleviation; and support for environmental protection and sustainable use of natural resources[44]. While this list corresponds to a number of needs in India, it is clear that it is derived in good measure from the wider development agenda informing EU relations with the developing world. This is especially so in relation to its Asian dimension where there is the clear distinction between economic cooperation and development cooperation. In the Indian case, economic cooperation has been an accelerating element. Support is directed toward the private sector and includes cooperation through established instruments such as ECIP, Asia Invest, European Business Information Centres, and Asia-Urbs (a cooperation programme between the EU and Asian local authorities). In contrast, development cooperation, while it is still very much the largest element of direct assistance, is a declining one. Although India remains the single largest recipient of EC aid in Asia its share of the total almost halved 1991-1995 (at 462 million ECU) compared to 1986-90 (471 million ECU)[45]. It has also been re-directed since 1993 away from rural development towards human resource development (particularly primary education programmes encouraging female participation) and poverty alleviation (access of the most deprived to productive resources and basic social services).

The 'EU-India Joint Statement on Political Dialogue' commits both sides to defending democracy, human rights, peace and a stable, just international order in line with the UN Charter; reinforced cooperation to promote prosperity, economic reform, liberalisation, free trade and economic stability as well as social progress and cultural links; allowing each others' interests to be taken into account in decision-making procedures; and a better mutual understanding to increase cooperation on international questions such as non-proliferation, the fight against terrorism, drug trafficking, money laundering and issues linked to international peace and stability[46]. Some of these issues have proven contentious. The EU has criticised India on its human rights record at the UN and over its policy on nuclear weapons. The latter has become especially sensitive since the nuclear test explosion in May. Almost immediately following it the EU issued a statement under the CCSP that condemned the Indian action as "a grave threat to international peace and security" and called upon India to take a number of actions it had long urged on her, including to become party to the Treaty on the Non-Proliferation on Nuclear weapons and the Comprehensive Nuclear Test Ban Treaty. It also explicity linked the political/security dimension with the economic/ development one, stating it would review India's actions with regard to the accession to these treaties along with its "continued eligibility for GSP preferences"; and work with member states "for a delay in consideration of loans to India in the World Bank and other international institutions".[47] In so doing, the EU indicated that India, despite its size and importance, was to be subject to similar conditionalities that it imposed on others.

This perspective permeates the most recent Commission overview on India endorsed by the European Council in December 1996. In acknowledges India's important position in regional and global affairs. But it qualifies support for India's greater engagement stating that while the EU is "ready to be a partner in India's integration into appropriate international bodies" it will do so only if "India accepts the international responsibilities and treaties that befit a major world power".[48] On trade and economic issues it states that "despite recent changes, India's tariffs remain high"; that direct public sector intervention in many industries, along with subsidies, distort the market and deter investment; and that liberalisation in government procurement, agriculture and financial, telecommunications and transport services are needed.[49] The implication of this is that accelerated changes in all these areas, as well as changes towards improving the protection of international property rights, are essential to involving EU companies more directly in India's economic development. Finally, on development cooperation the EU states that it is committed to social development and that it has "a fundamental interest in India making a success of its structural adjustment process".[50] It will therefore continue to make development assistance available: "However, European development cooperation must fit into an overall concerted policy framework if it is to be effective. For this reason a detailed sector dialogue on the policy lines, linked to the cooperation, needs to be maintained".[51] In sum, in all three dimensions - political, economic and developmental - the EU is exerting pressure and seeking to determine agendas. It is flexing economic and political muscle. It is very much part of the new development policy in which, despite a rhetoric of mutual interests, the EU is selectively determining content, pace and direction.

Conclusion

The final element of the EU's new development policy is being put in place in the current Lome negotiations. When these are completed the EU will have fundamentally revised its objectives and approach to the developing world. Geographic differentiation will no longer be the main criteria determining policy as common instruments are increasingly brought into play in furthering economic cooperation with the developing world. Within such programmes the economic interests of the EU will be more visible and the demands for reciprocity more pronounced. The favoured regions and countries will be those with which the EU can do business or in which it has a direct security interest. The Mediterranean, South America and East and South-East Asia are those most likely to benefit. Outside these regions, the focus will continue to be on more traditional forms of development cooperation. Here conditionalities will apply and development assistance will be more selectively targeted. The ACP will no longer be as privileged and Central America and South Asia will be in danger of increasing marginalisation. India may escape this face since it is large enough to be considered an exception, but it will not escape the wider trends that are shaping EU development policy. Among these, the assumption of a world role by the EU is of paramount importance.

The political, economic and even security objectives of the CFSP are becoming more pronounced to which development policy is now subordinated. It follows that the likely future of development policy as a distinctive element of the EU presence in the world is thus increasingly bound up with the future of the CFSP itself. To date, the CFSP has been slow the develop and even Jacque Delors, when President of the Commission, "stopped short of predicting the development of a common European foreign policy".[52] Nevertheless, as the recently concluded Treaty of Amsterdam has demonstrated, the momentum is still forward and the CFSP has been further strengthened as a result. Development policy must necessarily reflect such incremental change, with its vocation of a more integrated Europe and accompanying stronger global presence.

Notes

1. For a recent exploration of this concept in relation to the Lom_ Convention see Majorie Lister, *The European Union and the South: relations with developing countries* (London and New York: Routledge, 1997).
2. See Commission of the European Communities, *The Europe, Asia and Latin America Dialogue* (Luxembourg: Office for Official Publications of the European Community, 1991)
3. Enzo Grilli, *The European Community and the Developing Countries* (Cambridge: Cambridge University Press, 1993), pp. 337-38.
4. Michael Davenport with Sheila Page, *Europe: 1992 and the Developing World* (London: Overseas Development Institute, 1991).
5. Commission of the European Communities, *Development Co-operation Policy in the Run-Up to 2000* (SEC (92) 915 final. Brussels, 15 May 1992).
6. *Ibid,* paragraph 42.
7. *Ibid,* paragraph 45.
8. Commission of the European Communities, *The Future of North-South Relations* ('Cahiers' of the Forward Studies Unit) (Luxembourg: Office for Official Publications of the European Communities, 1997).
9. *Ibid.* p. 11.
10. *Ibid.* p. 16.
11. *Ibid.*
12. *Ibid.* p. 17.
13. See European Commission, Directorate General for Development, Lome IV *Revised: Changes and Challenges 1995-2000* (DE 89) (Luxembourg: Office for Official Publications of the European Communities, 1996).
14. This summary is taken from European Commission, Directorate General for Development, *Information Memo* (Coordination Group, Lome IV Review).

15. *Ibid.*
16. Carl Greenidge, Deputy Secretary General of the ACP. "Return to Colonialism? The New Orientation of European Development Assistance" (Speech to the Association of German Non-Governmental Organisations, Bonn, 17 September, 1996).
17. *Ibid.*
18. See Commission of the European Communities, *Green Paper on relations between the European Union and the ACP countries on the eve of the 21st century* (COM (96) 570 final: Brussels, 20/11/1996).
19. See ACP Group, *The Libreville Declaration: Adopted by the First Summit of the ACP Heads of State and Government* (ACP/28/051/97 final: Libreville, Gabon, 7 November 1997)
20. *The Libreville Declaration* and "Statement by the Hon. Ms Billie Miller, President in Office of the ACP Council of Ministers, at the Opening of the Negotiations for a Successor Agreement to Lome IV" (ACP-CE 2169/98 (Presse 329), Brussels, 30 September 1998).
21. Commission of the European Communities, *Strengthening the Mediterranean Policy of the European Union: Establishing a Euro-Mediterranean Partnership* (Com (94) 427 final: Brussels, 19/10/1994).
22. In addition to economic and social objectives, including a desire to reduce migration to the EU, Jean-Pierre Derisbourg, a senior Commission official closely associated with the Euro-Mediterranean Partnership, has identified two other reasons behind the policy: (a) a desire to rectify the balance in favour of the Mediterranean countries, who have received less assistance than those in Eastern Europe and additionally cannot expect to accede to the EU; and (b) to integrate the Mediterranean more closely with the EU in the face of regionalization in the global economy as exemplified by NAFTA, APEC etc. See Jean-Pierre Deisbourg, "The Euro-Mediterranean Partnership since Barcelona" in Richard Gillespie (ed.), *The Euro-Mediterranean Partnership: Political and Economic Perspectives* (London: Frank Cass, 1997), pp. 9-11.
23. See "The Barcelona Declaration" in Gillespie, *op.cit*, pp. 177-187.
24. George Joffe, "Southern Attitudes towards an Integrated Mediterranean Region" in Gillespie, *op.cit*, pp. 12-29, at p. 12.
25. Grilli, *op.cit.*, p. 225.
26. Council of the European Union, *Basic Document on the Relations of the European Union with Latin America and the Caribbean* (31 October 1994), paragraph 1.
27. Commission of the European Communities, *The European Union and Latin America; the present situation and prospects for closer partnership 1996-2000* (Com (95) 495 final: Brussels 23/10/1995).
28. *Ibid*, Paragraph 1.6.
29. *Ibid*, Paragraph 3.1.
30. *Ibid*, p. 13.

31. *Ibid,* p. 16.
32. Grilli, *op cit.* p. 290.
33. Commission of the European Communities, *Towards a New Asia Strategy* (COM (94) 314 final: Brussels 13/7/1994).
34. *Ibid,* p. 1.
35. *Ibid,* p. 13.
36. *Ibid,* p. 2.
37. See "Statement of the Chairman of the Asia-Europe Meeting" 1-2 March 1996, *Bulletin of the European Union,* 3/1996; and "Chairman's Statement: Second Europe-Asia Summit", 3-4 April, 1998, *Bulletin of the European Union,* 4/1998.
38. *Towards A New Asia Strategy.* p.6.
39. *Ibid.* pp. 20-22.
40. Figures from Aidan Cox and Antonique Koning, *Understanding European Community Aid: Aid policies, Management and Distribution Explained* (Overseas Development Institute, London and European Commission, Brussels, 1997), Table 5.1. The total includes an unallocable figure of 470 million ECU.
41. *Towards a New Asia Strategy,* p. 24.
42. See, in particular, the recent in-depth study by Dusmanta Kumar Giri, *The Single European Market and India: a study in North-South relations* (Ph.D. thesis, University of Hull, UK, 1996).
43. See Jorgen Dige Pedersen, "India and the EC in a new world order" *Contemporary South Asia,* Vol. 2, No. 2, 1993, pp. 265-84.
44. Commission of the European Communities, *EU-India Enhanced Partnership* (COM (96) 275 final. Brussels 26/6/1996), Annex 1.
45. Cox. *et al., Understanding European Aid,* Table 5.2
46. *EU-India Enhanced Partnership,* Annex 1.
47. "Statement on Nuclear Tests in India" (CFSP 9/22. Brussels and London, 25/5/1998), *Bulletin of the European Union,* 5/98.
48. *EU-India Enhanced Partnership,* p.7.
49. *Ibid.* pp. 7-8.
50. *Ibid.* pp. 10.
51. *Ibid.* pp. 12.
52. Lister, *The European Union and the South,* p. 17.

5

India-EU Economic Relations: Problems and Prospects

Nimmi Kurian

The first-ever summit between India and the European Union (EU) in Lisbon, Portugal on 28 June 2000 was a reflection of the growing importance of their ties. The Summit provided a forum for an exchange of views and problems on a range of issues related to trade, which forms an integral component of the relationship. But the ambit of the discussions was also broadened to include other common global concerns such as cross-border terrorism, drug trafficking, environment, nuclear disarmament etc. The resolve to enhance the scope of the partnership was reflected in the Joint Summit Declaration which called for a "new strategic partnership founded on shared values and aspirations characterised by enhanced and multifaceted cooperation."[1]

India's association with the EU dates back to the formative years of the establishment of the European Community, with India being among the first countries to establish diplomatic relations with the newly formed Union. Bilateral cooperation has been formalised by agreements in 1973, 1981 and 1994 and is complemented by a host of schemes aimed at strengthening business cooperation, namely the EU-India Partnariat, the Asia-Investment Programme and the Asia Urbs Programme. EU's funding for economic cooperation programmes in India in the 1990s amounted to ECU 80 million.[2] The EU is an increasingly important partner for India since it is the largest foreign investor, the largest donor and the largest trading partner of India.

Investment Flows

India's liberalisation policies have provided an impetus to EU's investments in India. In terms of actual inflow, as Table 5.1 shows, investments from the EU between 1994 and 1997 were worth $ 925.30

TABLE 5.1: Foreign Direct Investment Actual Inflow Per Country

Country	Mn US $ 94/95 to 96/97	Mn US$ 96/97	Mn US$ 95/96	Mn US$ 94/95
4 Main European Union Investing Countries	925.30	405.20	283.10	237.00
United Kingdom	268.60	54.20	70.90	143.50
Netherlands	218.20	123.70	49.80	44.70
Germany	300.50	166.20	99.70	34.60
France (2 years)	76.90	N.A.	62.70	14.20

million and made up 21 per cent of total inflows of foreign direct investment. The top ranking investors from the EU have been Germany, the United Kingdom, Netherlands and France. Germany and the UK have provided more than two-thirds of EU investments during this period, with their combined share amounting to $ 568 million. It should also be noted that collectively, the EU constitutes the largest source of FDI in India as shown in Table 5.2.

The prospects of business cooperation between the two sides have also been brightened following a shift in priorities initiated by the EU to develop a new Asian strategy under its Asia-Invest Programme. The Programme seeks to provide a facilitating environment so as to enable small and medium-sized enterprises in both India and the EU to form partnerships and business collaborations with one another. Under the EU-India Partnariat 1999, financed partly by the Asia-Investment Programme, the focus is on providing information on potential partners as well as information on market and investment opportunities.

TABLE 5.2 : Foreign Direct Investment Actual Inflow Per Source 93/94, 94/95 & 95/96

Source	1995-96 Mn US$	1994-95 Mn US$	1993-94 MnUS$
EU	281.7	236.9	156.1
USA	192.4	202.8	98.8
Japan	60.9	95.0	36.9
Switzerland	32.6	26.2	22.5
Singapore	58.8	24.5	9.9
Hong Kong	98.5	21.4	6.1
Others	693.1	265.3	38.7

Source: SIA

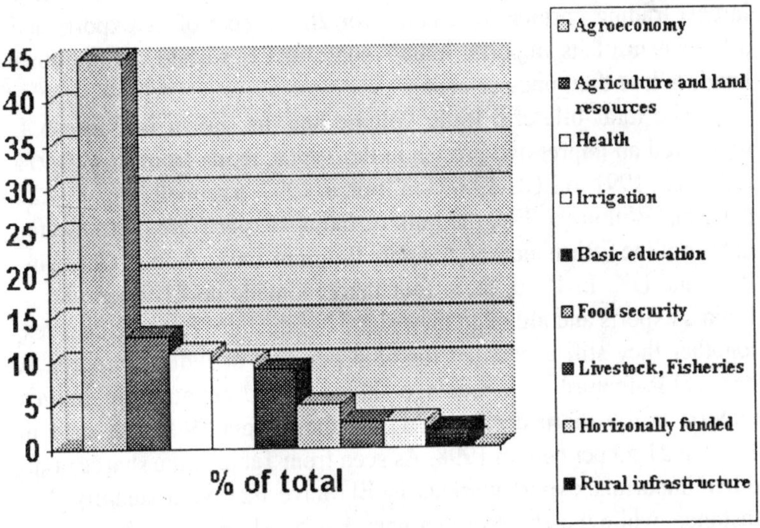

TABLE 5.3 :

Source. European Commission

Official Development Assistance

Taken together, the EU also constitutes India's largest bilateral donor. Development cooperation began in 1976 and by 1997, total development aid for India amounted to nearly ECU two billion.[3] The projects these have largely gone into are agro-economy, agriculture and land resources, health, irrigation, basic education, food security, livestock, fisheries and rural infrastructure. Their respective shares are given in Table 5.3.

Trade Flows

Bilateral trade constitutes the bedrock of the relationship between India and the EU. Their respective shares and contributions in each other's trade presents a picture of contrasts. The EU remains India's largest trading partner, accounting for 26 per cent of its exports and 30 per cent of its imports. India's share in EU's trade, on the other hand, is less than one per cent.

The total bilateral trade volume has, as shown in Table 5.4, registered an impressive growth in the 1990s, rising from ECU 9,975 million in 1991 to ECU 19,673 million in 1997, a growth rate of 97.22 per cent. Within the EU, the bulk of India's exports are concentrated in four of the fifteen markets, namely Belgium-Luxembourg, Germany, Italy and UK. In 1970, these four markets made up 81.9 per cent of India's exports and although their share has declined over the decades, together they still accounted for 68.8 per cent of India's exports. A noticeable feature of percentage shares of EU countries in India's exports is the sharp decline of UK's share from 59.52 per cent in 1970 to 21.53 per cent in 1998. As seen from Table 5, the shares of all other important export markets in EU have increased steadily. For instance, while the share of Germany has nearly doubled from 11.34 per cent in 1970 to 21.82 per cent in 1998, so has Belgium-Luxembourg's from 6.67 per cent to 12.67 per cent, that of Italy has more than tripled from 4.34 per cent to 12.82 per cent. The second strata of important markets whose shares have grown steadily are those of France, Netherlands and Spain whose respective shares are 10.32 per cent, 7.12 per cent and 5.09 per cent.

TABLE 5.4 : EU-India Trade

Year	EU Imports	% change	EU Exports	% change	Total Trade	% change
1991	4756	4.75	52.19	-12.97	9975	-5.33
1992	4878	2.56	5246	0.51	10124	1.49
1993	5880	20.55	6294	19.99	12174	20.24
1994	6912	17.63	7053	12.16	13965	14.80
1995	7794	12.76	9442	33.87	17236	23.42
1996	8588	10.19	9895	4.80	18483	7.23
1997	9465	10.21	10208	3.16	19673	6.43
1998	9790	3.43	9539	-6.55	19329	-1.74

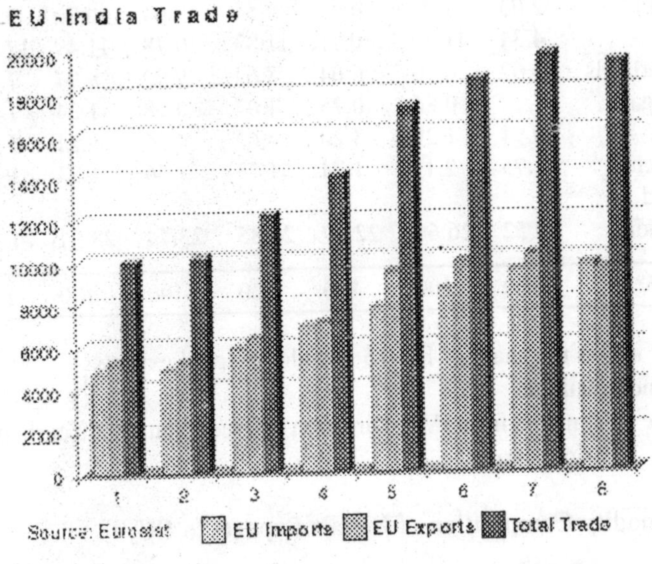

Table 5

TABLE 5.5 : Percentage Shares of Individual EU Member Country in India's Total Exports to the EU

Country	1970	1980	1990	1995	1996	1997	1998
EU-15*	19.48	26.13	27.71	26.96	26.21	25.41	26.32
Austria	0.15	1.01	1.72	1.09	0.99	1.05	1.38
Belgium-Luxembourg	6.67	9.24	14.16	13.47	12.48	12.86	12.67
Denmark	1.42	2.58	1.58	1.79	1.65	1.80	1.78
Finland	0.18	0.34	1.26	0.56	0.67	0.54	0.70
France	6.21	12.21	8.55	8.30	8.38	8.58	10.32
Germany	11.34	24.17	27.39	22.36	21.92	21.08	21.82
Greece	0.84	0.43	0.55	1.14	1.15	1.02	0.98
Ireland	2.03	1.01	0.49	0.56	0.64	0.70	0.81
Italy	4.34	11.39	10.11	11.83	10.78	11.49	12.82
Netherlands	4.62	6.70	6.04	8.64	9.90	8.97	7.12
Portugal	...	0.86	0.75	1.07	0.98	1.24	1.32
Spain	0.94	1.29	3.20	4.63	4.96	5.21	5.09
Sweden	1.75	2.11	1.74	1.71	1.76	1.84	1.65
United Kingdom	59.52	26.66	22.47	22.85	23.74	23.61	21.53
EU-15**	100	100	100	100	100	100	100

*Note** shows the share of EU-15 in India's global exports
**... not available

Source : Estimated from IMF, Direction of Trade Statistics Yearbook, Various Issues

Commodity Composition of India's Exports to EU

India's exports to EU are concentrated in textiles, clothing, leather and gems and jewellery. The top fifteen items which includes clothing, textile yarn and thread, agricultural products, semi-precious stones, leather, cotton fabrics accounted for the bulk of the export basket to the EU. Of this, textile and clothing alone accounted for close to 40 per cent of the exports.

India's basket of exports to the EU in 1997

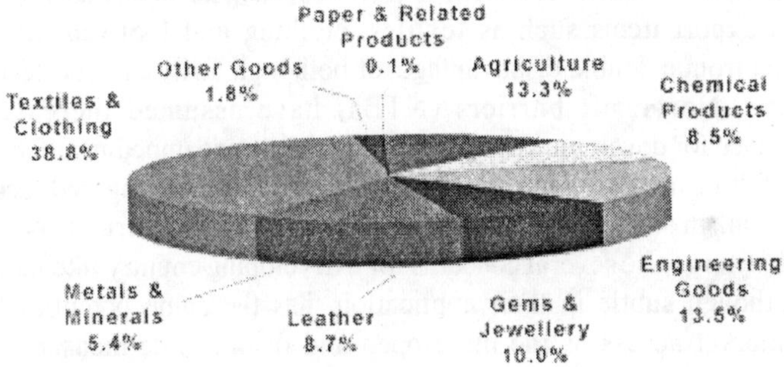

Source: Eurostat

India's Imports from EU

India's principal imports from the EU consists of machinery, precious stones, electrical machinery, chemicals and iron and steel. Engineering goods and precious stones together made up nearly three-quarters of total imports from the EU.

The EU's basket of exports to India in 1997

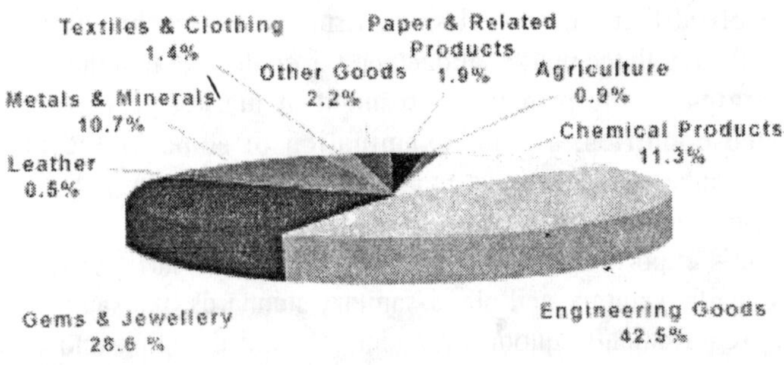

Source : Eurostat

Trade Disputes

An examination of EU's trade policy is vital since it has direct implications for India's exports to the EU which have been subjected to a slew of high tariff and non-tariff barriers significantly impairing market access. In this connection, it is important to note that major Indian export items such as textiles, clothing and footwear have suffered from a double disadvantage of both high tariff and non-tariff barriers. Non-tariff barriers (NTBs) have assumed increased importance for developing countries due to their trade impeding effects. Thus, while tariffs in the developed countries are being reduced, protectionism has emerged in the form of non-tariff barriers. Non-tariff barriers raise several concerns for a developing country like India and although subtle in their application, has the same potential to deny market access as the more open and quantifiable measure of tariffs. Thus, while Indian-made skirts and rayon scarves were banned in the US on the grounds that they were inflammable and, therefore, unsafe, exports of fresh and frozen shrimps was targetted on health and hygiene grounds and exports of mangoes were banned due to flies and weavels. NTBs allow a broad canvas of protectionist measures on diverse grounds. While not prohibiting access to markets, NTBs impose sufficiently high costs and exacting provisions so as to adversely affect performance and erode the cost-effectiveness of exports. Such measures present serious challenges for India's exports which are largely produced in the small-scale sector. As a result of the onerous provisions imposed by these measures and the attendant high costs involved therein, several small firms will often be forced to abandon the regulated market altogether. Given the fact that the NTBs are emerging as the primary instrument of market protection in developed countries, a brief examination of some of the most prominent measures becomes necessary since they have a direct bearing on India-EU trade.

India's exports to the EU face a spate of non-tariff obstacles such as health, sanitary and phyto-sanitary standards, packaging and labeling requirements, quota arrangements, anti-dumping and anti-subsidy investigations against Indian products. Quantitative restrictions in the form of Multi-Fibre Arrangement (MFA) quotas have been imposed on Indian textile exports since 1972. The quotas have increased to include almost all textile items and between 1986 and 1992, in the US market the MFA quota coverage has expanded from 16 per cent to 95 per cent by 1992.[4] Quotas have been a double-edged sword, which while providing an ensured market for Indian goods also worked as a clear disadvantage by capping exports at a certain level and working as a protectionist wall. Under the Uruguay Round of Trade Negotiations, it was decided to phase out the MFA quotas on textiles and clothing over a ten-year period, beginning in 1995. But although all quotas will be eliminated by 2005, the above-average tariffs have been kept in place. Two rounds of liberalisation have so far been carried out in 1995 and 1998, but these have not yielded any incremental benefits to Indian textile exporters since 30 to 35 per cent of exports of textiles and garments to the EU had already been outside quotas, even prior to the Uruguay Round. [5] Yet another problem is that of tariff escalation which acts as a disincentive against value addition. Thus, while exports of raw materials enjoy low tariffs, that of intermediatory goods face higher tariffs and finished products face the highest tariff.[6]

Under the Sanitary and Phytosanitary Measures Agreement, EU countries take protective measures on human, animal/plant life or health grounds with specific provisions that such measures are not inconsistent with the provisions of the Agreement; are applied only to the extent required; are based on scientific evidence; and their application does not constitute a restriction on international trade.[7] These measures have affected India's sea-food exports in a large way, and particularly with, EU's directive in 1991 that fish imports into the EU must conform to the sea food safety standards and procedures being harmonised across the Common Market. It enjoins upon all sea food exporters the responsibility of constantly keeping up with stringent hygiene and safety standards set by the EU. Besides harmonisation of standards and procedures, the EU has also introduced monitoring and inspections by its own authorities to enforce compliance and making exports contingent upon approval by the enforcement agencies. The EU imposed a ban on Indian sea-food exports in 1997 on the grounds that its processing plants did not meet prescribed quality standards.

Stringent regulations and measures also apply to foodstuffs which include maximum levels of pesticide residues that may be permitted in products and these are made mandatory in all member states. Products exported have to conform to the criteria set by the EU including nutrition labelling which binds all retailers to display the complete nutritional details on the packaging, including other relevant information for the consumer such as a 'use by' date which indicates the period within which a product is best consumed. Exports of peanuts, dried fruits, cereals and milk have been subjected to measures taken by the EU to reduce the.levels of certain contaminants (aflatoxin levels) in foodstuffs.

Another formidable non-tariff barrier to India's trade with the EU are the technical barriers to trade (TBTs) whereby there is a move towards greater harmonisation of technical standards and regulations.These measures have adversely affected the export performance of Indian products to the EU. The EU's stringent regulations on dyes is a case in point which has had a deleterious economic impact on the exports of two crucial product groups, namely textiles and clothing and leather. More and more products are required to conform to ecological standards, a process which entails expensive technological upgradation and importantly, increased compliance costs. The EU's ban on the imports of textiles and leather products treated with azo-dyes and pentachlorophenol puts at risk access to the entire EU market. A ban on these two vital chemicals also deprives producers of the important advantage of locally available low-priced dyes. The ban on pentachlorophenol, for instance, has forced Indian exporters to seek a replacement by importing a much more expensive substitute.

A related requirement which again raises costs and acts as an impediment is eco-labeling. Eco-labeling requires products to be labeled, with an undertaking that ecological standards are adhered to and a guarantee that these do not use chemicals or substances banned by the EU. Conforming to these eco-friendly standards have brought newer costs and problems. The financial burden on small firms has mounted as they confront problems of access to information and changes in the manufacturing process. These also increased the price of the final product, thereby eroding their price competitiveness. The eco-labeling scheme is applicable to all products except food, drinks and pharmaceuticals. Specific environmental standards govern the production process and give incentive for constant refinement so as to make products more environment-friendly. A label issued and approved by a competent authority under the EU Eco-Label Award Scheme allows an exporter to use the same label for his products across the EU.

Another trade related environmental measure is the EU's directive on reducing packaging waste. Stringent technical standards are to be followed during the production process so that environment damage could be minimised. Even the disposal of packaging waste is made the responsibility of whole-scale distributors, as is the case in Germany.

Anti-dumping and countervailing measures have also been frequently used as a protectionist means to safeguard domestic industry. Under WTO provisions, anti-dumping duties are allowed in cases where there is evidence of dumping and injury to domestic industry. The EU imposes anti-dumping duties on such products whose prices are significantly lower than the "normal value". The determination of the normal value raises fundamental questions as to what constitutes a fair price in international trade.[8] The EU has defined the 'normal value' of any product as the price of that product in its domestic market which is clearly a protectionist measure. It strikes at the price advantage of exporters in developing countries and the imposition of anti-dumping duties confronts the exporter with few viable alternatives as he has to either see his market access denied or accede to meeting the increased costs involved in adjusting to the 'normal value'. Indian steel exports to the EU have been subjected to anti-dumping and countervailing duties. Countervailing duties upto 25.5 per cent were imposed on Indian exporters of stainless steel bars to Europe, besides placing the export of hot rolled coils and plates under observation.[9] India's global steel exports amount to over 2 million tonnes, making up one-third of total production. India's steel exports have become more diversified in recent years as along with traditional items such as plates, bars and rods, the exports of hot rolled coils, cold rolled coils, pig iron and sponge iron too have been added to the export basket. India has taken both the EU and the US to the WTO for imposing anti-dumping and countervailing duties on its steel exports.

The EU has taken increasing recourse to anti-dumping investigations against developing countries. Even in instances where anti-dumping investigations do not find evidence of dumping and injury to domestic industry, the interregnum between the initiation of an anti-dumping case and its resolution imposes heavy economic costs on an exporter. Even when investigations are revoked for lack of adequate basis, the Indian exporter does not receive any compensation for the injury caused to his interests in lost sales and attendant damages.

Small units will be unable to sustain the waiting period and in many cases, would instead be forced to abandon such a protected market. Other delaying tactics are also resorted to by the EU to drive up these costs even further. One such method of prolonging anti-dumping investigations was used by the European Commission in 1996. Anti-dumping investigations against two product categories, namely unbleached cotton fabrics and bed linen from India were initiated in 1994. The investigations carried on for nearly two years and were terminated inconclusively by the Commission in 1996. But the European Commission once again resumed back-to-back investigations in the same year, effectively and blatantly prolonging the case and mounting the economic costs on Indian exporters. Another delaying tactic employed by the EU with regard to India and other developing countries and one which has clear protectionist overtones is the initiation of anti-dumping and anti-subsidy cases against the same product.

Thus, one can observe that the traditional export products of India have faced a combination of both above-average tariffs as well as suffer from several non-tariff measures. It is in these products where there is a high incidence of intra-EU trade, accounting for in many cases, nearly half of imports and in several others, nearly three-fourths. EU's trade defënce measures have thus allowed only a limited access to its highly regulated market in these products. As a result, imports from the rest of the world in these commodities have registered a slow growth.

Major Constraints

An examination of India-EU ties reveals certain distinct constraints.

— The EU and India share a very asymmetrical trade relationship. While the EU remains an important trade partner of India, accounting for under 30 per cent of its imports and exports, India represents a little over 1 per cent of EU imports.

— While the EU is the leading investor in India, these flows only represent 0.6% of the EU's global investments. In fact, the 1990s have seen a marked reduction in the EU's FDI flows to Asia in favour of Central and East European economies. EU's FDI flows to Asia shrank by half to $7 billion in 1997.[10]

— India's export market in the EU is largely concentrated in four of the 15 member countries, namely Belgium-Luxembourg, Italy, Germany and UK. These four markets account for upto 70 per cent of India's exports, with UK and Germany making up more than half.

— The present composition of India's exports to the EU represents product categories in which there is very strong intra-EU trade. Traditional items in India's exports to the EU are sectors in which EU's global imports have grown relatively slow.

— Indian exports are largely concentrated in a few resource-based categories such as textiles, leather and pearls. These constitute more than three-quarters of total exports. But their share in EU's total import basket is markedly low and in items like raw materials, pearls is negligible.

Future Policy Imperatives

Diversifying Product Composition

An examination of India's export pattern to the EU has revealed that major products face a host of trade barriers and, are sectors in which EU's global imports grow the least and one which is dominated by intra-EU trade. These two factors have effectively constricted the scope of India's exports to the EU as is evident from the low and in some cases, negligible market shares held by Indian products. To overcome this restriction and appreciably enhance exports, one needs to identify the fast growing categories in EU's global imports and India's capability to enhance its exports in these categories. The five rapidly growing areas of EU's global imports in the 1990s have been food, office machinery and telecommunicaiton équipment, auto products, chemicals, other non-electrical goods, and fuels. At present, India has a negligible share in EU's import composition in these products. These are at present as follows: food (0.61%); office, machinery and telecommunication equipment (0.002%); auto products (0.12%); chemicals (0.43%); other non-electrical goods (0.02%); fuels (0.08%).[11]

Increasing Access to Information

Access to timely information regarding changing consumer choices and preferences, new developments in EU's trade policy, regulations and directives all have a vital bearing on Indian exports and ability not only to maintain but also enhance access in EU markets. This calls for a synergetic effort on the part of government, industry associations and non-governmental organisations to create greater awareness of EU among Indian exporters.

Access to Technology

Cooperation agreements with EU will also play an important role in helping exporters to adapt to changing regulations and standards. Regular consultations, workshops and technical cooperation agreements can yield important gains such as accurate and timely information and making production processes more eco-friendly. Joint ventures in Research and Development (R & D) with EU partners should also be encouraged as a means to acquire and absorb better technology. Indigenous R & D efforts also needs to be bolstered so as to boost efficiency into every aspect of the production process and thereby enhance export competitiveness. Expertise, especially in the legal realm, needs to be developed in fighting cases at the WTO such as anti-dumping investigations against Indian products and also on products dumped in India.

Removing Infrastructural Bottlenecks

Rapid export expansion requires provision of infrastructural facilities such as uninterrupted power supply, rail and road connectivity and port facilities. For instance, complaints of inadequate infrastructural facilities such as fish / landing pots and water supply, makes sea-food exporters a vulnerable target for the EU's stringent provisions under the sanitary and phytosanitary testing measures. Lack of adequate testing facilities also results in higher overall compliance costs. Vital export sectors such as marine products are dependent on the availability of speedy and effective testing facilities and the leather and dye industry require common effluent treatment plants.

Improving WTO Dispute Settlement Procedure

The WTO's Dispute Settlement Procedure is defective as it severely compromises the interests of developing countries. India should oppose back-to-back anti-dumping investigations as well as the initiation of anti-dumping and anti-subsidy investigations on the same product, as these results in the Indian exporter enduring a high economic cost. The increasing recourse to anti-dumping must also be opposed as they often end without the charges being proved. India must demand that compensation be paid in such cases where an investigation fails to prove evidence of dumping. India should also strive for concerted action with other developing countries on such common areas of concern.

Conclusion

The liberalisation process initiated by India in the early 1990s has seen a strong thrust towards the external sector and the creation of a conducive policy environment aimed at export promotion. As a result of these policy measures, India's profile is in the process of a gradual but fundamental transformation. Foreign trade is becoming an "engine of growth" increasing its contribution to economic development and trade constituted 27 per cent of GDP in 1997. But India's global presence at present is a very modest one and with the share of its exports to the world at less than one per cent, remains a marginal international player.

The EU's importance as India's largest trading partner and as the largest source of investments, cannot be overstated. With the EU emerging as a trading bloc of increasing consequence, India is interested in broadening and deepening its ties with EU. The holding of the first-ever India-EU Summit at Lisbon in June 2000 was a clear indication that their ties have come of age and a reflection of its importance to both partners. The Summit highlighted for strong trade and investment opportunities in the fields of information technology, telecommunications, energy, infrastructure, financial services and bio-technology. And as India begins to realise the huge potential that remains to be tapped in its ties with the EU, it will redefine a largely

Notes

1. "EU-India Summit Declaration", *The European Union News* (Brussels), Vol. 10, No. 3, May-June 2000, p. 6
2. G. Srinivasan, "Indo-EU Economic Cooperation", *Portugal-India and the European Union, Commemorating the EU- India Summit*, Lisbon, 28 June 2000, p. 36.
3. "The EU and India: Trade and Economic Relations" at www.europa.en.int.
4. "Non-tariff Barriers or Disguised Protectionism" at www.cuts-india.org.
5. Bibek Debroy, "Negotiating a New Beginning" at www.indiatoday.btoday.com
6. Ibid.
7. "Non-Tariff Barriers or Disguised Protectionism", n. 4.
8. See Paramita Dasgupta, "Non-Tariff Barriers to Trade: The Issue of Technical Standards", *Foreign Trade Review* (New Delhi), Vol. XXX, No. 1, April-June 1995, pp. 46-66.
9. Gilbert Lobo, "EU Clamps Duties on Stainless Steel Exports to Europe", at www.expressindia.com
10. "Will India-EU Ties Reach Summit Now?" at www.hindubusinessline.com.
11. Paramita Dasgupta, "Enhancing Exports to the EU: A Product Based Approach", *Foreign Trade Review*, Vol. 22, No. 4, January-March 1998, p 45.

6

Role of NGDOs in EU-South Asia Relations

MICK WILKINSON

It is becoming increasingly obvious as we move towards the Millennium that we have entered an era in which democratic government, indeed, the nation state itself, is in many ways becoming a secondary player in areas of decision-making beyond its control. Globalisation, the IMF, the World Bank, the World Trade Organisation, transnational corporations, the very nature of these supra-national bodies and international fora and of the glabal financial and commodity markets has created a global democratic deficit. I would further argue that if those marginalised and disempowered by these developments are to further their interests, then there needs to be a concurrent globalisation of new social movements, a meeting of civil societies North and South.

After two decades of predominant free market prescriptions, North and South, the Northern countries totter on the brink of a new recession, the bubble has burst on the Asian economic miracle and the Soviet economy is in free-fall. For the developing world structural adjustment programmes have provided few solutions and have precipitated ecological disaster, burgeoning poverty and concomitant social and political unrest. In October 1996 in an open letter to the President of the World Bank the activist forum 'Citizens Against the World Bank' stated :

> "By the time you receive this letter you must be at the end of your visit to India. We hope that your visit must have

> revealed to you the impact of the World Bank's projects and programmes in this country. If you looked really beyond the superficial, we believe that the enormous environmental destruction and the social disruption will not have escaped you. Unfortunately, Mr. President, the World Bank. bears a significant part of the responsibility for this. Over the decades, the policies imposed by the Bank have significantly distorted development priorities, destroyed the resources and impoverished millions. And now, the 'new' policies that are being promoted by the Bank, under the Structural Adjustment Programme and in the name of Liberalisation, Privatisation, Globalisation are aggravating these impacts many times over".

At the same time the terms of world trade continued to be skewed in favour of the Northern industrialised countries. In 1990, referring to the GATT Uruguay Round negotiations Chakravarthi Raghavan wrote:

> "Thanks to (the) basic unity of the North against the South, and the aggressive neo-mercantilist policies of the major industrial countries, on the whole developing countries are now worse off in the Uruguay Round than when it was launched'. He went on to warn: "If there is no high level political effort in the South to confront and reverse these tendencies, the possibility has to be faced that the dominant industrialised countries would succeed in putting in place a New International Economic Order more unjust and more inequitable to the peoples of the South than even the present order".[1]

In many ways his worst fears were to be realised. The industrialised countries steam-rollered through their own agendas and the developing world saw few gains. During the Uruguay Round the Northern NGOs called for over-production and export dumping of farm products from the North to be eliminated by the abolition of all direct and indirect subsidies to Northern farmers.[2] They also called for compensation for those developing countries suffering increased global prices because of any such cuts in subsidies. Whilst large scale cuts in subsidies in the North were agreed, the EU continues to compensate arable farmers for cuts in support prices under the CAP reforms. The US does likewise with its farm support payments, export subsidies in all but name. Compensation to LDCs for increased market prices never made the agenda. On Northern protectionism the Northern NGOs called for the Multi-Fibre Arrangement to be phased out within a maximum of seven years, with no conditions placed on developing countries. The USA called for a 15-year phase-out. The compromise of a 10-year phase-out was hardly a major concession on the part of the industrialised North,[3] and made a mockery of the professed free-trade principles of the GATT!

Effectively the U.S and Europe continue to protect the products that they don't want the developing world to compete with whilst at the same time they are calling upon the developing world to open up their own markets to their products which are subsidised in diverse ways. When developing country goods collapse because they cannot compete with Northern-produced subsidised goods they are accused of being inefficient producers and told they need to be more efficient by reducing the wages of the workers and allowing peasants to go to the wall because they cannot compete.

Meanwhile on the 'new themes' put forward in the Uruguay Round, on Trade-Related Intellectual Property Rights (TRIPS) the Northern NGOs felt that any GATT rules should be "limited to trade distortions such as counterfeit goods", that "any extension of IPRs to life forms would reduce genetic diversity and threaten food security and must be prohibited".[4] The final agreement required countries to accept existing conventions. It extended them and brought them within the World Trading Organisation enforcement mechanisms. The end result is increased revenue for the industrialised countries, as developing countries, being net importers of technology, foot the bill.[5] The social consequences may be far- reaching, particularly on India's agrarian economy. In particular the powers the GATT gave to the multinational seed merchants enabling them to enforce copyright on scientifically improved seeds, which in theory means that farmers will no longer be able to gather seeds from these crops, but will have to buy seeds annually from the seed companies. The prospect looms of the displacement of local crops by genetically engineered varieties patented and marketed by global agricorps, with little interest in social or ecological sustainability. This will threaten food security and reduce genetic diversity.[6] In some cases the GATT will also require payment for the use of pharmaceutical formulae -both measures will impact disproportionately on the poorest. This also raises questions about national sovereignty, as under the Indian Patents Act of 1970, inventions relating to agricultural or horticultural processes were not patentable. The GATT obliged India to fall in line on patents or suffer retaliatory trade measures.[7]

On Trade-Related Investment Measures (TRIMS), the Northern NGOs declared: "The people of developing countries must retain their rights to develop their own service and manufacturing sectors in accordance with their development objectives. They must keep their rights to regulate investment and the behaviour of TNCs".[8] The Industrialised countries wanted to severely limit the use of TRIMS and have done so. The Least Developed Countries were given seven years to phase them out, other developing countries five. The agreements thus whittle away at the independence of national development strategies.

In a recent edition of Third World Resurgence Jayati Ghosh explains how these processes continue unabated with the WTO agreement on financial services: "paving the way for a handful of monopolistic firms in developed countries to seize control of the market in developing countries, which cannot hope to compete".[9] Global changes and the deregulation of markets, increasing foreign control over domestic production, both in industry and in agriculture, and the trap of export-led growth -one could be forgiven for believing this is merely another form of neo-colonialism cloaked in the terminology of globalisation. The direct consequences on local realities are becoming increasingly obvious, and increasingly severe: increasing poverty and ill-health, economic dislocation; increasing unemployment and population migration, ecological degradation, a breakdown in social cohesion, etc. Rural poverty is on the increase in India, over 40% of the population continue to subsist below the poverty line.

I recently discussed with an NGO representative in India the activities of the National Alliance of People's Movements, which is focusing on the impact of rapid economic change, international trade and investment regimes, large projects etc., and those of the India People's Movement, focusing on control over natural resources, land etc. I was informed of other groups such as CUTS who have done much work on international trade, GATT and the WTO and their impact on South Asia, and of the South Asia Watch on trade, ecology and environment. Just before I embarked for the 'International Conference on Europe and South Asia: 500 Years' ' I was e-mailed information on the "Declaration of Indian People against the WTO", made in Hyderabad on the 2nd of May 1998 which states: "We, the people of India, hereby declare that we consider the WTO our brutal enemy" and goes on to accuse it of "destroying our natural habitats and traditional agricultural and other knowledge systems. converting us into objects of Transnational Corporations' economy of consumerism" whilst proclaiming a "struggle against the WTO-IMF-World Bank trinity". The convention and rally in Hyderabad was taking place in a state where more than 400 suicides had taken place in the previous 5 months due to the impact of WTO-imposed policies. As the conference on Europe and South Asia: 500 Years convened there were decentralised ways of action taking place across India against the WTO in parallel to the WTO Ministerial Conference taking place in Geneva.

Whilst there may be ideological differences from region to region and an inability to unify struggles or at times to convert respective visions into alternative policies or effective strategies, it struck me that these movements suffered from a common dilemma — that of failing to get their arguments across in Northern economic and political decision-making fora. That is primarily for three reasons:

(i) the lack of a level playing field in international relations and the increasingly self-interested postures of Northern negotiators / decision-makers.

(ii) the failure of traditional negotiators for the developing world — the diplomatic staff — to make an impact. They are often overworked, with insufficient technical back-up, ill at ease with international fora and procedures of decision-making. Often official representatives are not necessarily the best people to fight for the needs of the poor and most marginalised in their countries.

(iii) whilst there are burgeoning new social movements in Europe- from the ecology movement to the women's movement, the average European citizen, whilst often well-meaning and generous in terms of donor activities, has little or no idea about what the various international fora do and even less idea of their adverse effects on the developing world.

My tenet is that Northern NGDOs can help bridge the gap between social movements North and South, they have the expertise to take on international negotiators in Northern fora, they have the financial power to facilitate direct representation by grass-roots Southern negotiators in those fora. As I prepared this paper some 50,000 people joined a demonstration organised by Christian Aid around the G8 Ministerial Meeting in Birmingham, England, to demand debt forgiveness for developing countries. Whilst the response of the Ministers concerned left much to be desired the demonstration nonetheless placed the debt issue firmly on an agenda which would otherwise been dominated by the India's nuclear tests and by attempts to stabilise global markets. In order to maximise the possibilities offered by such activities and it should be remembered at this point that one quarter of the world's NGDOs community conduct operations in India -it will be necessary to re-evaluate the role of Northern NGDOs in South Asia and to re-draw their lines of engagement both with Southern NGDOs and with civil society both South and North.

A New Grass-Roots Developmental Agenda

Post-war mainstream development thinking was built on the notion that development in the emergent post-colonial nations would best be achieved by the replication of Western models. As John Brohman points out: "in a highly normative and ethnocentric manner, Western values were universalised and linked with progress, while the values of traditional Third World societies were denigrated and tied to stagnation and underdevelopment".[10]

With the ascendance of conservative governments across the North in the 1980s official development thinking and practice followed the same tradition of paternalism and Euro-centrism but began to follow a new economic orthodoxy. The earlier consensus for an activist, interventionist state, had broken down.[11] Neo-liberals dominated the agenda. They pointed to the failings of corrupt governments run by self-interested elites and questioned the very notion of development being led by governments. Indeed, the state was suddenly the root of all evil. State intervention, far from promoting development, hindered it by restricting and distorting markets. It created a dependence culture, stifling independence and enterprise and limiting choice. It was a wasteful and costly exercise which met neither targets nor expectations.

Paying little attention to historical conditions, local cultural and social needs, neo-liberals used abstract economic models to offer up radical free-market alternatives. Market deregulation and 'rolling back the state' dominated the agenda. These prescriptions were enforced via the structural adjustment programmes designed and monitored by the Bretton Woods institutions.[12] The market was the new panacea to cure all ills. It would be supplemented by action to devolve public policy via private employers and the voluntary sector, the 'third sector' And so it turned out, as the reduction in state provision of health and education services saw those services become re-established in different forms under the aegis of aid agencies and NGOs.[13]

Development strategists in the North welcomed this 'third sector' with open arms. There were hard-headed financial reasons for official financial support to NGOs. In the 1980s, with continual recession and Northern governments falling back on tight monetarist solutions, support for voluntary organisations, charities, co-operatives and NGOs was seen as a pragmatic means of reducing government expenditure on personnel or private consultancy firms and of reducing criticism of government expenditure as being "inefficient and wasteful".[14] With the failings of the eighties and nineties there is a growing understanding that blind faith in the free market cannot be a sound basis for sustainable development, that "there is no reason to suppose either that the market can provide other than uneven development or that it can reliably improve the lot of the poorest regions and peoples".[15]

John Brohman argues that "like the older modernisation approach, the newer neoliberal framework also employs universalistic (ideal) theoretical constructs that are based on unrealistic assumptions and exclude much of the variability of Third World social formations". He elaborates: "The idealised neoliberal concept of the market neither reflects the diverse realities of Third World markets nor does it form a logical basis from which to compare Third World states as they exist in practice. Highly skewed power relations and structural inequalities within many societies produce real-world markets that are far removed from the ideal types of neoliberal theory".[16]

Paul Ekins, meanwhile, believes the basic tenet of free market capitalism -that trade promotes development because it is to the benefit of all parties concerned -is fundamentally flawed. That in reality there is anything but co-operative mutuality because one partner may hold all the cards, therefore achieve all the benefits, that high capital mobility means that Northern concerns can move production where they can achieve maximum advantage. He points to the effects of indebtedness, the need to earn foreign currency and countries being locked into the export of primary commodities by Northern protectionism against secondary activities. To industrialised country agricultural subsidies and dumping of surpluses which depress world market prices whilst protecting Northern prices. and markets.[17] He reiterates that trade can lead to dependency relationships — thereby removing the freedom not to trade and argues : "The global trading system, far from being a mutually beneficial voluntaristic system of exchange, has become a means of coercion, employed jointly by powerful institutions in the First World and their client elites in the Third, by which to force Third World resources into the global market on terms highly unfavourable to the vendor". Inevitably this process: "undermines traditional culture and social structures conducive to self-reliance, so that it generates a dependency on Western imports and Western lifestyles which becomes increasingly difficult to overcome".[18] Much is the same of international aid, Ekins believes it overwhelmingly serves the promotion of the domestic economy or foreign policy interests of the donors. It results in the personal enrichment and political dominance of powerful elites in recipient countries, the multiplication of bureaucracy, inefficiency, and waste. As a consequence he maintains that development disasters are the rule rather than the exception.[19] "In fact it is somewhat surprising that a relationship between governments of North and South should ever have been expected to benefit the Southern poor, because the majority of Southern governments are neither representative of or sensitive to the interests of the poor".[20] Instead, these "institutions of interdependence are fundamental contributors to unsustainability, ensuring that Southern environments are systematically ransacked of resources for the overconsumption of the rich, resulting in the marginalisation of the poor".[21]

There is an increasing awareness that for development policy to succeed it must reflect the needs of the poorest groups in Southern society. That is a normative judgement, but it is also a practical reality. According to Dharam Ghai and Jessica M. Vivian: "Sustainable environmental management, and, where necessary, environmental rehabilitation, can only occur where active local-level support exists", they assert that: "it is essential to recognise the critical importance of indigenous organisations of marginalized people for environmentally sound development under a wide variety of conditions", that: "such organisations can function both as vehicles of resistance to environmentally destructive practices and as agencies for the promotion of alternative, sustainable approaches to social and economic development".[22]

Similarly, Chadwick F. Alger criticises the continuing tendency to view global policy as: "product of a process that takes place in international conferences and organisations 'beyond the states' ". He believes instead that we should be looking towards a broader global policy paradigm, one which must extend "from small communities affected by global policies, sometimes referred to as the grassroots, to global institutions", because: "In the end, problems such as human environment, population, employment, desertification, and water are global problems because they affect thousands of local communities in all continents ".

"To be effective" he feels, "most global policies will require some degree of compliance in a multitude of communities spread across several continents" and that "This will be impossible if global policies do not have some degree of legitimacy based on local knowledge about, and acceptance of, global policies". Similarly: "the design of effective global policy will require that policy-makers acquire considerable knowledge about conditions and problems in a diversity of local places". He asks: "How can this be acquired except through drawing on the knowledge gained by local people through their everyday experience with ecology, food, empowerment, water and other problems?".[23]

Paul Ekins would agree : "In the South their approach to development tends to combine poverty alleviation with environmental concern because it is precisely through the regeneration of environmental resources that they hope to alleviate their poverty", He believes: "at a fundamental level the common thrust of the new movements for social and political change can be expressed by the word democratisation: democratisation of knowledge, democratisation of development, democratisation of the state. It is a democratisation based on a new articulation of people-to-people and people-to-nature relations". This, he feels, promotes cultural diversity as opposed to Western industrial hegemony; the fusion of humanity and ecology as opposed to ecological vandalism; the development of people in the round "both as individuals and members of social communities" as opposed to the "now dominant consumerist need of having"; and promotes "a mode of governance which promotes autonomy, initiative and capability, based on a commitment to social justice".[24]

It is not simply that new issues have come to the fore, it is that the failings of the current global political system have created a deep-seated desire for new forms of democratic expression. It is not merely that current political structures will not facilitate sustainable development, but that they cannot facilitate it; in part due to their distance from grassroots realities; in part due to the vested interests operating within them.

The growth of new social movements

In the 1970s new social movements sprang up across the developing world.[25] Those movements often rallied to nationalist, regional or continental aspirations and took up issues often ignored by conventional political channels - social issues, gender and ecological issues. They provided legitimate forms of dynamic and alternative grassroots, democratic participation. As they took on unofficial but organised forms the number of both Northern and Southern NGOs burgeoned. These NSMs include co-operative movements, church organisations, trade unions, self-help groups, lobbying groups, charitable organisations, by their very nature such movements are often loose coalitions around a central theme, taking on myriad of forms, embodying a variety of cultural, historical, political and social roots.[26] They invariably begin as a localised movement but they are increasingly forming into regional, national and international networks. There are single issue networks such as the Asian Human Rights Council and the Women's Reproductive Forum, grouping hundreds of NGOs from over 20 countries and broader networks working on an increasing range of issues such as, the Third World Network (TWN) created in 1984, which is growing apace throughout Asia, Latin America and Africa.

The growth of NSMs was a reflection of the dissatisfaction with traditional political forms per se and the desire to create more participatory channels of influence. They were also a response to new political realities; to the arbitrary nature of the global commodity and financial markets and the inability of states to control their own fiscal and industrial policies; to the growth of the global financial institutions, the World Bank and the IMF, perceived, as they were, to be far removed from the traditional democratic processes yet taking economic decisions affecting the lives of millions and impinging on national self-determination.[27] It was an attempt to counter the imposition of structural adjustment programmes, the destruction of natural habitats and the exploitation of resources by transnational corporations, all of which made serious inroads into local autonomy and self determination. Above all the growth in the NSMs can be linked to the calamitous effects of the debt crisis. Having been accrued in part due to the corruption and incompetence of unrepresentative elites, in part due to factors external to the individual countries themselves -hikes in world oil prices, the high interest rates of Reaganomics, the fall in the prices of developing country primary products on the world markets, etc, the debts were paid for by sequestrating the lands of the poorest for redirection to the export sector, or by cutting social provision. Ronnie D. Lipschutz terms this the 'global civil society', "the self-conscious constructions of networks of knowledge and action, by de-centred, local actors, that cross the reified boundaries of space as though they were not there", which are "challenging, from below, the nation-state system". This, he asserts, represents "an ongoing project of civil society to reconstruct, re-imagine, or re-map world politics", that "civil society is becoming global and therefore a political force to be reckoned with in a way that has not been the case since the medieval period".[28]

The grassroots imperative : NGDOs as advocates

As representatives of the grassroots and the NSMs, the NGO community are in many ways in operating in direct contrast to the self-interested agendas of international financial institutions and individual nation states, "NGOs are building new, horizontal bridges of co-operation between the peoples of North and South, independent of unequal official relations".[29] However, in the main Northern NGDO ambitions do not differ greatly from traditional development goals - tending towards paternalism, with Northern perceptions defining needs and objectives. They continue to hold their Southern counterparts in a patron / recipient strait-jacket in which they themselves define the objectives, control the design, implementation and evaluation of projects, nothing short of a form of cultural and developmental imperialism. Thomas cites even the most well-meaning NGOs setting up modern, formal, democratic and representative forms of 'people's organisation' such as co-operatives and unions, which often cut across pre-existing social and power relations in both village and urban communities.[30]

In recent years Southern partners of Northern NGDOs have displayed increasing disenchantment with the failure of Northern NGDOs to take on board an advocacy and facilitating role. There has been a growing disdain for those agencies which continue to concentrate on individual projects and problems -an approach which many Southern NGOs now see as short-sighted and piecemeal, and in some respects, patronising. They question the ability of Northern NGDOs to appreciate and identify with the true needs of the poorest in the South and by the very nature of Northern agendas, question their ability to respond accordingly. They have increasingly pushed for their Northern partners to focus on structural problems, consistently highlighting trade and debt, a new international economic order, human rights, militarisation and the environment as priorities.[31] The reluctance of many funding NGOs to take on board this "enhanced advocacy profile" is, according to leading NGO activist John Clark, leading to Third World NGOs moving away from their traditional partners and towards Northern advocacy organisations. "They are one step ahead of their funders in recognising that well placed pressure for international policy change is a more precious development resource than money".[32]

These views were formalised in the 'Declaration of NGOs on the African Economic and Social Crisis' which emerged from a meeting of Northern and Southern NGDOs at a Special Session of the UN General Assembly in May 1986. Their recommendations included: "We encourage Northern and International NGOs to recognise the linkages of many policies of their governments, corporations and multilateral institutions which their governments heavily influence and which adversely affect the quality of life and political and economic independence of African countries". They also called upon Northern NGDOs to "re-orient their activities so that they increasingly concentrate on development education, advocacy, fund-raising and facilitating information flows within the community" and to turn their efforts towards highlighting the economic and financial mechanisms by which the North continues to repatriate resources from the South.[33]

According to the Final Statement of the UN/NGO Workshop on "Debt, Adjustment and the Needs of the Poor", held in September 1987, "NGOs must support the efforts of the poor to empower themselves to give voice to the needs and aspirations of the poor at the national and international levels".[34] The 'Summary of Proposals for NGO Action' outlined how that would best be achieved: "NGOs in North and South should strengthen their networking activities to identify changes which need to be effected in Northern societies and economies in order to ensure effective design and implementation of development strategies NGOs should share on a global basis the information, data and analysis collected in their efforts to monitor the impact of adjustment policies and programs on the poor. They should develop a common agenda for a simultaneous international lobby on the issues".[35] There are growing demands in the South that the future administration of development projects, project approval, resource allocation and on-going oversight / project evaluation should be carried out wholly by Southern NGDOs, a move which would turn their Northern counterparts into mere fundraisers unless they, in turn, channelled their expertise into advocacy and lobbying on the macro-level.

Those views are gradually permeating Northern perceptions. John Clark writes: "NGOs are having to recognise that no matter how successful are the projects they support, the overall war against poverty is being lost. Poverty will not be defeated just by tackling it at the micro-level, important as that work is for the millions of people who benefit directly from grassroots development projects. To stem the mounting tide necessitates attacking the root causes of poverty at the macro-level".[36] Doug Hellinger of the Development Group for Alternative Policies, Washington, believes: "The misguided programs and policies of governments and large donor institutions can no longer be left unaddressed by NGOs. The latter should no more confine their attention to grassroots projects than they should quietly participate in projects that are designed by those outside entities without the participation of local populations". He continues: "While NGOs are still in fashion within the aid establishment, they need to move emphatically into those arenas in which the principal programs and policies that determine the direction of Third World development are being shaped".[37]

The European Union : An Open Door

The EC is the world's largest trading block, it is the largest importer of agricultural products in the world -approximately 60% of which comes from the developing world - and is the second largest exporter of agricultural products in the world. It also speaks on behalf of its members in international trade negotiations. Trade with the developing world represents almost one third of external EC exports and imports. It is therefore a very important forum to which the less developed countries need constant and influential access. The EC is the largest single supplier of aid and financial and technical assistance to developing countries. It is the biggest market in the world. As such it is imperative that countries in the South maximise their opportunities for dialogue and co-operation with the Community Institutions. In this the role of both Northern and Southern NGDOs could be crucial.

In many ways the European Union is an 'open door' .The Community institutions welcome advocacy as part and parcel of their own democratic dynamics.[38] The Commission, which is at the centre of EC development policy, has a limited number of staff -around 12,000, and is still what Mazey and Richardson term an 'adolescent bureaucracy' in that the limited number of staff within its technical services means it depends on the input of external experts for detailed information.[39] But their acceptance of interest groups also has a more directly political motivation, it is the Commission's concrete link with the democratic process. The Commission is not elected and therefore one of its chief means both to gauge public opinion and to reinforce its position vis a vis the Parliament and Council of Ministers is by listening to representations. It is also a means to filter national interests, a means to formulate a 'Community viewpoint'.[40] The Commission see this as an obligation based on the belief that its own initiatives could only be legitimated by obtaining the support of a large sector of public opinion, as expressed through interest groups. As such it has formally signalled its belief in the "preservation of the open relationship, open administration, and to extend it further," and to "ensure all special interest groups are given the opportunity of being heard by the Commission ".[41]

Brussels has therefore become a battle ground for ideas and influence. NGDOs can find common ground with other sectoral interests operating in Brussels, the trade union movement, church groups, women's groups, and consumer groups. NGDOs share common ground with the International Organisation of Consumers' Unions (IOCU) and the European Consumers' Organisation (BEUC). In the GATT negotiations, for instance, both the IOCU and the BEUC called for quick and substantive reduction of protectionism in agriculture and textiles, fairer anti-dumping rules, for no lowering of health and safety standards and for no intellectual property protectionism.[42] NGDOs also have the potential to forge alliances with trade associations, farmers' and business organisations. As one NGDO activist pointed out to me "the CAP isn't protecting small farmers either in Europe or in the Third World -allthe money is going to big farmers and agro-business and the consumers are paying higher prices -it's an absolute disaster".[43]

The NGDOs have a major factor in their favour -MEPs have expressed their anger recently at the vociferous activities of both the business and farming lobbies and object strongly to the idea that they can be bought by meals or other forms of inducements. NGOs, on the other hand, are perceived for the most part, as holding the disinterested/ high moral ground, and as such are ideally placed to move into that credibility vacuum. There is the general acceptance amongst politicians and the public as a whole of their political neutrality, their deep sense of commitment and selflessness.[44]

The main focus for NGDOs at the : European level is the NGDO-EU Liaison Committee, which provides the link between the European Union institutions and over 800 NGDOs and emergency aid organisations from the 15 EU member states. In its vision statement the Liaison Committee states: "The NGDO-EU Liaison Committee strives for a world based on just relationships between all peoples in which the European Union plays a full role in sharing the earth's resources equitably amongst the people of the world and makes available generously its wealth and expertise to those seeking to promote their own full development", whilst its statement of role is as follows: "By providing a channel for the views of civil society in the South to be heard in Europe, by encouraging a positive and progressive European approach to international affairs and by working to improve the quality, scope and impact of EU external co-operation and assistance, the NGDO-EU Liaison Committee aims to contribute effectively to the formulation and monitoring of EU development co-operation, emergency assistance and other policies that have a bearing on the Union's relations with the South".

The EC sees the NGDOs as a cost-effective tool in their overall development policy, enhancing its reputation for supporting the development process. They have become part and parcel of Community Development Policy. The nature of the Liaison Committee's relationship with the NGDO Division of the Commission DG VIII (Development), a permanent process of dialogue, co-operation and trust, gives the NGDOs direct access to the process of decision. In many ways it is a symbiotic relationship.

The Commission's Report to the Council for the 1990 financial year acknowledged the NGDOs' expertise in the development field: "the NGDOs have avoided many erroneous concepts and mistakes which have affected the development co-operation work undertaken by the public sector". Their work had "given rise to results which the experts unanimously regard as very positive". The co-operation between the Community and NGDOs had, according to the report: "been broadened over the years to include an exchange of views on development problems in general: trade, debt, demography, environment and migration, etc." It continued: "The Commission considers that this exchange of views is a useful addition to the discussions conducted within the Community, with the governments of the developing countries and in international institutions".[45]

And the Parliament? The Brussels-based NGDO networks have forged very good relations with MEPs. Eileen Sudworth of one such network, CIDSE explained to me: "I can't believe with MEPs how easy it is to actually lobby them, because they're so hot for information and for what they're supposed to be doing and they're in a kind of vacuum, they're captive in Brussels for three to four days and they're extraordinarily receptive".[46] As for the MEPs themselves, Alf Lomas MEP believes the NGOs are "pushing on an open door", he explained: "We welcome information which will enable us to raise the issues in a meaningful way", and cited several cases where lobbying the Development Committee and Parliament as a whole had met with measurable successes. Indeed, he criticised the NGDSs not for too much lobbying, but for not providing MEPs with sufficient back-up![47] For its part, the Development Council has consistently praised the activities of the NGOs and noted their essential role in both policy formulation and implementation. In May 1991 the 1049th Development Council Meeting put NGOs, for the first time, at the centre of European Ministers' discussions. Their resolution pointed to the 'essential role' played by the Liaison Committee in strengthening the Community's collaboration with NGOs and endorsed the Commission's effcrts to give support for their actions. It stated: 'Furthermore, in their campaigns to inform, educate and foster the awareness of the public about development matters, the NGOs play an essential part in channelling the energies of European citizens into this area. They thus foster public understanding and the support which is essential if a development policy is to succeed'.[48]

In January 1992 the Committee on Development and Co-operation stressed the "highly positive terms in which the three Community institutions view the relationship between the EEC and NGOs", it called upon them to widen their participation in Community action, it was its opinion that: "the competence of the NGOs of North and South and their knowledge of the real problems of the peoples could be turned to good account by the Community bodies, for instance by taking account of their opinions on matters effecting North/South relations (international economic and trade negotiations etc.) by involving them in meetings of the joint committees, etc, "It reiterated that :

"the role which NGOs, through their highest Community-wide representative body, the Liaison Committee, should be allowed to play with regard to exchanges of information and experiences and to assessing the impact brought about in the developing countries by the overall economic policies pursued at Community and international level, must be safeguarded and extended".[49] It would seem, then, that for the NGOs, with their unique reputation for selflessness and developmental expertise, the opportunities to influence European Community development policy will never be greater .

However, whilst the European Union is an open door that door must be knocked at. In many respects Northern NGDOs are not fulfilling their potential. The NGDO networks operating in Brussels suffer from self-inflicted constraints. Few Northern NGDOs spend over 10% of their income on advocacy and development education. The European networks are grossly understaffed and under-resourced, given the tasks they face and the weight of the transnational corporations often pitted against them. What successes there have been has been down to the determined efforts of a small number of experienced and dedicated Brussels-based NGDO practitioners. However, one is left with the over-all impression that this small pool of talented people is not being utilised to the full. My own studies found constant shortages, high levels of burn-out, rapid staff-turnover; with an ensuing short-term-ism, loss of institutional memory and of carefully nurtured connections. The lack of adequate resourcing leaves the networks unable to undertake the most basic of tasks. Hence, there has been a general failure to target the early stages of the process of decision, when parameters are often set, or even to identify the policy community, let alone attempt to integrate themselves within it.

There have been few overtures to other sectional interests operating in Brussels -the trade unions, business and farmers organisations and consumer organisations. That same lack of resources has seen the networks neglect the need for closer co-operation with ambassadorial and other diplomatic representation from developing countries. Much more could be done to bring Southern voices into the Northern political arena. It has also seen them failing to adequately service even the most supportive of MEPs or Commission officials. Whilst relations with DGVIII are very good, the networks have had only occasional contact with other Directorates General whose policies have a direct effect upon the developmental process such as DGs I, III, and VI, whereas those who might oppose development policies, the farming and TNC lobbies, are well entrenched there.

Because of the on-going day-to-day pressures of maintaining a presence with limited staffing, there were scant attempts to analyse previous lobbying campaigns and learn from them and few of the networks displayed a strategic, systematic approach to lobbying. They have failed to institutionalise even the most basic of press and publicity functions, tending towards exerting influence via clubability rather than exerting pressure via the media or by attempting to engineer concerted public protest. This is perhaps their greatest weakness, for if NGDOs are going to influence the process of decision it is, above all, important to make political leaders see activities on behalf of the developing world as a vote-catcher. To do this NGDOs need to "think about expanding their social bases in the North, especially, convincing other social movements to join forces on issues of general concern",[50] because the conquest of European public opinion is vital for real democratic pressure on governments, financial institutions and business confederations.[51]

My study of the Northern NGDO activities around the Uruguay Round GATT negotiations served further to highlight those financial, staffing and organisational inadequacies at the international level. The study found that in the case of the GATT negotiations the lobby was ill-prepared, ill-timed, fragmented, badly-targeted and under-resourced. It concluded that the failure to obtain anything other than peripheral concessions stemmed from the fact that by the time Northern NGDOs began to make their presence felt over the GATT, the Community position was more or less decided and resolute. Given these circumstances the ultimate weakness of the NGO-GATT Steering Committee was its failure to rapidly mobilise public opinion on the issues. As such what direct lobbying was undertaken lacked public support, perhaps the only factor which by that time could have made the European negotiators take a more pro-developing country stance.[52]

It is obvious, then, that if advocacy at the Community level is to be a serious objective of the Northern NGDOs they are going to have to commit far greater resources to the task. This will not be an automatic process. Northern NGDOs are made up of many different kinds of people, with varying agenda, they are still primarily focused on project work in the South. Even within the larger organisations, some of which regularly draw an annual income of some £40-£50m, those wishing to expend more resources on advocacy have to justify their case to the organisation as a whole. That is not an easy task, but the greater the demand, the greater the push from the South, the easier that task will become.

My intention here is not to unduly criticise Northern NGDOs, many of whom do good work, North and South, with the best of intentions. However, empirical evidence shows that project work alone is not solving the problems of the South. If NGDOs continue to go down this road it is likely that they will be made the new scapegoats for the failure of development. On the one hand the likelihood is that Northern governments will blame them if they fail to meet up to the demands of evaluators, whilst on the other hand in the South they will be perceived as too closely associated with the failings of Eurocentric development policies. Worse, NGDOs could be seen as a palliative to European consciences, window dressing by the Community to hide the inequities of the transfer of resour.ces from the South to the North! -the "tools of a new imperialism"[53].

Southern Input, Southern Agendas

For most developing countries globalisation and liberalisation have done little or nothing to improve their position, they are still on the periphery , they continue to move backwards in relation to human development and quality of life indicators vis a vis their Northern counterparts. Meanwhile the development assistance budgets of the OECD countries have been falling rapidly in recent years. The cornerstones of free-market prescriptions, the IMF, the World Bank and the World Trade Organisation are profoundly undemocratic institutions, lacking in transparency, decision-makers therein refuse to accept that there will be any losers from the process of liberalisation and globalisation, they insist that any setbacks will be of a temporary nature.

For those social groups in Southern societies who are marginalised and disempowered by these global economic and political structures to have their needs and aspirations heard and acted upon there must be a radical change in Northern public opinion, a change which will force the hand of Northern Ministers. That transformation will be advanced by the meeting of minds and the co-ordinating of activities of grass roots movements and civil society, North and South.

One means to that end is to highlight the complimentarity of interests— the effects of globalisation and liberalisation on the poorest communities North and South, the effects of environmental degradation South and North. In that the Northern NGDOs have a significant role to play. As of yet they are not fulfilling that role.

Northern NGDOs have their own agendas, their own priorities, relating both to donor expectations and organisational well-being; defined through and coloured by Northern experiences, based on Northern, often Eurocentric perceptions. Ultimately their activities on behalf of their Southern partners must be shaped and directed by those Southern partners and the NSM they represent. Genuine empowerment would entail Southern representatives arguing their own corner in Northern fora. European NGDOs can assist in that process by acting first and foremost as facilitators, in terms of ceding decision-making power over all areas of project work to their Southern counterparts; of helping to fund Southern research and information programmes; of financing the transportation of Southern voices into the relevant Northern economic and political fora; and of providing technological assistance and institutional know-how to their Southern counterparts, whilst themselves following closely, and acting upon, the demands of Southern networks. There is scant likelihood, however, of this transformation taking place unless significant pressure is exerted on Northern NGDOs from grass roots movements and their supporters in the South. That is the direction in which energies may now most fruitfully be directed. In this academics can play an important role, for whereas some Southern NGOs will shy away from demanding more control in the South for fear of losing funding altogether, academics can apply pressure from a disinterested and relatively secure position.

It is 500 years since the arrival of Vasco de Gama in India. If history is not to record globalisation as merely one more avenue for exploitation in the process of neo-colonialism the NGDO community North and South must take advantage of the globalisation of modern communications systems in order to press their case for a more equitable and transparent economic order based on principles of solidarity and equity. The cuuent global financial crises provide the perfect backdrop for that questioning of political and economic orthodoxy to begin.

References

1. Chakravarthi Raghavan : *Recolonisation : GATT, the Uruguay Round and the Third World*, London : Zed Books and Third World Network, 1990, p294.
2. *A People's GATT for World Development* – Hysel, 1st December 1990. NGO-GATT Steerign Committee, Brussels, December 1990.
3. Peter Madden & John Madely : *Winners and Losers : The Impact of the GATT Uruguay Round on Developing Countries*, London : Christian Aid, 1993. See also Peter Madden, *The Poor Get Poorer : The Impact of the GATT Uruguay Round on Developing Countries*, London : Christian Aid, 1994.
4. *A People's GATT for World Development, op cit.*
5. *Developing Countries in the WTO*, Overseas Development Institute, London, p3.
6. See John Rettie & Ruth Kelly "100,000 cought in Indian anti-Gatt riot," in *The Guardian*, 6.4.94 p12. See also Vandana Shiva, "Beware the Backlash" and Walter Schwarz, "Seeds of Discontent" in *The Guardian*, 11.3.94 p16 and David Belamy and Alastair McIntosh, "Getting away from the science of Dr. Strangelove", *The Guardian*, 9.4.96 p2
7. Peter Madden & John Madely : *Winners and Losers, op cit*, p17.
8. *A People's GATT for World Development*, op cit.
9. Jayati Ghosh, 'One-way street', *Third World Resurgence*, Issue 89, Jan 1998, pp36-37.
10. John Brohman, "Universalism, Eurocentrism, and ideological bias in development studies : from modernisation to neoliberalism", in *Third World Quarterly*, Vol 16, No 1, 1995, p125.
11. See Marc Wuyts, Maureen Mackintosh, and Tom Hewitt, *Development Policy and Public Action*, Oxford University Press 1992, Maureen Maureen, Introduction.
12. See Maureen Mackintosh, *ibid* p5-6. Also Bjorn Hettne, *Development Theory and the Three Worlds*. Longman Scientific & Technical, London/ New York, 1990, p138, and John Brohman, *op cit*, pp 134-136.
13. Maureen Mackintosh ibid p83
14. See OECD Directory of NGDOs in OECD Member Countries, OECD Paris, 1990, p21.
15. Alan Thomas, "NGOs and the Limits to Empowerment", in Wuyts, Mackintosh and Hewitt (Eds) *Development Policy and Public Action*, Oxford Univ. Press, 1993, p117. See also Ted Trainer, *Developed To Death : Rethinking Third World Development*, Green Print, The Merlin Press Ltd, London 1989, pp62-73.
16. John Brohman, *op cit*, p126.
17. Paul Ekins, *A New World Order : Grassroots movements for Global Change*, Routledge, London, 1992 p35.
18. *Ibid* p36.

19. *Ibid* pp36-37. See also Ted Trainer, *op cit*, pp97-101.
20. Paul Ekins op cit, pp36-37. See also John Clark, *Democratizing Development: The Role of Voluntary Organisations.* Earthscan Publications Ltd. London, 1991, Preface.
21. Paul Ekins *op cit* p38.
22. See Dharam Ghai & Jessica M Vivian, *Grassroots Environmental Action; People's participation in sustainable development*, Routledge, London, 1992, pp I and 17.
23. Chadwick, F Alger, Grassroots Perspectives on Global Policies for Development", in *Transnational Associations*, 6/1990, op cit, p336.
24. Paul Ekins, op cit, p39, pp208-209.
25. United Nations Development Programme, *Human Development Report 1993*, New York, 1993, p84.
26. See Joseph A. Camilleri, & Jim Falk, The End of Sovereignty? *The Politics of a Shrinking and Fragmenting World*, Edward Elgar Ltd. Aldershot, England, 1992, pp206-209.
27. *Ibid*, pp69- 77.
28. Ronnie D. Lipschutz, "Reconstructing World Politics: The Emergence of Global Civil Society", *Millennium: Journal of International Studies*, Winter 1992, Vol.21 , No 3, pp390-391.
29. "Social Movements and NGOs" in *Third World Guide 1990*, Instituto del Tercer Mundo, Uruguay, 1990, p138.
30. Alan Thomas, *Ibid* p124.
31. See Thierry Lemaresquier, "Prospects for Development Education: Some Strategic Issues Facing European NGOs," *World Development Supplement*, Autumn 1987: *Development Alternatives: The Challenge for NGOs*. Papers presented at the London Symposium on "Development Alternatives: The Challenge for NGOs". Co-sponsored by World Development and by the Overseas Development Institute (London), March 11-13 1987, p 194). See also Drabeck, Anne Gordon, in *World Development Supplement*, *op cit*, Editor's Preface, p.x
32. John Clark, Democratizing Development, *op cit*, p141.
33. "Declaration of NGOs on the African Economic and Social Crisis" which emerged from a meeting of Northern and Southern NGDOs at a Special Session of the UN General Assembly in May 1986. Cited in *World Development Supplement*, *op cit*, p83-84. These views were overwhelmingly endorsed by NGDOs in various NGDO fora in the latter half of the 1980s, most notably in the "Declaration of NGOs on the African Economic and Social Crisis" at the Symposium on Development Alternatives in London, on 11th-13th March 1987 co-sponsored by World Development (Washington) and the Overseas Development Institute with over 100 development professionals from 28 developing and 14 developed countries and a the South-South NGDO Co-operation Conference of ACP and Latin American NGDOs which convened immediately.

34. *World Development Supplement, op cit,* p257.
35. *World Development Supplement, op cit,* p261.
36. John Clark, *Democratizing Development, op cit,* p198 and see Clark in M Edwars and D. Hulme, op cit p200.
37. Doug Hellinger, "NGOs and the Large Aid Donors : Changing the Terms of Engagement", *World Development Supplement, op cit,* p137 and p141.
38. This was certaily the expressed opinion of every Commission official and MEP and most of the NGDO activists interviewed during my own research.
39. Sonia Mazey and Jeremy Richardson, "British Pressure Groups in the European Community : The Challenge of Brussels", *Parliamentary Affairs,* Vol 45, no 1, January 1992, p10, see also James N. Gardner, Effective *Lobbying in the European Community,* Kluwer, Boston, 1991, p72.
40. See Cecilia Àndersen, *Influencing the European Community : Guidelines for a Successul Business Strategy,* Kogan Page, London, 1992, p23.
41. See European Commission : "Communication on an Open and Structured Dialogue between the Commission and Special Interest groups", March 1993. As cited in *EURO-CIDSE News Bulletin,* EURO-CIDSE, Brussels, April 1993, pp12-13.
42. See *International Coalition for Development Action* (ICDA) Update No 6, Nov-Dec 1991 : p11, ICDA, Brussels, 1991.
43. Personal Interview with Peter Madden, Policy Officer Christian Aid and Member of the NGO-GATT Steering Committee.
44. See Bernard Ryelandt, "Why does the European Community work with NGOs?" in The Courier, No 152, July-August 1995, p64.
45. Report from the Commission's to the Council on co-operation with European non-governmental development organisations (NGDOs) in spheres concerning developing countries (1990 financial years). SEC(91)2263 final, Brussels, 3 December 1991, pp1-4.
46. Personal Interview.
47. Personal Interview.
48. The 1049th Development Council Meeting, 27 May 1991, Press Release 6379/91 (Presse 73 - G), Council of the European Communities General Secretariat, Brussels,, May 1991, pp7-11.
49. Report of the committee on Development and Co-operation on the role of NGOs in development co-operation. Rapporteur Mr Lucciano Vecchi. European Parliament, A3-0029/92, pp5-16. .
50. Anne Gordon Drabeck, "An Overview of the Issues", World Development Supplement, *op cit,* p xiii.
51. See Nigel Twose, "european NGOs : Growth or Partnership?" in World Development Supplement, *op cit.* p10.
52. See 'Lobbying for fair trade', M. Wilkinson, Northern NGDOs, the European Community and the GATT Uruguay Round; *Third World Quarterly,* Vol. 17, No 2, pp251-267, 1996.

53. See "The Declaration of NGOs on the African Economic and social Crisis" which emerged from the meeting of North and South NGDOs at the United Nations General Assembly 'Special Session on the Critical Economic and Social Situation in Africa', 26-31 May 1986. As cited in *World Development Supplement, op cit*, pp83-84.

7

India's Export Performance in Manufactured Goods to European Union with Special Reference to U.K.

O.P. SHARMA

This note primarily aims at an analysis of India's performance of export of manufactures in the United Kingdom (UK) in reference to European Union (EU) and world as a whole. The basic purpose of the paper is to investigate in a limited way whether India's good export performance at aggregate level has been reflected in similar performance in one of the major traditional and highly competitive markets, that is, the EU and with in it, UK. The note also touches upon very briefly the trends in foreign direct investment from EU and UK which have their bearing on export of manufactures. The analysis is mostly based on import statistics of EU, published by EUROSTAT. Comprehensive data on market share of India in EU and UK is provided at the end of the note

Section I provides an analysis of trends in imports of manufactures from India to EU and UK both sector-wise as well as by major product groups. In Section II, an analysis is provided of the factors underlying India's performance in UK and EU in manufactures. Finally, Section III touches upon other areas of co-operation such as aid and investment and provides concluding remarks on the emerging economic scene in India and EU.

I

Trends in Indo-EU and Indo-UK Trade in Manufactured Products

In the early 1980s, India experienced stagnation in its exports to the European Community, now European Union, and a decline in it's share in the imports of EC from the outside. For instance, India's share in import from extra EC declined from 1.1. percent in 1981 to 0.9 percent in 1985. Similarly in EC's import from developing countries, India's share declined from 6.2 percent to 5.4 percent during the same period. This was attributed mainly to the high instance of non-tariff barriers which was as much as 62 percent for India as compared with 41 percent for the developing countries as a whole and 43 percent for the newly industrialising countries.

As against this lackluster performance, there has been significant improvement in India's export performance in EU during the 1990s. Thus India's share in EU total imports increased from 0.96 percent in 1991 to 1.43 percent in 1995. Most of this increase was on account increase in share of manufacture exports. Share of agricultural items increased only marginally from 1.43 percent to 1.68 percent.

India's performance in the UK market is to be evaluated in terms of the strength of the UK market within EU as well as India's competitivity therein. Since 1992, EU became a single market whereby all physical, fiscal and technical barriers were abolished. This, taken together with the existence of Common External Tariff made the movement of the products completely free within the European Union. Evidence indicates that under these circumstances share of UK in extra-EU imports increased from 16.9 percent in1991 to 17.1 percent in 1995, largely because of increase in it's share in extra-EU imports of manufactures from 18 percent to 18.9 percent. The evidence further suggests that India improved its share in UK imports of manufactures from extra-EU from 1.3 percent in 1991 to 1.8 percent in 1995 despite the fact that India's share in agricultural products declined from 3.1 percent to 2.7 percent during the same period. As the data reveals, the improvement in India's share in manufactures was wide-spread. Except in some items, such as pearls and precious stones, machinery and vehicles, etc., in major items such as chemicals textiles, footwear and base metals, India improved its share considerably.

In a broader sense the strategic importance of the UK market for India lies in the fact that it absorbs a significantly greater proportion of imports from India. Thus while imports from intra-EU account for about 12 percent and those from extra EU account for 17 to 18 percent, UK absorbs about 22 percent of total imports from India by the EU. As suggested above while there has been a strong movement of trade away from UK market in agriculture products, in manufactures, the extent of market diversification for India's manufacture exports has been only marginal.

The greater importance of UK market for Indian products is also reflected in various groups of manufactures except pearls and precious stones, arms and ammunition and works of art. In these three items UK market is to a greater extent dependent on imports from extra-EU than India. Share of UK in imports of EU from India is much higher for plastics, wood articles, footwear, base metals, machinery, vehicles, instruments and miscellaneous manufactures. It is interesting to note that major exports items of India such as chemicals, leather goods, textiles, pearls and precious stones are not unduly concentrated in UK market. Chemicals, leather goods, textiles, base metals, stones and plaster products as well as miscellaneous manufactures together accounted for over 71 percent of total imports of manufactures from India to EU. These imports registered faster growth in EU market. Pearls and precious stones, however, registered faster growth in UK segment of the EU market.

The same story is revealed by the pattern of growth of imports from India and other areas into UK as well as EU. First, the evidence suggests that imports from India have been growing at a faster rate in the EU as well as UK both as compared to imports from Intra-EU as well as extra-EU during 1991 to 1995. Thus in the EU market imports from India increased at a compound growth rate of 13.1 percent per annum as compared with 7.2 percent from intra-EU and 2.4 percent from extra-EU. Similarly imports from India into UK market increased at the rate of 10.5 percent as compared with 2.3 percent from intra-EU and 2.7 percent from extra-EU. Another significant evidence is that the imports of manufactures from India have been growing at much faster rate both in UK as well as EU markets. It is for this reason that the share of manufactures in total imports of UK from India increased from 78.3 percent in 1991 to 85.4 percent in 1995. Similarly in the EU market, the share of manufactures in total imports from India increased from 82.3 percent to 85.3 percent during the same period. Looking at both the share of the manufactured items as well as the rate of growth of imports from India, it is apparent that most of the incremental exports have been resulting from high growth rates of manufactured exports particularly chemicals, footwear, base metals and machinery. Other items such as plastics, wood articles, vehicles and miscellaneous manufactures which have low share but registered high growth rates made added contribution to Indian exports to the UK market.

II

Factors in Performance of Exports of Manufactures to UK and EU

The broad trends described above indicate that performance in UK market has been in accordance with the performance in the EU market as a whole. However, the performance of exports to EU has shown some deceleration when compared with India's overall performance. Thus share of EU in India's exports increased from 27.5 percent in 1990-91 to 28.3 percent during 1991-92 but thereafter declined to 26.5 percent during 1995-96. Similarly, share of UK in India's overall exports declined marginally from 6.5 percent in 1990-91 to 6.4 percent in 1995-96. As would be seen, this is partly explained by significant dynamism in India's total exports during the last three years ending with 1995-96. During this period India's supply capabilities improved sharply resulting in increase in export/GDP ratio from 7 percent to over 10 percent. This has been partly due to the economic policy reforms, particularly in the areas of foreign trade, exchange rate, industry and foreign investment which are by now well documented.

The trends in share of EU or UK in India's overall exports conceals the performance of manufactures in general and of individual products in particular. Of particular importance is the sharp and significant decline in the share of UK in India's exports of leather and leather manufactures from 16 percent in 1990-91 to 11.2 percent in 1995-96, of gems and jewellery from 2.8 percent to 1.6 percent, ready-made garments from 11.9 percent to 10.1 percent, handicrafts from

11.2 percent to 10 percent and cotton yarn and fabrics from 12 percent to 9 percent. On the other hand, share of engineering goods increased from 5.1 percent to 7.8 percent. When taken together, the share of UK in India's total exports of these six major product groups declined from 7.9 percent in 1990-91 to 6.9 percent in 1995-96.

The adverse performance of the product groups mentioned above is particularly depressing in view of the fact that their share even in total exports of manufactures to the UK declined from 76 percent in 1990-91 to 62 percent in 1995-96. During the same period UK's share in total exports of manufactures of India increased marginally from 7.1 percent to 7.4 percent and that of primary products declined from 4.9 percent to 3.2 percent. UK's share in India's aggregate exports as mentioned above declined marginally from 6.5 percent to 6.4 percent during 1990-96. Obviously, India was diversifying its exports both in UK market as well as world as a whole.

Export performance basically depend, on the supply of exportable surpluses and demand in the international market. Supply of exportable surpluses in turn depend on capacity of production, domestic demand and relative domestic to international prices, the latter partly dependent on exchange rates. Similarly demand for exports depend upon purchasing power in export market, relative prices and the market competitiveness vis-a-vis trade rivals.

In large majority of products, India's share in world export is very small. Thus being a marginal exporter, India faces an elastic demand with respect to prices for it's products. There are exceptions like textiles where due to variable export restraints or other tariff/non-tariff barriers, competing rivals face discriminatory market access. However, in most other products, demand for India's export depends on world income or volume of world trade and relative prices in the external markets.

A major factor in India's export performance in recent years has been the recovery in word trade, which accelerated from 2.9 percent in 1991 to 9.4 percent in 1994 in terms of volume. Volume of import of industrial countries in particularly accelerated sharply from 2.1 percent to 10.5 percent. Even though the developing countries faced adverse trends in export prices, the over-all demand conditions were quite favourable in recent years.

On the supply side, it has been indicated above that the share of export in GDP has gone up sharply from 7.0 percent in 1990-91 and over 10 percent in 1995-96. Similarly, export/output ratio has shown increase in many agricultural products. In addition to these factors, except for a short period, movements in exchange ratio, as it affects profitability and competitiveness, as well as industrial production, which indicates the supply capabilities have shown favourable trends.

The factors and the determinants relevant to India's overall export performance are also applicable to the performance in the EU and the UK markets. As the trade policy decisions are largely taken at the EU level, factors-such as the tariff and non-tariff barriers, particularly the quota restraints on textile and other products have universal application in the member states of the EU. The more pertinent country specific issues which have their bearing on the export performance in UK market are the performance of their economy and the operation of the policies which are outside the ambit of EU.

While commenting on the export performance of India in EU, researchers and policy makers in Europe have emphasised the inadequate and inefficient supply conditions in India whereas the Indian researchers and policy makers have emphasised the constraints emanating from trade policy of the European Union, particularly in regard to tariff and non-tariff barriers. According to the former, in the post second oil shock period, when European demand for manufactured exports declined, India's competitiveness collapsed in zero sum game with China. Similarly, the European researchers and policy makers emphasised that inappropriate industrial and trade policies led to supply constraints. To buttress this argument, it is argued that there is substantial similarity between India's share in the EU market and in the world market and that India lost ground in both. On the argument that India lost heavily on account of the pyramid of preferences in favour of ACP countries, no evidence is found whereby ACP countries benefited greatly, notwithstanding the advantages they enjoyed in respect to non-tariff barriers (NTBs) like MFA.

These arguments are to some extent valid. It is nevertheless true that the recession in the early eighties and again in the early nineties not only led to the decline in the demand but also increasing rate of unemployment, which in turn enhanced the trade restrictions on cheaper manufacture imports from the non-ACP developing countries. In the UK, GDP growth rate declined to minus 0.1 percent per annum during 1991-93 as compared with 3.3 percent per annum during 1986-90. Similarly total domestic demand in UK declined from 4 percent per annum during 1986-90 to minus 0.1 percent per annum during 1991-93. Also unemployment rate further increased to 9.8 percent during 1991-93 from 9 percent during 1986-90. These trends explain the depressing performance of UK imports from intra-EU as well as from extra-EU. It is commendable, however, that India was in a position to experience a higher rate of growth of total exports as wells as exports of manufactures then from the other non-EU countries. Still, India's performance in the UK market was less satisfactory than in the EU market as a whole both in the total export as well as in the exports of manufactures.

The adverse export performance of the five major export product groups mentioned earlier was a major cause for comparatively slower growth of exports from India to EU as well as to UK as compared to total exports. This is partly explained by the less than satisfactory performance of the GSP scheme and partly by the stiffening of the NTBs on items such as footwear, cotton textiles, ready made garments, carpets and man-made fibres. The GSP coverage, the evidence suggests, has gone down substantially since 1988 both for textiles as well as for industrial goods. In case of industrial goods, GSP received as a percentage of GSP coverage declined from around 80 percent to around 65 percent between the late 80s to early 90s. Exports of India have also been affected by the continuance of high tariff rates. As compared to the average tariff rates of 3 to 4 percent in the EU, imports from India have attracted higher rates of tariff of 8 to 9 percent since the late 80s to the mid-90s. In fact, there has been substantial increase in the average tariff rates for leather articles, textiles and some other manufactures. On textiles, the tariff rates have accelerated during the 1990s itself.

Available evidence also suggests that the exports covered by NTBs as a percentage of total exports have been not only sustained at a high level on major export items but in fact increased further during the 1990s. On leather articles, footwear and textiles, the exports covered by NTBs as percentage of the total exports is even higher than 90 percent. As most of the products exported by India are labour intensive and as India has comparative advantage in their production, the stiffening of tariff and non-tariff barriers has directly affected adversely India's export performance in the EU and UK. Apart from the fact that investment planning for export expansion is not possible because of the unpredictability of benefits under GSP on account of its uncertain durability, rules of origin and proliferation of qualifying requirements, the GSP suffers from very poor coverage particularly in regard to processed agricultural products. Evidence suggests that if the GSP was fully liberalised, covering all products, without any limit, beneficiary countries would potentially enjoy over US$ 21 billion in additional trade benefits over and above the benefits from the present schemes. This would be even higher than the benefits arising from 100 percent cut in MFN tariff.

The GSP benefits lose their significance when the non-tariff barriers are applied with a view to effectively limit the operation of the preferential system. Anti-dumping measures, import surveillance and VERs have been applied with increasing frequency and uncertainty against successful exports stunting the growth efforts from exports and investment in the developing countries. It is in this regard that it becomes necessary to argue for trade liberalisation in the EU in the form of introduction of a GSP for NTBs as well rather than just for tariff preferences. This fits well with the insistence of EU for removal of quantitative restrictions on imports in India.

Contrary to these steps required, the EU has, in fact, introduced a new GSP scheme valid for the period January 1995 to end of 1998 whereby a large number of products of interest to India and other developing countries have been included under the categories "very sensitive" and "sensitive". These categories attract rates of duties of 85 percent and 70 percent respectively and allow a waiver of 15 percent and 30 percent only. The products under semi-sensitive and non-sensitive categories with rates of duties at 35 percent and zero percent are of much less importance. In addition, the new GSP scheme provides for he Graduation Clause by which countries on the basis of their per capita income beyond $6000 or 25 percent of more share in EU market would be excluded from GSP. By the criteria of specialisation India falls somewhere in the middle and is likely to be excluded from GSP beneficiaries along with China in due course. In case of textiles and leather, India might lose the preferences even sooner. In addition, India has been facing a host of anti-dumping measures in case of textile products. Finally, the new EU proposal for the first time envisages environmental and social concerns which could adversely affect India's exports.

III

Emerging Economic Scene and Prospects of Investment Co-operation Between India and EU : Some Concluding Remarks

Increased market access in the EU and increased inflow of capital are the basic requirements of improvement in the development co-operation between the EU as well as UK and India. Historical ties and the presence of a thriving Indian community in UK and other EU countries should make that task easy. Trends in foreign direct investment indicate that UK as well as EU have not taken full advantage of the opportunities provided by the economic liberalisation in India. For instance, the share of EU in actual total inflow of foreign direct investment in India has gone down substantially from 39.8 percent in 1991 to 11.6 percent in 1995. Similarly, the share of UK has gone down from 14.2 percent in 1991 to just 2.7 percent in 1995. While the actual inflow to India has increased consistently from around $1.1 billion in 1991 to $2 billion in 1995 the inflows from EU as well as UK have been violently fluctuating over the years indicating the instability in the investment pattern and it being limited to only a few areas. This is despite the fact that India has announced very liberal investment protection measures, significantly liberalised access to investment in infrastructure and other industrial sectors and even in some cases guaranteed a minimum rate of return on investment. A large number of projects/sectors/areas have been identified both for purposes of satisfying the local markets such as in food processing, agrobased industries, leather products, machinery and transport equipment, electronic and electrical equipments, chemicals, mineral and energy-based industries as well as exports.

Apart from FDI, the UK also provides economic assistance, mostly in the form of grants. Total aid utilised from UK has, however, shown falling trend from $160.5 million in 1991 to $84.5 million in 1995. The UK is the second major donor of aid to India after Germany. Also, aid assistance from the UK is mostly in the form of grant where as the grant element in total global aid to India has been only 7-8 percent. Still there are some adverse trends in external aid from UK to India. First, aid utilised from the UK has shown strong downward trend over the last five years even though there was some revival in aid authorised as well as utilised in 1995-96. Second, there is disturbing trend in that the aid utilised to aid authorised ratio has shown sharp fluctuations. Thirdly, share of aid utilised from UK to total has been low and shown downward trend even though there was some revival in 1995-96.

The emergence of single European market and the establishment of the World Trade Organisation have changed the basic perception of Indo-EU and Indo-UK relations in the sphere of international economic relations. In the context of regionalisation, there is, now increasing understanding between SAARC and EU as they have already signed a Memorandum of Understanding for increasing bilateral dialogue and exchange of information and contacts. Also, the conventional wisdom of the North pulling the South needs to be re-examined in the context of these developments. Developing countries will have gradually more and more impact on North in the 21st century. According to one assessment, if the developing countries continue to grow by 6 percent per annum and the developed by 2-3 percent per annum as have been the trends in the recent past, the share of global output provided by the developing countries could surpass that provided by the industrial countries by the year 2004. Recent trends suggest that the UK economy has now come out of recession as it experienced growth rate of around 3 percent last year. Similar trend are exhibited in the other Member-States of EU. The widening and deepening of EU is likely to accelerate within the next five years which will further increase the importance of this market to India. This will necessitate fresh trade initiatives in this area.

In the next five years India is going to implement it's Ninth Five Year Plan with the target GDP growth rate of 7 percent per annum and growth of exports by 12 to 14 percent per annum. This would require an investment rate of more than 29 percent and inflow of foreign capital of about $10 billion per annum by 2002. India is now gradually removing quantitative restrictions on imports and the tariff rate is likely to be reduced from the present peak of 40 percent to the level prevailing in ASEAN countries. The thought process of introducing convertibility on capital account has already been initiated.

These developments in India and EU described above provide an opportunity for enhanced trade and investment co-operation between the two regions. In recent period, EU policy towards India has been lacking in enthusiasm when compared with the same for ASEAN countries. FDI inflow has been at low level despite a number of bilateral investment protection measures. EU has taken several anti-dumping measures against India in recent period. India, on its part has not been responsive to the expectations of EU in matters regarding market access, investment measures and intellectual property rights. Other countries, such as Turkey and more recently MERCOSUR, have marched ahead of India in strengthening their relations with EU. Notwithstanding India's efforts in strengthening SAARC and ASEAN, greater possibilities for trade expansion within the Ninth Plan lie in exploiting the market opportunities in EU. For this, India should take fresh policy initiatives in it's dialogue with EU including the possibility of a free trade area.

Table 7.1: Share of India in Import from Extra-EU : EU and UK Markets

(In percent)

	1991	1992	1993	1994	1995
EU Market					
Agricultural Items	1.43	1.43	1.67	1.54	1.68
Total Minerals	0.25	0.27	0.41	0.33	0.34
Total Manufactures	1.06	1.09	1.28	1.40	1.59
Grand Total	0.96	1.00	1.19	1.27	1.43
UK Market					
Total Agricultural	3.11	3.29	3.28	3.33	2.74
Total Minerals	0.19	0.12	0.32	0.13	0.38
Total Manufactures	1.30	1.36	1.45	1.65	1.79
Grand Total	1.32	1.39	1.49	1.69	1.77

Table 7.2 : Importance of UK Market in EU Imports

SHARE OF UK IN IMPORTS OF E.U. FROM

		Intra-EU		Extra-EU		India	
		1991	1995	1991	1995	1991	1995
6	Chemicals	12.47	12.33	14.28	13.84	19.22	18.85
7	Plastics	12.81	11.26	16.11	16.75	21.18	22.36
8	Leather Goods	6.96	7.68	10.72	9.99	18.62	12.99
9	Wood Articles	11.52	12.31	19.42	13.91	20.78	26.81
10.	Wood Pulp	14.84	14.76	22.12	22.71	49.73	67.32
11	Textiles	11.76	10.64	14.53	14.51	23.52	20.79
12	Footwear	12.36	12.67	16.88	15.51	23.51	30.58
13	Stores, Plaster	9.02	7.70	14.88	13.68	38.92	16.60
14	Pearls & Precious Stones	9.65	16.72	22.43	33.45	8.08	9.12
15	Base Metals	10.41	8.62	14.19	13.60	36.37	28.81
16	Machinery	13.26	13.47	19.67	22.45	33.70	37.32
17	Vehicles	10.39	13.95	10.71	15.99	8.91	24.81

(Contd.)

Table 7.2 : *(Contd.)*

18	Instruments	12.93	11.60	18.37	18.28	39.02	33.80
19	Arms & Ammuni.	14.43	25.30	27.60	42.70	20.81	18.35
20	Misc. Imports	10.81	10.00	17.70	16.04	27.02	24.83
21	Works of Art	14.86	1.07	35.46	25.52	39.70	18.34
	Total	12.09	11.82	16.88	17.06	23.13	21.04
	Agriculture	12.94	11.65	15.67	14.71	34.10	24.09
	Minerals	7.95	6.37	12.25	8.98	9.54	9.91
	Manufactures	12.16	12.04	18.03	18.78	22.02	21.05

Table 7.3 : Rate of Growth of Imports into EU and UK: 1991-95

		UK			(Percent per annum) EU		
		Intra-EU	Extra-EU	India	Intra-EU	Extra-EU	India
6	Chemicals	10.38	7.02	20.02	10.69	7.85	20.62
7	Plastics	5.59	6.48	52.85	9.04	6.30	50.80
8	Leather Goods	5.51	3.14	2.18	2.95	5.42	11.79
9	Wood Articles	21.69	-9.88	20.33	19.69	-2.03	12.90
10	Wood Pulp	17.80	-10.15	32.09	17.97	-10.74	22.45
11	Textiles	-1.09	3.63	10.35	1.43	3.67	13.81
12	Footwear	2.65	1.87	18.72	2.27	4.05	11.16
13	Stores, Plaster	-0.37	1.99	8.59	3.64	4.17	34.39
14	Pearls & Pre Stones	22.25	20.92	11.45	6.56	9.42	7.66
15	Base Metals	4.39	5.23	17.49	9.41	6.35	24.53
16	Machinery	9.04	9.69	23.00	8.61	6.11	19.91
17	Vehicles	13.29	7.97	46.22	5.24	-2.33	13.19
18	Instruments	4.07	3.59	1.10	6.93	3.72	4.79
19	Arms & Ammuni.	31.03	36.34	-4.72	13.87	22.24	-4.79
20	Misc. Imports	1.83	3.41	29.63	3.82	6.00	32.40
21	Art pieces	-28.20	3.41	-16.44	38.52	12.28	2.64
	Total	2.33	2.72	10.47	7.19	2.45	13.13

Agriculture	1.62	2.57	-0.62	4.31	4.09	8.39
Minerals	-6.26	-9.28	7.31	-0.95	-1.95	6.29
Manufactures	7.73	4.19	12.88	8.01	3.13	14.17

Table 7.4 : Pattern of Imports from India into EU and UK: 1991-95

(Percent per annum)

		UK		EU	
		1991	1995	1991	1995
6	Chemicals	4.75	6.07	5.44	6.78
7	Plastics	0.51	1.71	0.53	1.61
8	Leather Goods	10.80	7.25	12.78	11.75
9	Wood Articles	0.40	0.52	0.42	0.41
10.	Wood Pulp	0.28	0.53	0.12	0.16
11	Textiles	47.92	43.75	44.87	44.31
12	Footwear	5.90	7.22	5.53	4.97
13	Stores, Plaster	0.92	0.79	0.52	1.00
14	Pearls & Pre Stones	5.31	5.04	14.72	11.64
15	Base Metals	6.37	7.47	3.86	5.96
16	Machinery	7.30	10.29	4.77	5.81
17	Vehicles	1.04	2.94	2.58	2.49
18	Instruments	2.17	1.39	1.22	0.87
19	Arms & Ammuni.	0.01	0.01	0.01	0.01
20	Misc. Imports	1.06	1.85	0.86	1.56
21	Art Pieces	0.63	0.19	6.35	0.22

Table 7.5 : Trends in Share of India in UK's Imports of Manufactures from Extra - EU : 1991-95 (In Percent)

		1991	1992	1993	1994	1995
6	Chemicals	1.04	1.18	1.36	1.65	1.64
7	Plastics	0.20	0.36	0.45	0.65	0.86
8	Leather Goods	1.45	1.30	1.36	1.43	1.40
9	Wood Articles	0.16	0.25	0.28	0.30	0.53

(Contd.)

Table 7.5 : *(Contd.)*

10.	Wood Pulp	0.05	0.08	0.10	0.15	0.26
11	Textiles	7.26	7.81	8.15	8.91	9.33
12	Footwear	5.61	7.14	10.22	10.96	10.34
13	Stores, Plaster	1.47	1.20	1.46	1.46	1.89
14	Pearls & Pre. Stones	1.40	1.01	0.53	0.92	1.01
15	Base Metals	1.31	1.57	1.67	1.41	2.04
16	Machinery	0.30	0.34	0.46	0.24	0.48
17	Vehicles	0.20	0.25	0.25	0.38	0.67
18	Instruments	0.52	0.45	0.38	0.53	0.48
19	Arms & Ammuni.	0.18	0.36	0.05	0.10	0.04
20	Misc. Imports	0.50	0.50	0.66	0.11	1.22
21	Art Pieces	0.26	0.17	0.12	0.13	0.11
	Total	1.32	1.79	1.49	1.67	1.77
	Agriculture	3.11	3.29	3.28	3.33	2.74
	Minerals	0.19	0.12	0.32	0.13	0.38
	Manufactures	1.30	1.36	1.45	1.65	1.79

Table 7.6 : Trends in Share of India in EU's Imports of Manufactures From Extra-EU : 1991-95

(In Percent)

		1991	1992	1993	1994	1995
6	Chemicals	0.77	0.64	0.98	1.11	1.20
7	Plastics	0.15	0.20	0.24	0.33	0.62
8	Leather Goods	8.50	8.87	10.00	10.07	10.75
9	Wood Articles	0.15	0.16	0.17	0.17	0.27
10.	Wood Pulp	0.02	0.03	0.04	0.05	0.09
11	Textiles	4.48	4.74	5.40	5.76	6.51
12	Footwear	4.02	3.76	4.51	5.09	5.75
13	Stores, Plaster	0.56	0.64	0.84	1.09	1.56
14	Pearls & Pre Stones	3.97	3.32	3.10	3.48	3.81

(Contd.)

Table 7.6 : *(Contd.)*

15 Base Metals	0.51	0.68	0.81	0.80	0.96
16 Machinery	0.18	0.18	0.21	0.23	0.29
17 Vehicles	0.24	0.18	0.22	0.32	0.43
18 Instruments	0.25	0.26	0.22	0.27	0.26
19 Arms & Ammuni.	0.24	0.24	0.28	0.12	0.13
20 Misc. Imports	0.32	0.39	0.51	0.68	0.79
21 Art Pieces	0.23	0.46	0.15	0.14	0.16
Total	0.96	1.00	1.19	1.27	1.43
Agriculture	1.43	1.43	1.67	1.54	1.68
Minerals	0.26	0.27	0.41	0.33	0.34
Manufactures	1.06	1.09	1.28	1.40	1.59

Table 7.7 : Share of UK in India's Exports of Major Items
(Rs. Crores)

Major Item	1990-91	1995-96
1. Leather and Leather Manufactures	329.2	648.2
	(16.02)	(11.25)
2. Gems and Jewellery	143.21	279.88
	(2.75)	(1.59)
3. Engineering Goods	164.92	699.44
	(5.12)	(7.75)
4. Ready Made Garments	410.47	1113.30
	(11.88)	(10.14)
5. Handicrafts	48.12	144.49
	(11.21)	(10.00)
6. Cotton Yarn and Fabrics	249.67	784.78
	(12.09)	(9.08)
Total (1-6)	1345.59	3670.11
	(7.95)	(6.86)
Total Manufactures	1768.79	5931.89
	(7.13)	(7.40)
Grand Total	2122.80	6717.04
	(6.53)	(6.43)

Note : Figures in parentheses indicate percent share in India's total exports of relevant item.

Source : DGCI&S - Monthly Statistics, March issues.

Table 7.8 : Trends in Foreign Direct Investment from UK and EU

		(Million US $) UK	EU	All Countries
1991	FDI Approval	10.03	59.79	166.91
	Actual Inflow	15.55	43.73	109.81
	Ratio	155.33	90.63	65.79
1992	FDI Approval	36.78	167.75	1214.86
	Actual Inflow	23.74	64.41	210.99
	Ratio	64.55	38.39	17.36
1994	FDI Approval	194.60	564.79	2768.54
	Actual Inflow	72.64	148.64	558.08
	Ratio	37.32	29.45	20.15
1994	FDI Approval	405.93	835.16	4433.47
	Actual Inflow	133.61	308.21	928.64
	Ratio	37.32	36.90	20.95
1995	FDI Approval	539.33	1883.21	10022.41
	Actual Inflow	54.56	231.74	1990.43
	Ratio	10.11	12.31	19.85
1991-95	FDI Approval	1186.72	3450.81	18606.19
	Actual Inflow	300.10	756.72	3797.95
	Ratio	25.29	23.09	20.41

Source : Ministry of Industry - Secretariat of Industrial Approvals

8

Indians in Europe

D.K. Giri

For more than 2000 years the Indians have been migrating to the different parts of the world. In ancient times, Buddhist pilgrims travelled to Central and South Asia. Indian dynasties expanded to South-East Asia. The Indian traders developed economic ties along the coast of East Africa. These contacts were largely political, cultural and commercial and did not result in heavy migration or establishment of Indians in foreign lands. The large-scale migration, is a product of British colonialism dating back to the days of abolition of slavery in British colonies in 1833-34.

About 12 million people of Indian origin are living in 160 countries of the world.[1] These Indians have migrated to these countries at different times, conditions and processes. On the basis of patterns of migration and settlement the Indian migration could be divided into the following five categories. First, the Indentured Labour migration (the West Indies, Fiji and Mauritius). Second, the Kangani/ Maistry Labour migration (Sri Lanka, Malayasia, Singapore and Burma). Third, the 'Free' or Passage migration (Africa, South of Sahara). Fourth, the voluntary migration to Europe and North America and the fifth, the labour migration to the West Asia.

This article aims at studying the issues of Indians in Europe. It is hard to get information on the EC countries except Britain and the overseas departments of France. However, on the basis of available information some broad generalisation could be made as most of the countries are characterised by a general pattern of migration from

India in the latest phase. The paper excludes the case of 'twice migrants' to Europe. I have taken a broad perspective in two parts of the paper. The first part examines the magnitude, causes and characteristics of the migration. The second section assesses the impact, immigration laws and the integration process. The causes have been analysed in the context of pull-push model and the impact in terms of remittances. The process of Indian migration to Europe has been complex and dynamic, its debate controversial. This paper attempts to join the debate by raising certain questions then answering any.

History and the Magnitude

The Indian contact with Europe goes back to 1,000 years when the Europeans came to India to trade in spices, textiles and carpets. In 1498, Portuguese set their feet in India when Vascoda Gama arrived in West Coast of India and they remained in Goa for 400 years. Not to be left out of this lucrative trade other European nations - the Dutch, the English and the French followed in the wake of the Portuguese. Subsequently, the British established their empire in India.

One of the major legacies of the British control of India was the planting of people of India all over the British empire[2]. The colonial contact brought the Indians to Britain also. The Indian migration to Britain dates back to nineteenth century. The early migrants to Britain were lascars (seamen), ayahs (maid servants), students, princes, businessman and politicians. The seamen worked for the British merchant navy, the ayahs were brought by the English families returning from India; the students came for higher studies and to take the Indian Civil Service examination which was held only in London; the princes visited as royal guests to show their respect to the Monarch; the politicians came to argue the case of Indian freedom; and the businessmen came to trade and participate in the business exhibitions held in London.

The number of these migrants was small as many of them returned after accomplishing their purpose. They were about 31,000 between 1921-45 and 33,000 between 1946-60[3]. Mr. Kondapi estimated about 5,000 Indians in 1945 living for a fairly long period in the United Kingdom[4]. It is hard to have a proper estimate of the

Indians in the pre-independence period as Pakistan and Bangladesh were part of India at that time and the governments did not keep any record of the people migrating. Harder still is to get any information about the Indian migrants to other European countries. Table 8.1 gives the number of Indian migrants to the French islands. These migrants were the Indentured labourers. The British colonies paved the way for recruitment to the French colonies. The recruitment took place at all the French trading posts especially Pondicherry and Karikal, later on it was introduced throughout India.

Table 8.1

Island	Period	Number
Guadeloupe	1854-89	43,326
Martinique	1854-89	25,509
Reunion	1829-1924	118,000

Source: Singaravelou (1975).

Most of these were Indentured labourers and were repatriated from the islands. The Indian migration to Europe has mainly occurred in the post-independent period, except in case of Britain which had colonial links with India for a long time.

After the Second World War and Indian independence important changes have occurred in the pattern of Indian international migration. The sixties saw heavy flow of migrants to the European countries. The migration to the United Kingdom was constrained after the passage of the Commonwealth Immigration Acts of 1962 and 1971; yet over 200,000 Indians migrated to the United Kingdom during the 1960s mainly because the law permitted the entry of professionals and skilled people and their dependents of the pre-1962 period residents. Other European countries were even stricter in allowing the Indian immigrants. During 1962-71 alone 42,440 Indians most of whom were professionals and skilled people and about 59,000 dependents arrived in the United Kingdom. Large inflows into Western Europe picked up when the immigration policies of those countries emphasised skills rather than national origin as the major determinants of admission.

While it is difficult to say exactly how many Indians have left the country and how many have permanently settled down in Europe, different estimates suggest that about 510,000 have become permanent residents in the European Community countries; with United Kingdom accounting for the majority followed by Netherlands.

The following Table 8.2 gives the estimate of the Indian immigrants in 12 countries of the European Community. It seems the Indian immigrants in Netherlands include those Indians from Surinam as well.

Table 8.2

Serial No.	Name of the country	Number of Persons of Indian origin residing in the country			Number of those who have accepted citizenship	
(a)	(b)	(c)			(d)	
		1970	1980	1984	1980	1984
1.	Belgium	377	400	313	5	11
2.	Denmark	256	637	1821	65	886
3.	France	1,400	500	40,000	6	37,000
4.	Germany	4,681	13,082	28,030	1,521	262
5.	Greece	13	300	250	-	2
6.	Ireland	150	6	427	6	27
7.	Italy	761	900	1,335	-	335
8.	Luxembourg	n.a	n.a	n.a.	n.a	2
9.	Netherlands	202	101,500	102,400	100,000	100,000
10.	Portugal	-	6,000	7,000	5,930	6,603
11.	Spain	1600	4,000	5,000	37	n.a.
12.	United Kingdom	321,995	392,000	719,000	250,000	359,000

Source: A.H. Helwes (1986:213-20)[6].

n.a.: not available

Who are the Migrants?

Information on occupational, educational, age and socio-cultural characteristics of Indian immigrants to Europe is scarce with the exception of United Kingdom. On the basis of available information the Indian immigration population could be broadly divided into six groups. The first group is the Indentured labourers to the French islands; the second three groups are in the United Kingdom and the third group of people are in the European Community countries.

The majority of Indian immigrants in the French islands were coolies and of Tamil origins. Others were the Indentured labours from Northern India who were called 'Calcutta' after name of the port of their embarkation. The South Indians were called the 'Malabare'. There were some of Muslim immigrants who came from North-West India mainly Sind and Gujarat and were called 'arabes'.

The second group consists of the people who were the first immigrants to the United Kingdom. They were mostly old people, Bengali Muslims and Gujaratis who worked as lascars. They came in the last quarter of the eighteenth century and the whole of 19th century. They numbered about 500, lived in the ports and hardly had any contact either with India or with the new immigrants. The third group came in the first-half of the present century. They were mainly Sikh ex-soldiers, pedlars and money changers and whereabouts 3,000 and 4,000 including their dependents.

The third and the largest category consisted of industrial workers who came around the beginning of Indian independence and the end of the second world war. The partition of Punjab at independence caused large population movements across and outside India. Some of the most enterprising among the dispossess and dislocated sought to build new lives overseas. They came to Britain to fill the labour-gaps created by the people leaving the old industries like textiles, iron works and public transport. Moreover, Britain was experiencing industrial growth providing new openings for the labourers from India. Indians saw these opportunities and migrated.

The Indians who came at this stage were mainly from two districts of Punjab — Jullunder and Hoshiarpur — and two parts of Gujarat — Central and Southern. Initially, these immigrants came alone with the intention of working hard, making money and returning home. Having accumulated enough money they returned and were replaced by their family members or relatives. This pattern of temporary settlement with one member of the family replacing another in the work place was stopped by the migration legislations. The migrants had either to stay or go back with no chance of replacement. Almost all stayed and called their wives and children to join them. Hugh Tinker suggests that during the partition many Sikh ex-soldiers were rejected from their villages. The ex-soldiers had often kept in touch with the former British officers of the Indian army who offered jobs to them. In the beginning they came individually and after settling down brought their relatives in 'chain migration'.

The fourth category is mostly professionals; the doctors, the engineers, academics and scientists. They migrated in two batches. First were the professionals from the metropolitan centres such as Bombay, Calcutta, Madras and Bangalore which supplied northern India with professional people during the 19th century and even later. Since these professionals had already migrated from their traditional culture, it was not too hard for them to migrate again for better prospects. Second was the migration as students. Majority of the students came to Britain as they spoke English and had similar patterns of education. Recently, many Indian Universities have introduced the teaching of major European languages enabling the students to go to other countries of the Community.

For two reasons, it is difficult to estimate how many of these students actually settle down. First the immigration laws have become very strict. Secondly the students with the sponsorship from government of India and other foreign foundations under various exchange programmes return to India as they have signed a bond to this effect before leaving India.

Factors Promoting Migration

There are a number of push-pull factors for migration depending on the categories, process and period. The first five categories of migrants had mainly the push factors; shortage of land, rural poverty and cultural dislocation. Aurora attributes their migration to 3 factors[7]. First the high pressure of population on the land. Second the tradition of travel and working away from home. Third the attraction of western culture. Desai gives almost the same reasons; the pressure on land, consequent unemployment and the tradition of migration.[8] Another factor was the dislocation of the village communities by fragmentation and administrative reorganisation of the Moghul empire by the colonial administration. In many parts of India migration was preceded by the loosening of the village community bond. The professionals had somewhat different pull-push factors in their migration.

Unemployment

One of the major reasons for migration is the high rate of unemployment in India. Table 8.3 gives some ideas of the educated unemployment in India in 1985.

Table 8.3

Occupational category	Number (in thousands)	Unemployed persons (in thousands)
Engineering graduates	266	19
Engineering diploma holders	430	86
Medical graduates	184	12
Dental graduates	12	Neg.
Nursing graduates	3	n.a
Agricultural Science graduates	90	10
Veterinary science graduates	24	1
Arts and Humanities graduates	2026	455
Vocation graduates	910	143
Basic science graduates	957	197
Commerce graduates	878	155
Under graduates	1290	316
Total graduates including		
Diploma holders	8492	1343
Matriculates and Higher		
Secondary school graduates	21375	3314
Total educated persons	30367	4657

Source: M.C. Madhavan (1985:470)

Neg. = less than 500; n.a = not available

These figures are based on the unemployed registered in the Employment Exchanges in different parts of the country. There are many unemployed outside the government records. Indian economy simply cannot employ all its professionals. Further, in India there is something called 'structural unemployment' which is responsible for migration. This has two aspects. First, the number of professionals in a particular sector is highly disproportionate to the requirement. Secondly, the mismatch between the Indian education and employment[9]. For example, the allopathic doctors in the country are found more suited to Britain and the United States. Jayaram goes on to say that some of the Indian medical colleges are maintained for the benefit of the other countries[10]. The rural masses of India cannot afford to utilise the high expertise of the doctors, and the consumers of health service found in the European countries their parallels in a few urbanised middle classes. On the other hand, when the Indian doctors find that they have the skills to find job in the European countries they find the Indian working conditions unattractive. The graduates from the prestigious institutions prefer high paying jobs in reputed institutions. The high expectations of these graduates and their frustration in not getting them also prompt them to migrate.

India has more than 200 medical and Engineering colleges which produce 6,000 medical graduates and 9,000 engineering graduates per year. Although the Government is spending considerable amount in Research and Development only a small number of professionals are employed in the 'key institutions' identified for the purpose. The private and the public sectors do employ scientists in their laboratories, but they are very few in number compared to the developed countries. Out of the total immigrant population of India 24 per cent were professionals in the United Kingdom, 27.9 per cent in Community countries and 73 per cent in United States[11].

Colonial links

Most of the nation-states which are affected by high rates of migration are former colonies. India, a former colony of Britain followed the educational pattern established by the British. More importantly, the university education in India is synonymous with learning of English. So the Indian migrants were familiar with the educational system of Britain and almost all the professionals knew English which is also the second language in any Community countries. Apart from language, religion also, to some extent facilitated the migration. Large number of schools and colleges in India are run by the christain missionaries. They naturally follow the western pattern and the dominant language is English. Thus, the language and religion makes it easier for the migrants to interact in their place of migration. Another curious argument found in Desai's research was that the English exploited the homeland of the immigrants for so long that they had a right to come here and earn an honest living.

Material Benefits

The wage differences that exist between India and the European countries seem to exert the greatest pull towards emigration. The income that a highly skilled professional can earn in a Western country could be more than five times what he could earn in India. The salary of a petty worker in the West is more than a college teacher, office clerk and many lower ranking officials in India. Many of the material benefits that he could easily get in Europe would not be available to him in India for a long time. An average middle class Indian family could not afford many modern technical conveniences that most people in the West take for granted. These conveniences hold an attraction for these professionals eager to have them and they can easily have them by migrating.

Working Conditions

The facilities in the European countries are generally superior to those in India. For high research in science and technology, better equipment and atmosphere is available in Europe. The migrants, by working with the outstanding experts, acquire superior training and prestige. This helps them to get better job opportunities at home.

The push factors in working conditions are many. Because of these factors many professionals refuse to return home. Those who returned to India after their training wanted to migrate to avoid professional isolations, loss of contact with colleagues through inability to travel and to have access to journals and other specialised materials. Most of the scientific establishment and government departments are headed by the civil servants who do not have expertise in the area. They may not take the advice of the technical experts and in decision-making and implementation — resulting in frustration and conflict with the experts. Moreover, these heads of the departments have control over the experts. They expect their juniors to comply with them because of their position in the institutional hierarchy although they may lack competence and authority on the subject. The patron-client relationship exists in many departments in India. Dissatisfaction arises out of lack of professional recognition, scope of promotion and professional autonomy. Thus, a slow progress up the professional ladder, over-staffing of particular departments and desire to be independent are some of the factors contributing to the migration from India.

Red-tapism

Most of the institutions in India are bound by excessive bureaucratic procedures. The civil servants heading the institutions can make things difficult for those engaged in research. Only a few Universities in India are autonomous while the rest hardly provide any academic incentives of freedom.

Conditions in the European countries are seen to be far more superior with less bureaucratic interference and recognition of talent irrespective of age and status.

Impact of the Migration

The impact of migration could be seen in the context of its population, socio-economic conditions, inflow of the foreign capital through remittances, and involvement of the migrants in her development process.

On population

Migration can affect the population of the sending countries. To some countries, it could be a loss and some it is a necessity. For instance, it is difficult to imagine how Ireland or Italy could have survived in last hundred yeas without the safety valve of mass emigration. Without emigration, these countries would have been overwhelmed by an excess of population. Even small societies like Malta and Barbados depended on emigration for some kind of equilibrium. But, to India it hardly made any difference. To her nearly 800 million, another 12 million would not make much difference. Besides, the rate of migration from India in any of the recent decade was only around 2 per cent of the decennial population growth. The studies show that the impact of overseas migration on the labour market was hardly felt in India. So, the migration of the professionals which are fewer in number would not affect the population so much.

On Society: A developing society like India is affected by the large-scale migration of the professionals. The impact is not only felt in terms of the costs involved in training them, but also in terms of the long-term developments of the country.

Indian Society needs the services of the professionals to cater to the vast needs of its people in terms of health, education, communication and so on. Most of the professionals in India are either concentrated in the few urban areas or migrating out of the country. One realises the need of the emigrants in view of the underdeveloped economy of India, but the loss of talent to the society should be seen in the emigration of the professionals. Large population and consequent unemployment seem to be major factors of emigration. In order to tackle the twin problems India needs many committed doctors and other scientific know-how's.

On Economy: The economies of the man-power exporting countries are deeply influenced by the remittance of the emigrants. The question of remittances in India is becoming increasingly significant. It not only influences the economic development and its international balance of payments, It also affects its local, economic and social process.

Precise data is not available for the remittances of the emigrants from the European Community countries, although most of the remittances come from the developed countries because of their high wage rates and economic status. In the United States, the Indian emigrants are said to be the richest. The table 8.4 below gives the amount of the remittances India received from 1977 to 1980.

Table 8.4

Year	Amount Rupees in millions	Amount Pound in millions
1977	19,083.3	1122.5
1976	22,187.5	1305.1
1979	27,752.8	1632.5
1980	44,672.8	2627.8

Source: A.H. Helweg (1983:435)

a : the pound is equivalent to 17 Indian rupees.

This capital from abroad has considerably reduced India's international balance of payments deficit. In fact, the remittance enabled her to have surplus balance of payments in 1976.[12] The remittances covered 49.4 of the trade deficit in 1980 and 39.3 per cent in 1981.[13] The potential contribution that the overseas Indians make at different levels has been recognised by both Central and State governments in India. The two states which have most benefited from the remittances are Kerala and Punjab. In Kerala, the remittances account for 15 per cent of the personal income of all house holds.

So much was the need of the foreign capital for the development programmes that the Communist Chief Minister of West Bengal made frequent visits to the European Capitals for inviting the non-resident Indians to invest in the States. The former Janata Chief Minister of Karnataka Ramakrishna Hegde made different schemes to attract NRI investments from the West.

The Central Government in India has also adopted several liberal policies concerning the use of remittances. The foreign currency has priority over the native currency in the purchase of government houses, vehicles and shares etc. to encourage remittances through banks India has allowed the non-resident Indians to have a choice of opening non-resident external rupee account or a non-resident foreign currency account. The accounts are exempt from income and property tax and draw a slightly high interest rate than domestic deposits.

It is argued that the remittances could cause an increase in aggregate demand and consequently contribute to inflationary pressure. But, the benefits in terms of savings and investment outweigh the inflationary costs. Besides, most of the savings are in cash only as the migrants bring them in the form of jewelry and consumer durables. In the United Kingdom alone Indians saved 13 per cent of their income and transmitted to India one third of it.[14] So, the overall prosperity that remittances bring do benefit large number of families.

On the whole, the remittances have contributed to the Indian economy; at the same time the erosion of human resource also has affected the productivity and growth. The balance requires a closer examination than possible here.

Immigration Laws and Indian Migration

The fact that the Community countries differ culturally, economically and politically and have different immigration policies has influenced the migration. British policies have influenced more than those of the other countries that have been favourable to the migrating professionals.

The British perception of the migrants was that Britain with limited resources was overcrowded with the limitless inflow of immigrants from the Indian sub-continent.[15] Between 1948 to 1962 immigration was uncontrolled because the migrants were British colonial and commonwealth citizens. In 1950, British government put pressure on Indian government to control the migration by restricting the issue of passport. It was ineffective. The first Commonwealth Immigration Act of 1962 sought to control the migration by imposing the need to obtain employment vouchers. This changed the nature of Indian migration although, ironically, the number continued to increase.

The Act changed the nature of the migration in as much as it increased the number of women and dependants who came to join the existing wage earners. It also affected the performance of settlement. Under the voucher system many skilled workers began to arrive to fill the short supply of the skilled jobs. The number increased because the punjabis realising that the windows of opportunities were going to be closed secured as many vouchers they could. In 1965 the voucher system was abolished, the Act of 1971 imposed further restrictions allowing only dependants to migrate. Roger Ballard argues that it will be quite difficult to achieve total control on migration however draconian the curbs may be because of kinship network of Indian migrants.

The Single European Market which is already in operation within EU will have far reaching consequences in terms of migration into and within the Community. The relaxation of frontier controls within the European Community will mean tightening the external border through a common visa policy. This would mean that the nationals of the non-EC countries will find it hard to make even a short visit to an EC country. Paul Gordon[16] argues that if the British experience is anything to go by many people will be prevented from making visits either because of delay in processing their visa or without any effective means of applying against the refusal of visa. However, it will be hard to say how much the Indian migration will be affected until a common migration policy of the Community is evolved.

Immigration and Integration

By the 1930s virtually all migrants have become permanent residents of the host countries. Have they adapted themselves into their new habitat? If any thing, their differentiation gets more pronounced and cultural make up more strengthened. Tagore once commented that the Indians going abroad take their India with them and try to recreate it in the land of their adoption.

There have been attempts at assimilation when the Sikhs for example shaved their beard and cut their hair. In other places, there have been some degree of assimilation as well. In the French overseas departments except in the reunion the Indians have almost integrated and assimilated into the socio-cultural system. Of late, the Indian immigrants are being more assertive of their cultural identities sometimes taking the form of militancy. Having got uprooted from the parent culture and failed to integrate into the new one, the Indian immigrants are characterised by a phase of cultural revivalism and militancy. The gurudwara, the mosque and the Hindu temples become the main focus of the community activity. What is worse, is their strong emotional and substantial financial support for the militant Hindu religious causes be it Hindu Parishad or Khalistanis.

Desai says that integration as far as working and staying peacefully in the host society has been achieved. He attributes the relative failures to the sense of community built as wall around the immigrants. This community will gradually disappear as the second generation would break this barrier and secondly, the greater dispersal and the restriction on immigration would weaken it. On the other hand the resistance from the host community may sustain it. Hugh Tinker endorses the latter and places the onus on the host community. Rosetal does not disagree with the same view point. Helweg is bit uncertain about the question of integration and envisages basically two scenarios. First that the Indians would like to make a contribution to their host society and would like to be recognised for that. Second the Indians would no more take it lying and would claim a fair share of the fruits of progress. Before one makes a value judgement about the process of integration it will be necessary to look at the positive and negative aspects of it. The positive aspects or the factors of integration are as follows:

The media: Every household has a television which is the main meeting point. Through the television the foreign culture seeps through mainly to the younger generation. The Indians develop English style of living 'keep pets, have perks and take holidays'. Intermarriage : many new generation immigrants are going into marriage from outside the community which is undoubtedly the best way of integration. Most of the Indian immigrants work in the different organisations. 40 per cent of the immigrants join ethnic or cultural associations; 10 per cent the bridge organisation and 20 per cent the indigenous British organisations[17]. This samples were taken for the elite immigrants. Most of the community relation bodies are containing the Indian immigrants.

Participation in politics: in the early the number of immigrants was low and their participation in politics was less. In the initial phase before the independence the migrants were more interested in the politics of the countries of their origin. Branches of major political parties were established in Britain. In 1936 an Indian Political Conference was held in London to discuss the ways and means of furthering the campaign of Indian independence. Another point of view is that the Indians in the western countries are a small group forming less than 3 per cent of the population. In numerical terms which, in democracy, also dictates the political terms — Indians are marginal to the rest of the community. Accepting their political position of powerlessness they quietly pursue their occupation preserving the family structure and family code of life. Anwar shows that the Indians are increasingly participating in the British political system to buttress their sense of security.[19]

The indians have benefited from continuing residence in the country in terms of financial security etc. The difficulties of returning to their homeland also leads them to integrate.

The negative aspects of the integration are:

The racial discrimination: the racial discrimination the Indians experience in the host country in getting jobs and positions commensurate with qualifications is a major disincentive for integration. In Britain this has been a major problem. The 'myth of return' and the transient mentality of the immigrants shape their attitude and perceptions. Since they expect to return some day they would like to preserve the cultural ethos and identity. In that sense they perceive their culture a statistic and change detrimental. Added to this is the fear of submergence of their culture with the beginning of mixing. Aurora talked about the 'cultural distances' of both the communities. Vijay Laxmi Pandit noticed this aspect when she was the High Commissioner of India in Britain. She writes in her memoires about how the Indian workers coming after independence encountered a different culture and style of living. She noted that none of them was speaking English and were slow to learn and therefore slow to integrate.[20]

The mutual prejudices often distance the communities. The common place-image of Indians being money-minded and not taking part in any popular events like sports is one instance of such prejudices. Some Britain may not like the Blacks but all appreciate the contributions of John Barnes and Linford Christie to the British sports and games.

Indian communities are in a transitional phase. One opinion points at the cultural confusion of the Indian immigrant youth subject to intense pressures from opposite directions; one from the village India and another of the West. Most youth try to have a middle path and suffer from both. Dennis Brook and Karnjit Singh argue that the first generation may have the sense of nostalgia but the second and the successive generations are getting absorbed. The diminished intensity of visits and remittances home is a sign of increasing assimilation.

The issue of integration is a contentious one. In order to have correct perspectives, it is necessary to clarify the terminology. I would like to take it as 'participation' of the immigrants in the socio-economic and political process of their country of adoption. In that sense, the Indian immigrants are fairly integrated. They are an integral part of British trade and business. They do take part in social and political movements. The activism of Indian Workers Association is a good example. The contribution of the professionals to the British Society is beyond doubt, especially the Indian doctors constituting a significant part of National Health Service. It is estimated that Britain spends 80,000 pounds to train doctor. In that case 11,000 Indian doctors working for the National Health Service are subsidising the British economy.

The integration is a two way process. While the 'hosts' realise and respect the legitimate right and contribution of the immigrants, the latter should stop raising walls around them. This would facilitate the social interim leading to a greater integration.

Conclusion

Large population, high rate of unemployment and wide spread poverty has been the main causes of Indian migration. Even the 'voluntary migration' to the West had been mainly influenced by the economic considerations. Given adequate opportunities and reasonable income, many Indians would not like to migrate. A survey among the overseas Indian professionals found that 34 per cent definitely wanted to return to India, 14 per cent said it was probable that they would return, 22 per cent were uncertain, 21 per cent said they might settle abroad and only 9 per cent were definite to migrate[21]. Another important variable is the Indian policy of human resource development. If the orientation is to develop western skills, the Indian professionals would like to come to the West.

The increasing 'skill drain' is going to cause concern to India. The debate on the 'skill drain' seems to be eased by the positive impact of the remittances on the economy. But, out of world remittance to India three-fourth comes from Gulf, rest one-fourth accounted by the rest of the world of Indian immigrants. Should India develop an active emigration policy? How will that be compatible with the democratic right of the citizens to move for better life? Can India negotiate the question of labour with the EU? Some of these questions assume great significance in the interesting turn of events in EU. Finally, in view of the current rate of unemployment in the EU countries, the kind of migration policy that will eventually emerge in the EU will be of tremendous significance to a major-labour supplier like India.

Notes and References

1. For the statistics of the Indian migrants all over the world see Prakash C Jain (1982) and A.W. Helweg, 1986. *Sikhs in England*. (Delhi: Oxford University Press). pp. 214-20.
2. For the details of labour migration under colonialism see C. Kondapi (1951) and Hugh Tinker (1974).
3. N.C. Madhavan (1986: 439)
4. C. Kondapi. p. 360.
5. Rose *et al*. pp. 85-66
6. These statistics include the twice migrants. The Indian immigrants include those from Surinam and in France from former colonies.
7. G.S. Aurora (1967) p. 33.
8. R. Desai (1963), p. 2.
9. See Glasser, William A. and Christopher Habers. 1978. *The Brain Drain* (New York: Pergamon press) pp. 502-7.
10. Jayaram. H. 1977. "The social implication of medical education in India" *Journal of Higher Education*, 3(2). Pp. 202-20
11. See K.C. Madhavan
12. A.H. Helweg (1983). P. 435
13. Mr. Abella. 1984. P. 496.
14. Rose *et. al*. 1969. P. 194
15. See Zig Layton - Henry in Thomas Hammar (ed) *European Migration Policy* (Cambridge: 1985).
16. Paul Gordon. 1990. *Fortress Europe? The meaning of 1992* (Runnymede trust).
17. V. Robinson. "An Indian elite in 1985", in G. S. Pradhan (ed) *Who's Who*.
18. R.M. Lohia. 1938. *Indians in Foreign Land* (Allahabad, India) p. 35
19. Muhammad Anwar, "Participation of Asians in the British Political System", in Colin Clarke. Ceri Peach and Steven Vertovec (ed.). 1990. *South Asians Overseas* (Cambridge)
20. Vijay L. Pandit. *The Scope of Happiness* (New Delhi, 1986)
21. Glaser and Habers. *op.cit.*

9

Political Set-up for European Union: Relevance of Indian Experience

ANKUSH B. SAWANT

Since its first step, the formation of the European Coal and Steel Community in 1951, over the past fifty years or so the members of the European Community have succeeded, in spite of many setbacks, in advancing on a long way towards their declared and cherished goal of European integration. Naturally, in view of the primacy given to the process of economic integration, the achievements in this area are greater than in other fields. As a result of this, the European Community today is the world's largest trading group.

Although the achievements in economic field are most striking, the achievements in political terms are not negligible. In the political field, in the first place, the Community brought about a profound change in the relations between its members, particularly between France and Germany, converting old enemies into partners in progress. In the process, Europe has been transformed from being a cockpit of conflict into one of the most secure and peaceful areas of the world.

Organisationally, the European Community's work is collectively carried out through the institutions, set up by the member states to govern the Community. A novel system of government has been created in which there are significant federal type institutions. They are the Commission, the European Parliament and the Court of Justice. These institutions co-exist alongside the European Council and the Council of Ministers which represent the member governments and in which the ultimate power is still firmly vested. These institutions played an important role in this transformation.

However, it must also be admitted that the nature of these bodies has restricted the role of the Community in relation to the rest of the world. As a result, the European Community has so far rarely been able to take effective initiatives in the field of foreign policy. It also lacked effective means of actions in these areas where it has not been able to bring its economic muscle power to bear. As a result, they could not take any effective action even on their doorstep in former Yugoslavia.

This was, in fact, in contrast to the intentions of the founding fathers. In creating the European Community, its original six members set out on a more ambitious course, the eventual aim of which was described in the 1950 Schuman Plan as a federation. They chose this path mainly for political reason. Aware of the destruction and the bloodshed caused by the two world wars, they wanted some restrain against forces of nationalism – as a way of embracing Germany and preventing renewed Franco-German hostilities. It meant aiming at not only economic but an eventual political union.

But inspite of this even original six founder members of the Community moved cautiously towards a union. They also subsequently showed great forbearance in accommodating the concerns of new members – especially Britain and Denmark. However, as negotiation leading up to the Maastricht Treaty (1992) showed that a majority of them wished to see a federal type of union.

The Maastricht Treaty on European Union, which became operative in November 1993, is but one step further, and a very important one at that, on the road of European Integration. The Treaty makes amendments and additions to the three existing Treaties* - ECSC, Euraton and the EEC. Under this Treaty, the European Economic Community has now been officially designated as the European Community (EC), although in practice the term EC had been used for several years to describe the three communities together.

The new treaty established a European Union (EU) which introduced citizenship thereof and aimed to increase intergovernmental co-operation in economic and monetary affairs, to establish a common foreign and security policy, and co-operation in justice and home affairs. According to the preamble of the Treaty the purpose of

Common foreign and security policy is to reinforce "European identity and independence in order to promote peace, security and progress in Europe and in the World". The EU Treaty stipulates that every European State with a democratic government system may request accession to the union.

The Maastricht Treaty by laying ground for the monetary union also took an important step towards a political union and by creating the European Union it took further significant step forward in dealing with common problems in the field of the economy, security, the environment and the polity – a far reaching step.

Though the Maastricht Treaty was a step towards closer political unity in Europe, the treaty itself proved to be a source of controversy at ratification stage. The United Kingdom, Denmark and France have ratified it after a prolonged and acrimonious debate. The commitments to a common foreign and security policy and even on eventual common defence policy, have become controversial. But more controversial is the structure of new European Union. Though the majority of member states wish to see a federal type union "in which the role of the Community is limited to those policy areas where common action is absolutely necessary" the opponents raised hue and cry blaming them of creating "Centralised European Super State". The result is the new European Union, with two intergovernmental "pillars" – Council of Ministers and European Council, alongside, the original Community. Some like the British Government fought for these as a way of heading off a federal Europe. Others accepted them only with reluctance. The treaty, therefore, represents also an uneasy truce between the two sides. The battle was again joined in 1996. But the Amsterdam Treaty is largely seen as failure in this regard and already there is a talk of new treaty negotiation next decade.

The nature and future of the Union, now formally created at Maastricht, depend on the settlement of this issue. Considering the past experience, the Community has enough patience and skill to overcome such problems. The Community has travelled cautiously a long way with such obstacles and objections and overcame them. The same, hopefully will happen in case of the political set up of the European Union. However, the issue itself will be settled by the socio-economic forces now prevailing in the Europe. Europe had waged two World Wars in earlier part of this century and suffered from the resultant bloodshed and destruction. The end of World War II saw the emergence of the cold war which though was not equally devastating, was more tension ridden and damaging to economic welfare. The end of cold war gave way to old tensions, but Europe is now beset with other problems, including a bloody conflict in the Balkans, recession and high unemployment and the growing concern about the region's long term economic prospects.

If the Maastricht Treaty was Europe's answer to these problems and was designated to take Europe further along the road to an ever closer union, then the Treaty and its spirit will prevail. Again if the union is to be succeeded in its objectives, the strengthened union is crucial for the future peace and welfare of Europe and for its contribution to a better world order. The present curious hybrid structure is not a structure that will enable the European Union effectively to pursue the tasks its members have assigned to it.

The members of the European Union are in search for ways in which a group of states can more effectively work together to meet the challenges of the contemporary Europe and the world. That search implies a mutual willingness to accept the constraint on the excessive national sovereignty in exchange for collective good. In fact the original intention of founding fathers of the European Community were not merely co-operation but integration.

And here the Indian federal experience will be of some relevance to the European Union. Federalism is one of the most important aspects of modern constitutionalism. Federal state is the fusion of several states into a single state in regard to matter affecting common interests, while each component state enjoys autonomy in regard to other matter. This form of political organisation suited to communities with a diversified pattern of objectives, interests and traditions, who seek to join together in the pursuit of common objectives and interests and the cultivation of common tradition.

India is a living example of centralised federalism. Indian Constitution says "India...shall be a union of states". It is worth noting that although the Indian Constitution is federal in structure, it does not say that India shall be a federation of states. Of course as it is rightly pointed out federalism anywhere in the world is more a 'functional' than 'institutional' concept and the Indian Constitution is no exception to this.

The essential features of Indian Constitution are : (i) Dual Government: The union as federal government and a government in each component state; (ii) Division of Powers: In keeping with fundamental characteristic of federalism powers have been divided between the union government and the state governments. Both union and state governments draw their authority from the same source – the Constitution. (iii) Supremacy of the Constitution: Since both union and state governments draw their power from the same source that source – the Constitution – is supreme. (iv) Independent Judiciary: Indian judiciary is autonomous and independent. Its major role is to interpret the Constitution, administer justice and protect the rights of individual.

Apart from these major characteristics Indian federalism also has some unique features. They are : (i) there is no equality of state representation in union parliament; (ii) There is only one single common citizenship; (iii) There is single integrated judiciary, (iv) The constitution has established All India Services. (v) There are emergency provision which, in case of emergency, will give federalism almost all the benefits of unitary state. This provision was made mainly because inspite of federalism the national interest ought to the predominant.

As regards the distribution of legislative powers, unlike the USA and Australia, where there is only a single enumeration of power (only the power of federal legislature being enumerated), and Canada where there is double enumeration, the Indian Constitution provides for threefold distribution of legislative powers between the Union and the States (Article 246). Union Parliament has exclusive power to make laws with regard to any matter enumerated in the "Union list". These include defence, foreign affairs, banking currency, coinage, union taxes and duties (total 97 items or subjects). The legislature of any state has exclusive power to make laws for such state or any part thereof with respect to any of the matter enumerated in the "State list". These include police, public order, public health, sanitation, local government, agriculture, forest, fisheries, education, state taxes and duties (62 items or subjects). States are autonomous within their own sphere as allotted by the Constitution.

Both Union Parliament and State legislature have power to make laws with respect to any matter enumerated in list III, namely the concurrent list. These include criminal law and procedure, marriage, contracts, torts, trust, welfare of labour, insurance, economic and social planning (total 52 items or subject). In case of overlapping of a matter as between three lists, predominance has been given to the Union Legislature. In the concurrent sphere, in case of repugnance between a union and state law relating to the same subject, the former prevails.

Unlike USA and Australia and following the precedent of Canada, the Indian Constitution gives residual power to the Union parliament to make laws with respect to any matter not enumerated in the concurrent list or state list (Article 248) and the final determination as to whether a particular matter falls under the residuary power or not is that of the courts.

Now, if we turn to European Union, we find many similarities in circumstances, objectives and purposes. First of all by coincidence the European Community decided to call its political structure European Union and not European federation or association or anything else. In keeping with the objectives of the Community – to reinforce European identity and independence in order to promote peace, security and progress in Europe – the term union is more appropriate and positive. Now if the union is to achieve such objectives it should be given sufficient power and must be strengthened.

So following the Indian example, the main provisions of Maastricht Treaty – economic progress, ultimately leading to the adoption of single currency, co-operation in the field of justice and home affairs, provision on common foreign and security policy and special rules on social policy – can form the part of the union list.

Since again the members are sceptical about the excessive centralisation of the union government and wants "that decision should be taken as closely as possible to the people they affect" the doctrine of subsidiary powers which have been discussed in the European circles can become a part of the state list. The federating units will have autonomous action in such areas.

To cushion these two lists, there could be a third list – the concurrent list – where both the union and state governments can legislate with overwhelming weightage for the union legislature. Also in keeping with Indian practice, the residuary powers could be given to the union.

To conclude, the way European Community is constructed – to create a permanent and indestructible community – a proper and healthy political institution is a must. That is the real challenge before the builders of new Europe. It is suggested that Indian Federalism could be a model for the European union for its political set up. It is only in such a federal structure that sufficient elasticity can be obtained, which is what the European Community wants.

Reference

Andrew Duff, John Pinder, Ray Pryce (eds.), *Maastricht & Beyond: Building of European Union* (London, Routledge, 1994).

Durga Das Basu, *Shorter Constitution of India,* Tenth Edn. (New Delhi, Prentice Hall of India, 1988).

G. Wyn Rees (ed.), *International Politics in Europe* (London Routledge, 1993)

H.M. Seervai, *Constitutional Law of India – A Critical Commentary* (Bombay, 1993).

Hidayatullah, M., *Constitutional Law of India* (Vol.2) (New Delhi, The Bar Council of India Trust, 1986).

K.K. Bhargava and Ross Masood Husain, *SAARC and European Union* (New Delhi, Har-Anand, 1994).

Wim F.V. Vanthoor, *European Monetary Union Since 1848: A Political and Historical Analysis* (Cheltenham, U.K. Edward Elgars, 1996).

* The European Coal and Steel Community.(1951), the European Economic Community (1957) and the European Atomic Energy Community (1958).

10

Multilateralism and Regionalism in European Union and South Asia Relations

MARIO TELO

For two decades, but particularly after the end of the cold war, Asia, Western Europe (EU) and Latin America have more and more been emerging as new global actors, especially as trade and economic growth are concerned. The growth of Latin America and of South and South-East Asia is particularly flabbergasting. For instance, the Asian share of world trade for the first time surpassed that of the EU in 1993 and it reached in 1996, 13.4 per cent compared to EU's 12.7 per cent and USA's 10.5 percent.

Such new economic performances take the form either of a regional or of a national pattern: ASEAN, MERCOSUL[1], European Union (EU) are examples of the first type and India, Japan, China, of the second type. Let us first of all examine it in Asia.

In this framework, in 1994, the EU Commission launched a new policy called "Towards a new strategy for Asia" and stressing the importance of both economic cooperation and political dialogue, in view of a multilateral and peaceful management of the international system. In spite of the past difficulties, linked to the geographical distance, to the Anglo-saxon hegemony in Asia (UK joined the European Community only in 1973), to a conflict inside the EC-EU between protectionists (for instance as agriculture is concerned) and trade liberalizers, a new era was to start after this strategic statement.

Actually, we do know that Asia, even more than Europe, is a very differentiated continent. South Asia has been so far the most neglected partner of Europe (and this is not imputable to Europe only), in spite of limited aids and economic assistance since the end of the 70s. This minimalist approach is impossible to defend after the end of cold war, because of the interest of the EU to strengthen new potential actors of the globalized economy and new political partners for the common goal of a peaceful and multipolar world.

In spite of its relative weakness, EU is very much interested in reinforcing regional cooperation in South Asia: on the one hand the SAARC[2] and, on the other hand, the ASEAN[3].

However, first of all the international low profile of the EC before 1989 and, secondly, the political conflicts of South-Asia, affected the progress of such relationship, in spite of the long and good bilateral relations of the EC-EU with India that started in 1973[4], followed by cooperation agreements with Sri Lanka (1975), and with Bangladesh and Pakistan (1976) and other East-Asian countries[5] later on. As the relationship to ASEAN is concerned, the first economic agreement was reached in 1980, and gave rise to a growing mutual trade relationship.[6]

The Asean-European Meeting of 1996 was an important turning point which made the development of the bilateral relationship more fit to the post-cold war era;

- — on the one hand, in spite of its trade deficit, Europe would like to reduce barriers to free trade in order not to be weakened by the American initiative of APEC (Asian Pacific Economic Cooperation);
- — on the other hand, Europe is looking to develop political dialogue with Asian countries, increase the cooperation between both regions in the common perspective to manage peacefully the international affairs.

In the 90s we are witnessing a positive change, as the relations between Europe and South Asia are concerned. Such a new scenario cannot be understood but if it is analyzed both in its inter-regional and bilateral dimensions, even though the bilateral relations, especially with India, seem to be up to now the best possible framework for cooperation.

Of course, in front of the huge differences between geographical regions of the world in terms of economic development, traditions as well as degree of political stability, we have to stress the fact that Eurocentric visions are out of the realistic agenda and more particularly:

(a) The European integration process is absolutely exceptional and impossible to export as such elsewhere in the world. However, as a matter of fact, the international interest for the European way of achieving it in fifty years through regional cooperation, peace, democratic stability and socio-economic prosperity, is more and more increasing among political observers both in the business world and in the scientific community. As a consequence, a comparison between different regional organisations has been proposed by many scholars and inter-organisational relationships are improving everywhere.[7]

(b) The international role of the EU has been growing dramatically after the end of the cold war and the birth of the common currency, the Euro. As a civil actor and an economic power, Europe is more and more interested in drawing consequences from its trade relations. As the relations to South Asia is concerned, we have to mention the potentialities of the fact that Europe is the first trade partner of India, the first foreign investor and the first in aid to development as well.

On the other hand the decreasing security needs in South Asia, after 1991, and on the other hand the openness of Asian countries, namely India, to global trade, could improve the European-South Asian relationship both politically and economically in the framework of the common multilateral vision of international affairs.

Europe is conscious of the huge potentiality of India as an international economic and political actor and the European institutions are very far from the patterns of past Eurocentric European national colonial powers. The common stake for Europe and South Asia, namely India, is to cope with the new challenges of economic globalisation and political international disorder.

This paper entails three main parts:

(a) a theoretical investigation of the main trends of international relations in the globalized world after the cold war in the light of the concept of "asymmetrical multilateralism";

(b) a critical analysis of the evolution of the European Union as an international actor, stressing its feature of "civil power";

(c) a comparative analysis of regionalism in two areas of the world, South Asia and Latin America and some final considerations concerning the current and wishful evolution of international relations.

Theoretical Approaches to the Post-cold war World

International studies and European studies are often characterized by an astonishing division between economic and political approaches, which makes it hard to understand that the connection between such two levels of the international system is growing after the end of the cold war. Economists emphasize the markets globalisation process, analyze deeply its technical side and ignore at the same time huge implications in terms of power, of new security hierarchies, of hard politics. Political scientists, on the other hand, both realists and idealists, often simply don't care about the fantastic implications of the economic and financial globalization process, namely in terms of weakening traditional Nation-State's power and deterritorialisation of regulating authorities[8].

Our object precisely is to measure the impact of globalization and regionalism on the redistribution of world power, in other words their influence on the international system after the end of the bipolar order. We are of course aware that our analysis doesn't cover but a limited part of the international system, leaving aside not only the poorest countries of the world but also those numerous countries which are not members of some regional organisation, that is the great majority of the States.

Let us start by a definition of the main concepts, and more particularly those of globalisation and regionalisation.

"Globalisation" is of course something else than a main economic internationalization; furthermore, we would like to stress the fact that it is also something else than a growing interdependence between sovereign States.

There are in fact four new data inducing substantial changes:

— technological progress allowing multinational companies to organize their production globally (communications...);

— increasing international trade (not only intra-firm), cross-border capital flows, restructuring corporate activities (Reinicke, 1997);

— developing international organisations as well at quantitative as at qualitative level;

— political implication of economic global processes in terms of declining States sovereignty.

With the notion of "ambiguous regionalisation" we mean to emphasize the difference between, on the one hand, a societal phenomenon (associations, informal trends, etc), and, on the other hand, what should more appropriately be called "regionalism" as intergovernmental organized cooperation at the scale of the regions of the world. Such a cooperation entails policies by member states, better-structured organisations and strategic expectations as well.

Actually, in several cases, one should rather speak of sub-regional organisations (such as EU or EFTA in Europe, Mercosur in Latin America and Asean in Asia), but in spite of that, the world "regional" is generally accepted. However, regional/sub-regional organisations on the one hand, interregional ones on the other hand (APEC for instance, including American, Asiatic and Oceanian countries) are in fact a different phenomenon. We will deepen this aspect later on.

Does regulating power concentrate or decentralize in the new international context following the break of the bipolar order? Which role can regionalism play in an international environment, characterized by a hierarchisized state-system: one superpower, a number of middle-range States, growing international organisations and diffused private and public networks? We would here only take into account four answers to these questions, that should help us to have a better understanding of the possible evolution of the regionalisation/regionalism phenomenon and in particular of the role of the EU.

A. The most important feature of neo-realistic approaches is not only their emphasis on renationalisation of great states' foreign policies in the uncertain framework of the post-bipolar world: they do take into account the new regional organisations, but they consider them as an instrument of stronger national interest[9], in the framework of the "new international disorder"[10] and of the declining hegemony.

What seems hardly acceptable to us in this neo-realistic approach are the two following points:

1. In their analysis of regional and international organisations neo-realists often underestimate the change of domestic political factors and their implications in terms of foreign policies: interpretation of national interests, priorities, political will, for instance, can change consequently to a political evolution, democratisation, a strengthening lobbying, political elections or a changing balance in traditional cleavages (right-left; public-private; free traders-protectionists, and so on). Not only does the stronger or weaker engagement of elites in regional organisations often depend on the impact of domestic factors but also public opinion, fears, reactions to globalisation, etc., are taking an increasing part in the new regionalism.

2. Neo-realists underestimate the historical dimension of the current change as for international relations and especially for regional integration process. History doesn't mean continuity. Crucial events like 1945 and 1989 do deeply structure the "long term" of the historical change of regionalism. The huge difference between the old regionalism (for instance between the wars) and the new one is the decreasing role of hard power politics and economic protectionism.

   Let us take the example of Europe and emphasize the difference between the 30s and the 50s. Even the difference between the French leadership in the 50s and the emerging German leadership of the 90s should be more heavily stressed, as far as the European integration is concerned.

   Now-a-days, only a very small part of the international framework (East-West conflict, Franco-German couple, and so on) which characterized the success story of the European Communities subsists. A new era is about to start as far as regional integration is concerned: its roots are to be found in the cold war time (decline of the US hegemony in the 70s and 80s), but we are now witnessing a further development in the framework of both the political and economic challenges of the post-cold war period and the economic challenges of the globalised economy.

B. Neo-institutionalism is a useful analytical approach, focused on the international law and oganisations, and not only a kind of cobdian or wilsonian utopianism identifying economic liberalism, democracy and peace.[11] The European regionalism often plays the role of preferred example of successful regime international regulation. What about the new challenges after the fall of the Berlin Wall?

The book by R. Keohane, J. Nye et S. Hoffmann, *After the Cold War*[12] argues that European institutions played a crucial role in the stabilisation (at international and domestic levels) of post-communist Europe. They provide information, manipulate states' foreign policies in a common juridical framework. They not only offered successfully a "regime oriented" choice to small countries, but were also able to become, for some major states, a matter of "preference" (Germany for example). In spite of limitations and failures, it is largely true, as empirical researches about OSCE, Council of Europe, NATO, EU, WEU will confirm[13]. International organisations can (by their multiple roles, according to the book's conclusions) change the self-interpretation of Nation-States and their practical behaviour too. Sometimes, they use conditionalities and pressures in order to push states to bargain and cooperate; in Europe they sometimes succeeded (remind you, for example, the relations between Hungary, Rumania and Slovakia). It is not yet clear which trend can take the overlapping evolution of international and regional organisations, like EU and NATO for instance, when hegemony is at stake.

One should more take into account two contradictory elements:

— on the one hand regarding the comparison between world-regions, the difference there is between intergovernmental regional organisations and supranational organisations. For instance, can the EU become the core of pan-European regimes? European Union's institutions are a particularly interesting example of a regional organisation going beyond international interdependence and intergovernmental cooperation. Not only do they negate the theory of international game as a zero sum game, and explanations in terms of short-term costs-benefits help at all to understand supranationality, majority vote procedure and supranational law (J. Weiler 1985): the deepening process is going so far in macroeconomic harmonisation, social regulation, pooling and sharing of sovereignties, monetary union, that the question of the international significance of the West-European experience is becoming of sovereignty when crucial policies are concerned (security, defence, police, currency, social aspects, etc.) the European Union is quite unique;

– on the other hand, the potential institutional impact of new challenges and dynamics of international political economy, should not be underestimated. They are far from being neutralized by the strength of regional organizations. On the opposite, regionalism can directly be affected by new demands (social, industrial, etc.) for a more competing trade and industrial policy.

C. *Transnationalist approaches* are very useful in so far they are putting on the table the general question of the reorganisation of authority and powers in world economy. Almost two decades of international and infranational deregulation (production, finance, labour, market, welfare state, knowledge, technology, internal security, and so on) aggravated the decline of Nation-States' authorities. The new element is the fact that a too wide and weak regional organisation could be unable to build up a new central authority and be the victim of the same decline. How and where is decision power about to move?

Technology enables more easily both disintegration and concentration of world powers. The very problem is to understand the new balances between functional deterritorialisation trends (private companies, networks, lobbies, NGO's, etc) on the one hand, and on the other hand, the development of both new international (WTO, IMF, etc) and new original regulations. States and territorial dimension risk to be reduced to compete in offering fiscal paradises to international investors[14]. Called the "New Middle Ages", it shows huge problems in terms of legitimacy and democratic control[15].

Rosenau proposes to complete such a scenario by a counterpart balancing fragmentation: on the one hand, disintegration of the powers of national and regional authorities, on the other hand, concentration of power in the field of high politics and hard security.

Which are the new power-hierarchies in an international system influenced by transnational network? Neither the state authorities in the world, nor the regional ones, would decline at the same speed: the answer is that fragmented multilateralism is unavoidably hierarchical and asymmetric. Is such an answer satisfying? Only partly. Its weak point is security where concentration of power, military technology and the existence after 1991 of a unique political world leadership, legitimate new unipolar theories to emerge.

D. New regionalism arose as a consequence of international uncertainties due to the decline of some of the main features of the US hegemony of 1945-1971, in particular the Bretton-Woods system. It is a matter of fact that the debate of the '80s about the declining hegemony of the USA (P. Kennedy, R. Keohane, etc) is largely over and that, after the period of 1989-91, we are more and more witnessing a revival of both an economic-technological and a political leadership of the USA[16]. At the end of the century, it seems to many scholars, that, in spite of important domestic and international obstacles, a new kind of American leadership is about to be established. It hasn't much to do with the past or with past opposite theoretical cliché's. R. Cox likes the expression of "imperial system" in order to include the G-7, the FMI but also the new above-mentioned transitional pluralistic networks, private companies, epistemic communities, charged to justify inside and abroad the advantages of liberalisation, globalisation, setting stable security organisation.

The USA would gather both, the disintegrating and the concentrating systems mentioned before[17].

Of course, many observers admit that, almost ten years after the fall of the Berlin wall, the ability of unipolar approaches to contribute to the explanation of the post-cold war international system increased. In this framework, regionalism is about to be completely transformed in the regional side of a "globalism" that is of a strategy directed by the USA.

However, our critical remarks rest on the very simple fact that the present world is far from being stabilized and that *no single approach* seems fit to say a final world in the present time of uncertainty. Regional organisations are far from being adjusted to a globalist scenario. The real tendencies towards the stabilisation of an imperial system are balanced by other tendencies, namely the growing number and increasing heterogeneity of actors.

Our second critical remark focuses on the historical process of strengthening of regional organisations, subregional blocks, territorial cooperation associations in the framework of a more globalized world: in Latin America, in Asia, in Africa, in Europe, and so on. The very important question to be deepened is the kind of impact the regional organisations have on the economic and political international systems, in a period of uncertain hegemony.

3. Regionalisation and Globalisation : Main Tendencies

What stays behind the existence of large and important regional organisations like ASEAN, MERCOSUR, NAFTA, EU, and so on[18], is not only the will of member states. The "Yearbook of International Organisations" makes it clear that, since 1980, governments and NGOs are about to increase their commitment to many types of regional and subregional associations; their weight, compared with that of global organisations, is growing.[19] Various factors could explain such an evolution, namely internal dynamics: the spillover effect of sectoral and functional cooperation, the fear to be marginalized in a more interdependent world, especially if many states of the region have joined; economic competition with (and reaction against) external powers, the weight of common values.

It is a matter of fact that regional trade organisations belong to major economic actors of the world.

In the long term, as far as the development of great regional organisations is concerned, one can observe some similar trends in quantitative strengthening and in qualitative evolution from economic cooperation to political and cultural concern. The very first degree, as simple meeting forum, is often overcome towards sectoral cooperation and then towards more general intergovernmental cooperation, in terms of common policies.

Of course pressures coming from the international system also play a very important role: globalisation hurries and deepens both regionalisation and regionalistic reactions. During the cold war, regional cooperation used to be overdominated by systemic East-West confrontation and sectorialised, depoliticised, or even stopped. Regionalisation can better express itself as regionalism after the break of communism.

Thirdly, as J. Nye pointed out[20], regional leading-states are particularly interested in reinforcing and strengthening the development of regional organisations (respectively: Germany and France, Brazil, Japan, Malaysia and so on). Minor powers could be interested in joining, either with economic goals (to accede to larger markets) or in order to create an institutional cooperative framework allowing to brake and embed potential regional hegemonic powers (for instance Belgium, Holland and Denmark in the EU)[21].

As for the international factors, which are in favour of neo-regionalism, one mustn't forget the foreign policy of the European Union. The debate on the international significance of the EU as regional integration model is, of course, still open[22]. However, the success story of 50 years of European integration in one of the richest part of the globe can for sure create rivalry and emulation. Moreover, the EU did and still does actively promote regionalisation in other places in the world, such as Latin America, Northern Africa and Asia: Lome Convention, framework agreement with Mercosur, Bangkok agreement (ASEM) with South-East Asiatic countries have to be seen as attempts to strengthen regional partners and regional organisations as wishful partners.

Such an ambiguous and multiform regionalisation process was unexpected for almost all international theories: as well for the neo-realistic as for the institutionalist, marxist, dependence-theorist or any other theory. R. Gilpin is often quoted as a forerunner, which is true! But even R. Gilpin's vision (and also P. Kennedy's[23] vision, though via another approach) of a kind successors of the American hegemony is not fit to cope with real current developments, and not only because of the above-mentioned weakness of neo-realistic approaches. Just like the trilateral debate of the 80s, it was too closely linked to the cold war and to an over-estimated of US's declining role[24].

Our early definition of "ambiguous regionalisation" has also been deepened in two main points:

(a) the territorial logic of authority is in crisis in its traditional from because of the globalisation process but it is about to revive in a new form: the regional one.

(b) We are witnessing a kind of dialectic between asymmetric development of heterogeneous kinds of regional organisations in the post-cold war world on the one hand, and, on the other hand, the attempt of the USA to strictly link regionalisation to their globalisation strategy.

The international literature is focused on following questions:

- is the territorial logic of authority unavoidably pushing to a kind of neo-mercantilist bias (separate units fighting for hegemony)? Or can different issues possibly be foreseen, including different types of neo-regionalism?
- which relations are possible between the unipolar globalism pattern and regional organisations? Pure subordination? Compromise and balance in the framework of a multilateral world?
- what role are the big regional states going to play as regionalism is concerned? The priority of the need to guarantee their economic security at regional level will unavoidably have a spillover effect towards political and military security, a kind of "regional nationalism" (a Fortress Europe, emphasis on "Asian values", etc.)?
- on which conditions can regionalism strengthen international cooperation regimes?

In order to make a step forward, we propose to classify the various tendencies of regionalisation in three main trends:

— regionalisation as a subordinate step of market globalisation;
— regionalism as a reaction to globalisation;
— open regionalism.

(a) Regionalisation as a part of market globalisation

It is not only a spontaneous trend, on the contrary, it is merely the result of a conscious long term policy, namely the American strategy of "emerging markets": regions are conceived as part of trade liberalisation, consistent with the worldwide implementation of a high strategy, started by the Bush-administration and continued by Clinton. Such a vision underlines the risks not only of traditional protectionism but also of every regional regulation.

It focuses on the necessity of building, bilaterally, new interregional structures, including and absorbing previous regional and infraregional organisations.

Just like APEC includes the "Network" based ASEAN, AFTA should subordinate MERCOSUR and transatlantic structures – for instance, NTM (New Transatlantic Market) – should integrate and brake the EU and its tendency to fix its own priorities in terms of monetary union, social union, etc[25].

In spite of sub-regional financial crises of 1997-1998, so far APEC certainly is the best "success story" of such a pattern linking regionalisation and globalisation[26], while the EU is faced with more problems to be fully integrated. Other experiences, like Mercosur, can be considered as intermediate.

The main problem is the contradiction between the global rules such a vision needs to be implemented everywhere in the world and the heterogeneity of the main regional practical tendencies. Secondly, the compatibility between bilateral interregional agreement and multilateralism (WTO) is not clear at all.

Thirdly, while its economic logic is very coherent, the political and institutional conditions to implement and stabilise a unique model are still missing. In the two main areas indicated by Brzezinski as crucial for the American geostrategy, Europe and Asia, they are particularly missing. The lacking institutional precondition can hardly be substituted by a new unipolar global hegemony.

As a conclusion, the risk of unstability is remarkable[27].

(b) Regionalism as policy in reaction to globalisation

Such a trend too is linked to real cultural and political moves. The idea of a post-cold war international system, characterized by competing cooperation and potential economic and trade conflicts between regional blocks, is becoming appealing for many scholars. For some of them, economy will more and more be at stake in geopolitical/geoeconomical conflicts. According to this vision, the main States in fact created regional organisations in order to cope with such overwhelming challenges. Can the 21st century's world witness a revival, in a new form, of the 17th century's concept of mercantilism? Mercantilism has been defined as "the attempt of governments to manipulate economic arrangements in order to maximise their own interest, whether or not this is at the expenses of others. The interest can be related to domestic concerns (full employment, prices stability, etc) or to foreign policy (security, independence, etc)"[28]

It seems to be generally accepted to adapt the modern concept of "neo-mercantilism" not only to national governments but also to regional blocks.

In 1897 already, Robert Gilpin proposed a distinction between malevolent and benevolent forms of neo-mercantilism[29]. The first one is characterized by State power attitudes but at supranational level, emphasizing the military dimension of sovereignty, while the second one is exclusively defensive and based on the background of domestic social demands: employment policies, defence of welfare and economic traditions in order to keep internal socio-political stability. In the second case, the goal is a peaceful cohabitation between several capitalist regional system in a multipolar world. However, the emergence of the territorial democratic logic of interest representation and of feeling of belonging could entail contradictions with globalization and spillover into political and military security.

But in fact, regional neo-mercantilism reduces the room for nationalism and national protectionism and, at the same time, it rejects pure deregulation and anonymous trans-nationalism by defending traditional republican and welfare values. Its cultural dimension is linked to the vision of a multicultural world, where each civilization needs an independent material background and a certain degree of external sovereignty in order to grow or even to survive. Openness to the world market is not excluded, but it is subordinated to such strategic priorities.[30]

Malevolent neo-mercantilism, beyond impossible revival of List's protectionism, has been re-elaborated by political scientists in France, Italy and USA studying the post-cold war world.

In this vision, existing economic imbalanced regions of the world could provoke geoeconomical conflicts between regional blocks ("logic of war and grammar of economy"[31]). Regional entities would not only defend their economic security, but also strengthen their international competitiveness and weaken the concurrence from other blocks. While North-North military conflicts are excluded because of the importance of common interests, trade wars could be the main form of such a conflict, either with pure trade goals or with the political goal to impose the will of a regional or global power. Even strategic goals might step in when the very matter of the conflict is the access to strategic resources or technologies.[32]

Can the European Union possibly be interested in such a geoeconomic conflictual strategy, even in soft version? In spite of its present difficulties with its trade competitiveness towards American and Asiatic capitalism and in spite of the fact that, in view of the "Euro", the EU is interested in creating an obligations and capital market, in concurrence with the American one, such a question cannot be answered here and demands a further paragraph. But the European Union, as first trade power in the world, is much more interested in diminishing than increasing trade conflicts at international level.

(c) Open regionalism is currently nothing more than a draft. It needs to be deepened, to avoid the feeling of something too vague and based on contradictory definitions. It shared with globalisation the priority of a growth of international trade worldwide. But an international and global stabilisation is not conceived as a spontaneous thing; on the contrary, it should rather be considered as a gradual learning process, created by a common willingness of the actors to bargain multilaterally and to cooperate. This approach shares some of the doubts raised by benevolent neo-mercantilists about the potential

conflicts linked to existing asymmetries and unbalances in the world economic and political system and the unability of the simple markets globalisation to overcome such unbalances. But it doesn't share with neo-mercantilists the scepticism about the possibility of managing conflicts (and creating a positive sum game) through common rules and strengthening international and regional regimes.

The favourite trend is the reform of international economic and political organisations (WTO, IMG, G7, Security Council of UN), in order to ease the representation of regional entities and to set common rules for everybody, superpowers included. Under certain conditions, transnationalism and networks could be consistent with open regionalism. But it should be stressed that it needs a high degree of economic and political governance.

In such a vision, regional blocks could constitute the main pillars of a multilateral and multipolar world allowing the political government of the globalisation process and the reinforcement of international peace:

— regionalism could have stabilizing and homogenizing effects inside the region, strengthen the respect of international law and of democracy, increase economic integration, under certain conditions, and even diminish center-periphery conflicts in the same region (example: US-Mexico; EU-Central-Eastern Europe), avoid mass migrations, and so on.

— as far as its external effects are concerned, regionalism could reduce the number of players in international game, easing agreements, stability and, following P. Taylor, even the chances of a positive sum game. Regional organisations bargain more efficiently, create a special inter-organisational bargaining know-how, strengthen international regimes, often have a positive impact also on the countries outside the blocks.

In conclusion, one could fit open regionalism in the two layers model of Rosenau: on the one hand, it is compatible with the pluralistic and transnational elements of globalisation. On the other hand, open regionalism is a trend linked to the idea of a world government, but it stresses the importance of its preconditions, first of all of a reduced number of actors, of political will and of a parallel reform process of international organisations.

European Union as a Special Kind of Open Regionalism

Open regionalism can be considered as consistent with the trend of European integration since its very beginning, with both its value and practical institutional developments, But some important transformations, occurred during the 80s and the 90s, inside and outside Europe, are about to make such a conclusion more problematic and demand for a deeper analysis.

— The increasing impact of internal factors, namely of social and political domestic troubles: the mass unemployment, the decreasing consensus of national public opinions brake the further deepening of the European integration and weaken the federalist pattern.

  The diverging perceptions by national governments of the European responsibilities in the post-cold war world are breaking the development of the common foreign and security policy and raising the question of the changing nature of Europe as international actor: structurally subordinated entity or post-modern civilian power? As far as the globalisation is concerned, all of the three above-mentioned trends are present in the European public sphere even if, of course, the French-speaking are rather influenced by the neo-mercantilist and strategic culture while the English-speaking are rather influenced by the globalisation-euphoria.

- The European Union is particularly affected by transnational factors: on the one hand, the supranational institutions seemed in the past able to take advantage of the weakening of Nation-States; on the other hand, lobbying, growing institutional complexity of the system (due to the original but problematic mix of supranational and intergovernmental procedures), its internal efficiency and effectiveness of decision making. Instead of strategic orientated foreign policy, we often are the witnesses of fragmented, overlapping, sometime even contradictory, external relations.

The European Union is facing a new challenge after the end of the bipolar world: the political Union and European Monetary Union apparently not only express the will of concentration of authority but also of strengthening of external sovereignty. However, it is more and more evident that the form of such an external sovereignty cannot be that of a federal superstate. If a new institutional pattern is not developed in the next years, on the one hand the disintegration tendencies, and, on the other hand, the revival of old conflicts between protectionists and globalizes might weaken the Union and its regional strength[33].

As far as external relations are concerned, the European Union's first challenge is to make more consistent and coherent the multiple dimensions of its action, both worldwide and at continental level: cooperation with developing countries; humanitarian help; trade policy through agreements and sanctions; interregional agreements; Mediterranean cooperation process; Common Foreign and Security Policy (CFSP); action in international organisations and conferences; and more particularly, Ost-Politik as a help to democratic transition, economic recovery and peaceful settlement of minorities and border conflicts in Eastern and Central Europe; preparing the Eastern enlargement; partnership with Russia and special relation with Turkey (association and customs union).

The European Union already is an international actor, a civil and trade actor namely. As political power, I mean in traditional terms of military power, EU's performance in former Yugoslavia and so on, confirmed that its weakness in overcoming in national divergent visions and its dependence on the US leadership has increased a lot, the Madrid summit (1997) of NATO has proved.

However, three factors allow to leave the question open whether or not Europe can develop as a — even "postmodern" and "postwestphalian[34]" — civilian power : the objective of huge political implications of its trade and cooperation policies, the external pressure by a general transformation of the international system and the current strategic debate on foreign and security policy.

The IGC and the negotiation before the Treaty of Amsterdam as well as the current discussion did show the evolution of three divergent visions of the future of the European region in the framework of a globalized world :

(a) The British conservative government has been for many years the upholder of the *status quo* in terms of deepening the political integration, which actually meant to consider regional integration as a subordinated component of the globalisation.

Even the Monetary Union and the CFSP decided in Maastricht used to be considered as dangerous steps towards "fortress Europe" and regional neo-mercantilism, and the arising of a supranational superpower as a threat to both transatlantic relations and national sovereignty.

In fact, the British conservative did raise a real question: a large part of the "*acquis communautaire*" is not directly compatible with the globalisation imperatives and has to be drastically reformed or even abolished if the EU accepts the US idea of globalism. In terms of type of relationship between globalisation and regionalisation, such an approach fits very well the first scenario mentioned above and would entail a dilution of the process of European construction as a simple free trade area.

The weak points of such an approach are: the isolation of the conservative UK and the so-called "domino effect", namely the interest of eurosceptical countries to join the others, if the EU goes on with the Maastricht programme, in order to avoid marginalisation (which explains why almost all the EFTA countries, but Norway, Switzerland, Iceland and Liechtenstein, joined the EU between 1973 and 1995). This also explains why recently UK and Scandinavian countries increased their involvement in EU-affairs conditioning the future evolution of the EU "from the inside".

(b) Neo-mercantilist and "strategic" visions are very largely diffused in Europe in both their forms. France is particularly affected by such trends, since its old and recent history (De Gaulle-Mitterrand)[35]. The shared idea is to develop a political and military power allowing to overcome the present weakness of European Nation-States and gradually substituting American leadership in the European security. The concept of sovereignty is rehabilitated at regional level, both as economic and trade security and as greater political independence of Europe, even in the framework of an alliance with the US.

Concretely the Franco-German cooperation should create the hard core of a new world power, working for a multipolar world. The military organisation Western European Union (WEU), the Eurocorps, the Monetary Union and the external relations are conceived as a means for attending that goal. The changing balance between France and Germany after the German unification (1990) gives the latter the role of crucial actor in such a project and makes such a vision more problematic.

The paper of the German Christian-Democrats, Lamers and Schauble, in 1994 tried to harmonize that idea with the challenge of the unavoidable Eastern enlargement[36]. It became clear that such a project only possibly can work under one precondition: the creation of a hard core made up of some of the member states, federal or confederal[37].

Furthermore, the increasing weight of Germany is about to cause three main changes: firstly, as a junior partner of NATO, Germany doesn't share anti-Americanism; secondly, because of its history, Germany is much more prudent as far as military assertiveness is concerned, and that will influence the nature of international common actions; thirdly, Germany is strongly against protectionism and trade conflicts. This tends to exclude malevolent neo-mercantilism as far as the EU of the year 2000 is concerned.

However, the benevolent version of neo-mercantilism, or better, the strategic visions of regionalism, largely spread beyond the French borders, are linked to the upholding of the so-called "Rhenan model of consensual capitalism". In the framework of the accelerating globalisation, that means that deregulation is accompanied by "re-regulation" at supranational level. The Social Charter of 1989, the Social Protocol of 1992, the Amsterdam Treaty's employment and social chapters, plus the common policies, the single market rules, are typical examples of new regional regulation. Research, industrial and social policies, programmes for common infrastructures, internal social consensus and so on, are considered as parts of an improved ability of the EU to complete worldwide as a consistent and compact system.

In the 80s the expression of "fortress Europe" has been critically used to disqualify such a scenario.

The Monetary Union will probably increase this peculiar feature of the EU: an open regionalism, but at the same the will to give common and independent answers to globalisation and to defend the European industry and in general terms, the European interests.

(c) We are indeed witnessing the fact that, on the one hand, the pressure of globalisation, and on the other hand, the multiple strategic and neo-mercantilist pressures issued from internal factors are making the European open regionalism more problematic than in the past. The "acquis communautair" and the Amsterdam agenda are clear enough in fixing a third way between protectionism and pure globalisation strategy.

It is a matter of fact that the construction of a kind of transnational society and market, the Monetary Union and supranational institutions have been seen as the European answer to global interdependence. That is largely happening, even if deregulation is voted by unanimous votes; even if the main supranational "Keynesian" plan, J. Delors's White Book of 1993, has not been implemented; and even if the Amsterdam Treaty and the Luxembourg summit against unemployment (1997) confirmed that employment policies are a matter of national commitment and national responsibility. However, Europe is the highest regulated region in the world and many kinds of regulating forces are acting after Maastricht and Amsterdam: the Monetary Union, central directives, social dialogue as a way to a kind of supranational neo-corporatism, coordination of national policies.

The Swedish sociologist Goran Therborn proposed the pattern of a "Scandinavian Europe" as an alternative to both the French model of a hard political superpower and the weak pattern of the nice German Bonn Republic of the 50s-80s.

The Amsterdam Treaty has to be understood as a compromise between two visions: a very prudent step towards a social and trade power, but still keeping the door open to further progress towards political hard core policies. A submilitrary, civilian, humanitarian power, a kind of "self-styled foreign and security policy", but at the same time, increasing pressures towards a stronger political assertiveness.

The real problem is that such a new kind of regional power has to cope with the real challenges of international politics. Two extreme scenario are possible: either Europe is able to reform gradually the international system towards a more modern and comprehensive vision of security in a multilateral world, or the European "*sui generis*" power will be amongst the victims of the return to traditional power politics partly combined with the current fragmentation of political authorities.

That is why a further development of the European integration is hardly conceivable without the parallel expansion and the strengthening of other regional organisations to have a chance to credibly assert the idea of a possible "capitalist diversity" and to succeed in reforming the international relations in view of a new multilateral system.

SAARC, EU and International Relations

The first internal problem of the SAARC is regional animosity provoked as well by ethnic, religious, political factors. Another main structural problem of the SAARC (just like MERCOSUR) is to transform the internal asymmetry (if we compare for example the Indian giant and the microstate Bhutan, as far as the size of the member States and the population is concerned) into a positive resource for the regional development.

Regional organisations include everywhere smaller and larger countries, minor States and big powers. In many parts of the world the smaller countries are playing since the very beginning a particularly active role in the building process of regional organisations: Brussels (Belgium) is the capital of the EU, Montevideo (Uruguay) is the seat of the secretariat of the MERCOSUL, and Katmandu is the seat of the secretariat of the SAARC.

As a matter of fact smaller States have a particular economic and political interest in developing regional organisations, in diminishing the weight of traditional power hierarchies in international relations, in helping conciliation between former enemies. However asymmetry is a problem and no regional organisation can succeed unless the bigger powers become the trainers of the building process: France and Germany in Europe; Brazil and Argentina in MERCOSUL; Indonesia and Malaysia in ASEAN; India in SAARC.

Big powers are interested in reducing regional conflicts and historical problems only if, on the one hand, the international framework helps keeping stability and, on the other hand, if their economic and political weight as international actors can be improved through regional cooperation. Only under these two preconditions, the huge internal brakes and obstacles can possibly be overcome.

As the SAARC is concerned, it is interesting to observe that in many parts of the world important steps towards regional cooperation have been made during the 80s especially in the period of the so-called "decline of the USA" as an international superpower[38]. In the particular South Asian context, the beginning of the Soviet intervention in Afghanistan (1979/1980) contributed to a new perception of the evolution of the international system and the need of regional cooperation.

What seems most astonishing to international scholars, is the important gap between programmes and realisations.

The "SAARC Charter" of 1985 has been very poorly implemented. The Charter mentions following objectives: strengthening economic, social, scientific, cultural and technical cooperation. Many sectoral cooperation programmes have been approved concerning twelve non-controversial cooperation areas: agriculture, post, meteorology, transports, telecommunications, arts, sports and culture, fight against drug traffic, cooperation for woman development, for health and demographic problems. These subjects became Integrated Programmes of Action (IPA). Why did regional cooperation loose very soon its original impetus and didn't it progress very much, in spite of the relaunching by the Bangalore Summit of 1988?[39]

The scholars do agree that many factors explain such a failure:

a) the economies of SAARC member States are not complementary enough to take advantage of intraregional trade, which remains very underdeveloped (compared with Mercosul and Asean) the long experience of national economic models like the imports-substituting economic plans (suggested by ONU commissions in the 60s, with the effect of similar exports by every country of the region), the trade tariff, the too timid liberalisation, the very limited intraregional trade, the lack of diversification of exports, have been more important obstacles to regionalism.

b) the external factors didn't help very much in regional organisation. In spite of international instability and Soviet threat, the world stayed bipolar until 1991 and India, on the one hand, and

Pakistan, on the other hand, kept very different perceptions and links as security is concerned. The Chinese potential threat didn't play at that time the same integrating role as it did for ASEAN countries from 1967 up to now.

c) The lack of political bilateral understanding made it impossible (at least between 1985 and 1991) to provide a stable political framework for economic cooperation and for the implementation of the SAARC Charter. It is matter of fact that all of the successful experiences of new regionalism are based on bilateral confidence building measures between the main partners (not necessarily in the framework of the Treaties). In spite of the whished "atmosphere of good neighbourly relationship and rational behaviour" (Rajiv Gandhi, Dhaka Summit, 1985), the bilateral mistrust hasn't yet been overcome.

Does the situation change after 1991? The Colombo summit of December 1991 and the following meetings allow a moderate optimism.

Our conclusion is that the improved international framework, the initiative of the European Union, the openness of the South Asian economies, can provide better conditions for both regional and EU-Indian cooperation.

As the regional cooperation is concerned, we are witnessing the diminishing military external uncertainty, due to the decreasing interest of the USA in supporting Pakistan's nuclear capacity (and the weakness of alternatives) on the one hand, and, on the other hand, the improving India-USA relationship. More than in the recent past, the building up of regional cooperation as a third way – which means neither as a "security community" concerned above all with military aims, nor as an "economic fortress" based on economic protectionism, nor regionalism as a pure optimistic adaptation to the economic globalisation as conceived by USA – can be considered as realistic.

The defense budget could be reduced and a new atmosphere of peaceful cooperation is perceptible as bilateral relations are concerned (namely India-Bangladesh and India-Sri Lanka relations). The perception of the globalisation as a threat has been partially competition, to avoid to be marginalized by the neomercanitilist strategies of the global traders. The Preferential Trading Arrangement (SAPT) of 1993 is a good step in a right direction and a Joint Economic Commission can help in this context. To increase economic complementarities is a further step. To make the secretary and the administrative machinery of regional organisation stronger could strengthen the effectiveness of the cooperation and the EU is very interested in exporting its know-how in this matter. The Colombo Summit of 1998 will be an interesting opportunity to strengthen regional cooperation.

Second positive change: the steps accomplished in the domestic democratisation of all the states of the region but Bhutan. The international comparison links regionalism, economic liberalisation and democratisation.

As the bilateral relationship between India and the EU is concerned, the good pieces of the news are the Cooperation Agreement of 1994, a very advanced text, proposed as a model for other international agreements (it includes a mixt commission meeting once a year, three sub commissions on trade, economic cooperation and development, many important working groups on energy, software, satellites, research and so on). The 1996 communication by the European Commission "strengthening EU partnership" deepens such a new approach, linking economic and trade cooperation with political dialogue. On the one side India realizes that EC-Indian relations are more important than bilateral relations with single European states. On the other hand, the EU can more easily play an international role in the region, consistent with the fact that it is the first trade partner (30% of Indian trade), the first foreign investor and the first in aid to development.

Even if the institutionalization of the inter-regional cooperation could take more time, India and the EU are making important progresses as the "second track" is concerned, namely the civil society and business cooperation at India-EU level[40].

Second example: the relationship between EU and Mercosul as a crucial test in the evolution of the post-cold war international system.

For many of its historical and present features, both internal and international, Mercosul constitutes something completely new as far as the Latino-American regionalism is concerned. During the last decade we did witness either a stagnation or a decline of the Andis

Pact of the CACM in central America, and of the CARICOM, while the tremendous success of Mercosul as a sub-regional bloc is flabbergasting for observers and scholars.

Created in 1991 (Treaty of Asuncion and Protocol of Brasilia) as a liberalisation programme (to be achieved in 2000) for the first 4 member states, the Mercosur has been institutionalized in 1994 with the "Ouro Preto Protocol" and the customs union[41]. Led by an intergovernmental institution, the Common Market Council, the Mercosul disposes of an articulated institutional structure, which has been gradually strengthened by a parliamentary commission, a socio-economic forum, a secretariat in Montevideo, a protocol for the juridical conflicts (Brasilia 1994). Mercosul is widely considered as a success story in terms of increasing internal trade and strengthening Mercosul countries' competitiveness in the world: with $ 850M in 1995, Mercosul became the fourth regional block worldwide after the UE ($73000M), Nafta ($6.800 M.), Japan $4.500M) and before Asean ($7 M.) and Russia ($400 M.).

The success of Mercosul is appealing for Latin-American neighbours and the perspective of a "great Mercosul" is not excluded even if its form depends on international and domestic factors and could also be that of a "variable geometry". It is a matter of fact that association aggreements have been established in 1995-96 with Chile and Bolivia and a dialogue started with Venezuela and Columbia.

The international literature and the Latin-American scholars as well are divided on the nature and significance of Mercosul: some comments see Mercosur as a simple training to globalisation, a kind of subordinate sub-regional adaptation to the Northern American agenda; other comments, on the contrary, analyse the Mercosul as a reaction to the threats of the American way to conceive liberalisation. Others are looking for a less simplified interpretation. Everybody agrees that we are witnessing a break with the old Latin-American protectionism and a new trend as the economic and trade extroversion is concerned, but its direction is still ambiguous. A debate is open with participation of business people, politicians, intellectuals.

The discussion has got two main poles: liberal globalizers and strategic globalizers. Between them, a more and more differentiated and complex discussion is about to deepen the search of the Latin-American formula to open regionalism, where both the priority of the linkage with democratisation and importance of defending the place of Latin-America in the worldwide globalisation are more particularly stressed.

Actually, the current evolution of Mercosul is partly a sign of the international interest for the European pattern of regional integration for following reasons :

— the customs union goes beyond simple liberalisation and negative integration and concerns policy, active common policy in a crucial sector of both external and internal relations; it can provoke a kind of spillover effect and push to other common policies;

— the importance of the political dimension since the very beginning (Alflosin and Collor) and the first agreement on nuclear security (1985, Iguazu Declaration) is quite exceptional. The common goal of stabilisation of democracy and human rights has been confirmed by the common experience of 1995 stopping Paraguay's General Oviedo's golpe. Mercosul "creates a regional arena for support for new and fragile democracies"[42]

— the shared idea to give a stop to previous habits of trivial reversibility of weak regional agreements and the importance given to common experience, to the "acquis" (successful conflict management, collective discipline, care of the external image) and to the common agenda as deeper integration and external relations are concerned. To see the current evolution in terms of a kind of spill-over effect seems not unrealistic.

— beyond pure utilitarianism, a part of the social and cultural belonging has been mobilized at level of civil societies and already contributes to the strengthening of regional associations and organisations, more particularly after the end of the cold war.

Last but not least: a similar debate is growing in Europe and Latin America on the limits of the past republican model of national democracy on the one hand, and on the other hand, on new orientations towards regional entities, toward a major place of interest-organisations and ideal communities in the framework of a better balanced globalized economy and a more symmetric multilateral international system (reinforcing ONU, but also WTO and so on).

After the "Interinstitutional Cooperation Agreement" of 1992 (including information, technical assistance, institutional support; mixed commission on agriculture, customs, liberalisation and so on), an important "Framework Agreement" between the EU and Mercosul was established in 1995. The European investments are increasing and the inter-organisational dialogue is supported by strong bilateral relations with Mercosul settled by Spain, Germany, Italy, Portugal and France[43].

Why is Mercosul also a mirror of the weaknesses of the European Union as interesting a pattern for other regional organisations?

The first fact to be taken into account is of course the obvious and deep heterogeneity of the Western European and the South-American integration processes.

The liberalisation of trade in Mercosul is very different from the high regulated European common market (only 24 articles in the Treaty of Asuncion, compared with the Treaty of Rome). The internal asymmetries of Mercosul (Brasil represents 80% of the total GDP) hinder strongly, partly supranational, central institutions; the macroeconomic divergences between the member states, in particular the two giants, are still huge and explain why common policies are so poor; the social and cultural dimensions are only embryonic and the substantial legitimacy risks to be too weak in case of conjunctural crisis.

The second problem has to do with the international relations. The domestic and international weight, the real content, and the consequences of the AFTA (ALCA) project, launched by the USA in Miami in 1994 and signed at the Summit of the Americas of Santiago (Chile) in April 1998, to create a Pan-American Free Trade Area before 2005, are far from being clear. Clinton's trip in Latin America in October 1997, the meeting of San Jose de Costarica in March 1998 and the Pan-American Summit of Santiago in April 1998, do show how crucial and flexible the new American Presidency's strategy in Latin America is, but also the remaining uncertainties concerning the final exit of such an ambitious project: important domestic constraints, for instance affecting the "fast track" procedure in USA, the Latin-American demand for intergovernmental and "international" guarantees, like veto-right, gradualism, real compatibility with deeper integration concerning only some countries, linkage between different issues, namely agriculture and so on.

The process is on the way, the stake is clear, the issue though remains uncertain: AFTA (ALCA) could either fail or become a part of a worldwide unipolar strategy of USA or a new kind of trade agreement where both parties, South and North, would better find their mutual strategic convenience, fight against fragmentation and fundamentalism, building stability at continental level.[44] Of Course the economic integration wouldn't be so deep as in Mercosul, and Nafta would also keep its particular role and features in the new framework. It would be a new historical step towards a more egalitarian relationship between the Americas.

Many Latin-American intellectuals are about to conceive the transatlantic relations as a triangle, where Mercosur can also use the opportunity given by trade differences and conflicts between USA and Europe: the bargain about timing and contents of AFTA, the 1999 meeting between EU and Mercosul, the next WTO round (Millennium Round) including agriculture and services will be the next steps of such a vision.

Second open question: as far as the future of the transatlantic triangle is concerned, free trade could be considered as a means or a weapon in the hand of three strategic global traders. Many scenarios are open, even if it would be wrong to analyze it simply in terms of fight for sphere of influence: either a competition for Latin-American markets between European Union and USA, or, perhaps, new ways to a more symmetric multilateral world.

One should not forget that the transatlantic triangle a part of the world economy and the general dynamic of the world system will play a major role. On the one hand, Mercosur doesn't represent but 1 5% of the world trade (the European Union 37.4%, Asean 6.8%, Nafta 18.7% and Apec 45% of the world trade). The USA and Western Europe have other important strategic matches to play: in Asia, Southern East Asia and even in Africa. European Union has urgent answers to give to its East-South borders crisis[45].

On the other hand, to make steps forward towards a more symmetrical multipolar world is certainly vital as well for Mercosur as for the EU, but much less for the USA. In conclusion, the real matter of discussion is not the existence of the transatlantic triangle, but the possible nature of such a triangle, its internal symmetry, the weight of both domestic and international factors concerning its evolution, its place in the world. Indeed it would be absolutely irrealistic to analyze the EU-Mercosul-USA relationships independently from the global political and economic system after the cold war.

Conclusions

The evolution of the relationship between European Union on the one hand and SAARC, ASEAN and MERCOSUL on the other hand namely with regional great powers like India and Brazil, is a crucial test for a less asymmetrical multilateralism, as concerns the international system. In spite of the new American leadership in Europe and worldwide, it seems inconceivable to return to American hegemony of the three post-world-war-two decades. In "After Hegemony" (Keohane) times, new regionalism and multilateralism could not only be a strong objective tendency developing in parallel with globalisation, but also give birth to both new trade and economic policies and political strategies fit to a multipolar world after the cold war and the bipolar system.

The role and the responsibility of the EU as international actor, on the one hand, and the evolution of India, on the other hand, are important as far as the evolution of the process is concerned. The current relationship, mirror of international strength and weaknesses of a multilateral world, should avoid both, neo-mercantilist and protectionist regional blocks and regionalisation as a subordinated part of current American globalism. Only at this condition, EU and India will be able not only to develop as global actors, but also to offer new patterns of civil powers contributing to a "regime oriented" and peaceful evolution of the international system.

Notes

1. The regional organisation created by Brazil, Argentina, Uruguay and Paraguay with the Asuncion Treaty of 1991 can be called either Mercosur or Mercosul, following the Spanish or the Portuguese/Brazilian language.
2. Formed in 1985, the South Asian Association for Regional Cooperation (SAARC), includes India, Nepal, Bangladesh, Bhutan, Sri Lanka, Maldives, Pakistan.

3. The ASEAN, created in 1978 includes in it eight countries — Indonesia, Malaysia, Brunei, Phillippines, Vietnam, Thailand, Singapore, Myanmar.
4. After the mutual diplomatic recognition in 1962, making lower the import tarif for important Indian products like tea and the Cooperation agreement of 1973, increasing the European aid, creating a framework for joint research and development programmes in the sectors of energy conservation environmental protection.
5. With Japan in 1974, with China in 1975 and 1978, even if very affected by domestic troubles in China.
6. The trade balance of the EU with ASEAN and Japan is affected by a huge deficit.
7. See K. Eliassen/K. Borve Monsen 1997 and A. Quddus 1996; A. Ahsan, *SAARC: A Prospective,* Dhaka 1992; R.G.C. Thomas, *South Asian Security in 1990s*, IISS. London 1993; V Marston Hewit, *The International Politics of South Asia*, Manchester U.Press, 1992; S. Mansingh, *Regional Cooperation in South Asia*, S. Chopra (ed) *Studies in India's Foreign Policy*, 1992.
8. S. Strange, *Territory, State Authority and Economy: a new realist Ontology of global political Economy* in R. Cox, the New Realism, London, MacMillan, 1997; *The Retriate of Nation State.*
9. Ch. Hill, *The Actors in Europe's Foreign Policy,* London, Routledge, 1996
10. Eric Hobsbawm, in M. Telo and P. Magnette, *Repenser 'Europe, I* Editions de I'Universite Libre de Bruxelles, 1996.
11. Simon Bulmer, *Four Faces of European 'Union Governance: A New Institutional Agenda.* Paper 1995, E.P.R.U., Manchester et *Analyzing the Governance of the Single Market, in K. Armstrong and S. Bulmer, The governance of the Single European Market,* Manchester 1997 (forthcoming), W. Wessels, *European Union and National Institutions in The European Union and Member States Toward Institutional Fusion?* Manchester 1996 and *Die Europapolitik in der Wissenschaflichen Debatte, in Jahrbuch der Europaischen Integration, 1995/1996.* Bonn, 1996 pp. 25-36, B. Kohler-Koch, *The Strength of Weakness. The Transformation of Governance in the E.U.* in S. Gustavsson, L.Lewin (ed) *The Future of the Nation State,* Stockholm, 1996.
12. R. Keohane, J.Nye et S. Hoffmann (ed), *After the Cold War International Institutions and State Strategies in Europe, 1989-1991,* Harvard Cambridge, 1993.
13. See F. Algieri, J. Janning, D. Runberg, *Managing Security in Europe,* Bertelsmann Foundation Publishers, 1996; V.Y. Ghebali, *L'O.S.C.E. dans l'Europe post-communiste*, 1990-1996, Bruxelles, 1997.
14. The Risse-Kappen(ed), *Bringing Transnational Back In. Non State Actors, Domestic Structures, International Institutions,* Cambridge, 1995 and especially the article of St. D. Krasner, Pp. 257-80.
15. Lester Thurow 1996 and also S. Strange (pp. 3-18), in R. Cox (ed), *The New Realism,* London, 1997. For the point of view of J.N. Rosenau, pp 57-81.

16. P. Kennedy, *The Rise and Fall of the Great Powers,* Random House, USA, 1987.
17. J.N. Rosenau, "The Person, the Household, the Community and the Globe: notes for a theory of multilateralism in a turbulent world", in R. Cox, *The New Realist,* cit, pp. 57-80.
18. As subregional security organisations are concerned, the SADCC (South African Development Co-ordination Conference, later SADC) has been founded in 1980, the GCC (Gulf Co-operation Council) and the SAARC (South Asian Association for Regional Cooperation, including India as leading power) in 1985, but without any integrationist pretensions.
19. P. Taylor, *International Organisation,* pp, 25-45.
20. J.S. Nye, "Regional Institutions", in R. Falk, S.Mendlovitz (ed), *Regional Politics and World Order,* San Francisco, 1973.
21. See the very interesting book by A. Gamble-A. Payne: *Regionalism and World Order,* Macmillan, London, 1996.
22. W. Wallace in his book, *Regional Integration: The West European Experience,* (Washington 1994) argues in favour of the thesis of the European exceptionalism, while P. Taylor points out of the common trend of regionalism (cit, p. 252-54).
23. P. Kennedy, *The Rise....,* and R. Gilpin, *The Political Economy of International relations,* Princeton, 1987; see also P. Taylor (p. 34).
24. R. Keohane, *After Hegemony: Cooperation and Discord in the World Political Economy,* Princeton, 1984; S. Huntington and M. Crozier, 1974 on the Trilateral Commission (USA, Europe, Japan) and St. Gill, *American Hegemony and the Trilateral Commission,* Cambridge, 1990.
25. C.F. Bergsten, *Globalizing Free Trade,* in "Foreign Affairs" n. 3., 1996, pp. 105-120.
26. APEC, as interregional free trade project, includes the three NAFTA countries, the eight ASEAN countries, Australia, New Zealand, China, Japan, and will include Russia.
27. A. Gamble and Th Payne pp. 250-60). Z. Brzezinski, *Le grand Echiquier. L'Amerique et le reste due monde,* Bayard, Paris, 1997 and in "Foreign Affairs" *A Geostrategy for Eurasia,* vol. 76, n. 5, 1997.
28. R. Gilpin, *Three Models for the Future,* in Smith and others *Perspectives in World Politics,* London 1981, p. 402.
29. R. Gilpin, *The Political Economy of International Relations, Princeton* 1987 also see: B. Buzan, *Economic Structure and International Security: the Limits of the Liberal Case,* in "International organisation", n. 38, 1984.
30. Bjoern Hettne, *The Double Movement: Global Market versus Regionalism,* in Cox(ed), The *New Realism* 1997, Tokyo, New York, Paris, Hettne quotes K. Polanyi (*The Great Transformation,* 1944) as forerunner for such benevolent mercantilism.
31. Edward Luttwak, "From Geopolitics to Geoeconomics. Logic of Conflict and Grammar of Commerce", in *National Interest,* summer 1990.

32. C. Jean, *Geopolitica,* Bari, 1995. Geoeconomic strategy consists in attacking the *niches* uncovered by common international rules in order to avoid reactions. The formula "high tech Colbertism" has been proposed.
33. Ph. C. Schmitter, *Imaging the Future of Euro-Polity* in Marks, Schmitter, Schrpf, Streeck(ed*), Governance in the European Union,* London, 1996.
34. The concept "postwestphalian" is actually current in the framework of the literature of international relations: after the Westphalian system (started with the treaty of Westphalia, 1648, giving birth to an international system based on the principle of the balance of power between sovereign states) a new international system is at stake, going beyond the rules and the constraints of the simple power politics.
35. J.L. Quermonne, *Le systeme politique de l'Union europeene,* Paris, 1994, pp. 148-149.
36. K. Lamers – W. Schauble, CDU/CSU, *Reflexions sur la politique eruopeenne, in "Europe Documents"*, 7 September 1994.
37. Schmitter, *Le federalisme est-il la seule solution?* in M. Telo (ed.). *Democratie et construction europeenne,* Bruxelles, 1995.
38. P. Kennedy, *The Rise and Fall of Great Powers,* 1987; R, Keohane, *After Hegemony,* 1985.
39. Five new areas of regional cooperation has been approved with the aim of improving people relations at the level of civil society: a broadcasting programme, a documentation centre, SAARC Chairs, fellowship in the South Asia universities, promotion of tourism, a SAARC Youth Volunteers programme.
40. Communication de la Commission, Partenariat reinforce UE Inde, 26.6.1996; Direction generale 1 b, Alleviating poverty, 20 years of EC support to Asia, Brussels 1997.
41. Brazil, Argentina, Uruguay and Paraguay. *Open Integration. The EU and the Mercosul and the International system.* IEEI Lisbon march 1995; *Alem do commercio. Ampilar as relacoes Europa-Mercosul,,* Forum Latino Americano, Lisboa 1997; M. Bekerman, Mercosur. *La Oportunidad y el desafio,* Buenos Aires, 1992; F. Pena, *Previsibilidad y Eficacia, Una perspectiva para la cuestion institucional en el Mercosur,* Julio 1997. O. Dabene, L'integration regionale en Amerique latine: Le Mercosur, CERI, Paris, 1995; IRELA "la Union europea y el mercosur", informe de Irela, octubre 1994. OCDE, "Integration regionale et systeme commercial multilateral: synergie et divergence", Paris, 1995; A. Toledano Laredo, *Les relations entre l'UE et le Mercosur, in "Revue du marche Unique europeen,* Paris, 4, 1995; barahona de Brito, A., "The political dimension of cooperation between the European Union and the Mercosul" in *Open Integration,* 1997 Lisbon.
42. Jean Grugel, *Latin America and the Remaking of the Americas,* in A. Gamble and A. Payne, *Regionalism and World Order,* 1996, p. 151.
43. *El apoyo internacional a la democracia en America Latina,* in "Sintesis", n. 21, decembre 1993.

44. F. Pena, paper presented to the Lisboa Euro-Latino American Forum of May 1998.
45. Commission de la CE, "Proposition de decision du 25.10.1995 relartive a la conclusion de l'accord cadre interregional de cooperation entre la CE et ses Ettas membres, d'une part, et le Mercosur et ses Etats membres d'autre part, "Journal officiel, 19.1.1996, Luxemburg. Parlement Europeen, "Resolution due 16.5.1995 sur le renforcement de la politique de l'UE a l'egard de Mercosur" Journal officie 19.5.1995, Luxemmeburg; W. Wessels – U. Diedrichs, The role of Mercosur in European Union Priorities after the IGC, Forum Euro-latino americano, Sao Paolo, october 1997.

REFERENCES

F. Algieri, J. Janning D. Rummel, *Managing Security in Europe*, Bertelsmann, 1996.

APEC secretariat, *A Vision for APEC. Towards an Asia Pacific Economic Community*, Singapore, 1993.

APEC Secretariat, *Implementing the APEC Vision*, Singapore, 1995.

E. Baron-Crespo, *L'Europa all' alba del millenio*, Italian edition including contributions by G. Amato and M. Monti, Marsilio, Venezia, 1997.

C.F. Bergsten, *Globalizing Free Trade*, in "Foreign Affiars" n. 3, 1996, pp. 105-120.

L. Bizzozzeor *Paz y Seguridad en el mundo post-muro*, Institut Goethe-Fac. de Ciencias Sociales, Montevideo 1997.

L. Bizzozzero y J. Grandi *Hacia una socieda civil del Mercosur* in "Integracion y comercio" n.3, 1997.

Boyer and others, *Mobdialisation, Au dela des mythes*, La decouverte, Paris, 1997.

F. Braudel, *Civilisation matérielle. économie et capitalisme (XV-XVII siécle)*, Paris, Colin, 1979.

S. Bulmer and A. Scott (ed), *Economic and Political Integration in Europe : Internal Dynamics and Global Context*, Blackwell, 1994.

J. Clark, *Globalisation and Fragmantation*, Oxford 1997.

E. Cohen, *La tentation hexagonale, la souveraineté a lépreuve de la mondialisation*, Paris, 1996.

Commission of the European Communities, *Towards a New Asia Strategy*, Brussels, 1994.

R. Cox (ed) *The New Realism, Perspective on Multilateralism and World Order*, 1997, London.

T. Dos Santos, *Nova Etapa de uma Veha Polemica, F.H. Cardoso e a Theoria de la Dependéncia*, paper, 1993.

G. Duprat (éd.), *L 'Union européénee*, Paris, 1996 (see the chapter written by J.L. Quermonne).

Kjell Eliassen and Catherine Borve-Monsen, *Institutions and networks: a comparison of European and South East Asia Integration*, paper Brussels, 1998.

ECSA, World Conference, Brussels, September 1996, papers by A. Sbragia, R. Seidelmann and others.

G. Edwards and Á Pijpers, *The Politics of European Treaty Reform*, London and Washington, 1997

L. Fawcett and A. Hurrell (eds), *Regionalism in World politics: Regional Organisation in International Order*, Oxford, 1995.

J.P. Fitoussi et P. Rosanvallon, *Le nouvel age des inégalités*, Paris, 1996.

Forum Problems Peace and War, Florence, Conference "The Future of European Union", June 1996

A. Gamble and A. Payne, *Regionalism and World Order*, MacMillian, 1996.

St. Gill, *American Hegemony and the Trilateral Commission*, Cambridge, 1990

R. Gilpin, *Politcs and Economy in International Relations*, 1987.

Hashimoto, *A Caring Society*, Speech at the "G7 Conference on Social Problem", Lyon, 1996.

R. Higgott, D. Camrous, *Regionalism, Identity and Ideas. The Regional Political Economies of Europe and Asia Pacific in comparative Perspective*, JPSA, Kyoto, Dec. 1996.

P. Hirst & G. Thompson, *Globalisation in Question*, Cambridge Boston 1996.

E. Hobsbawn, *The Age of Extremes*, London, 1995.

G.D. Hook, *Japan Leader in East Asia*, in A. Gamble and A. Payne, *Regionalism and World Order*, cit.

S. Huntigton, *The Clash of Civilisations*? in "Foreign Affairs", n. 72, 1993.

C. Jean, Geopolitica, Bari, 1995.

IEEI, Lisbonne, *Politique externe et de sécurité commune de l'UE*, paper, 1996.

M. Iokibe and others, *Towards a more effecive UN (Japan Options)*, Tokyo, New York, 1996.

R. Keohane et R. Nye, *Power and Interdependence*, Harvard, 1989.

R. Koehane et S. Hoffmann, *The New European Community*, 1990.

P. Krugman, *Regional Blocs : The Good, the Bad and the Ugly*, in "The International Economy", Nov. 1991.

Edward Luttwak, "From Geopolitcs to Geoeconomics. Logic of Conflict and Grammar of Commerce", in *National Interest*, summer 1990.

E.D. Mansfield, H.C. Milner (ed), *The Political Economy of Regionalism*, Columbia Univ. Press. 1997

Michelmann et Soldatos, *Federalism and International relations*, Claredon, 1990.

OECD, *Regional Integration and the Multilateral Trading System, Synergy and Divergence*, Paris, 1995;

O.N.U., Rapport-Programme des Nations-Unies pour le développement, juillet 1996

I. Otake, *Interpretating the Emergence of Neo-Liberal Reforms in 1980s. Japanese and French Experience Compared*, paper for Kyoto Conference, 1996.

S.H. Park, *The Current Status and Future Prospects of Regionalism and Multilaterlism in the World Economy. A case Study of Ec. Relat. between EU and APEC in the WTO Era*. Paper to ECSA World Congress, Brussels, Sept. 1996.

A. Quddus, *European Union's emerging relations with Asia*, post doctoral research, IEE, ULB, Brussels 1997.

E. Remacle, *L'U.E.O.* Thése de doctorat, ULB, 1996.

Y. Sakamoto, *The Role of Japan in International System*, in "The International System After the Collapse of East-West Order", Luxemburg, 1993.

Modijitaba Sadria, *Le Japan peut-il avoir politique indépdendante*? in "Le Monde", 22. 11. 1996.

A. Sbragia, *Instituion-Building from Below Above The E.C. in Global Environmental Politics*, Irvine, California, 1996.

Klaus Schwab and Claude Smadja, "Davos: mondialisation et responsabilité sociale", in *Le Monde*, 17. 7. 1996.

G. Schiavone, *Western Europe and South-East Asia, Cooperation or Competition*? MacMillan, 1989.

G. Schiavone, *Asian Pacific Economic Cooperation and the Role of the European Community*, in "The EC after 1992. A New Role in World Politics? Norms, Baden-Baden, 1991

R. Seidelmann and M. Telo' (ed), *Where is Germany going?* (in Italian), Rome, 1996.

S. Strange, *The Retraite of the State*, 1997.

R. Sturm. *Economic Regionalism in a Federal State. Germany and the Challenge of the Single Market*, Tubingen, 1994.

A. Tanka, *Contending Models of International Security in Asia Pacific: Modern, Traditional or Neo-Medieval?*, paer for Kyoto Conference 1996

A. Tanaka, *Regional Arrangements, the UN and Security in Asia*, paper, Oct. 1996

P. Taylor, *International Organisation in the Modern World, New York 1993*

M. Telo' - P. Magnetter (ed.), *Repenser l'Europe*, Brussels, 1996

M. Telo' - P. Magnette (ed.), *De Maastricht a Amsterdam. Le nouveau Traite et l'Europe*, Brussels, Complexe, 1998

G. Therborn, *Europen Modernity and beyond*, London 1995

L. Thurow, *The Future of Capitalism*, 1997

A. Vasconcelos, M.F. Durand (ed.), *La PES* C, Paris P.U.F., 1998

W. Wallace, *Regional Integration: the West European Experience*, Washington, 1994

I. Wallerstein, Geopolitics and Geocoluture. Essay on the changing world system. Cambridge 1991

S. Wilks, Regulatory Change (and Corporate Governance) in Europe and Japan, Freer Markets, More Rules?, Paper for Kyoto Conference, Dec. 1996

WTO Secretariat, Regionalism in the World Training System, Geneva, 1995.

D. Wurfel (ed.), *South-East Asia in the New World Order*, MacMillan, 1996.

11

The West Viewed From India

B. VIVEKANANDAN

Viewed from India, conceptually the 'West' presents the picture of a hologram of overlapping circles — each circle representing a distinct dimension of the whole. Geographically, the frontiers of the West was initially confined to Europe. But the colonial expansion of the West, followed by large scale emigration of people of European stock, enabled the West to widen its political and cultural frontiers to far flung areas of the world. The expansion of the cultural frontier was clear and sharp in North America, Australia and New Zealand, and less sharp but still conspicuous in many other areas which came under the ambit of the colonial expansion of the West. However, besides specific pockets of European settlers, a large number of people in other parts of the world, particularly in the metropolitan cities across the globe, the Western cultural influence is a recognized fact of life. Many countries have also patterned their political system and jurisprudence after the models provided by the West. As a result, this multi-layer and multi-dimensional concentric circles of this hologram makes it hazardous to clearly demarcate the geographical frontiers of the West today as it blends with a more nebulous and expansive concept where it is in perpetual competition with other socio-political and cultural entities elsewhere in the world. The inroads the West made in this context is notable in the dual or split societies in a large number of developing countries where, to a considerable extent, the West is viewed as a synonym for influence, modernization, industrial and technological advancement, permissiveness, etc. Indeed, today every society, in the developing world particularly, has become an arena of intense and perpetual competition between the Western values and the Eastern values, leaving that larger question of which one, on balance, is superior to the other unresolved. However, in a broad sense, the Western attitude and way of Life have made considerable inroads everywhere — in Asia, Africa and Latin America. It is possible that eventually for mutual benefit a synthesis between the finer aspects of the two value systems and their cultures may emerge in future. However, if, unfortunately, the emphasis turns the other way round, it would be disastrous for the whole humanity.

India's perception of the West evolved out of its constant interaction with Europe ever since the Portuguese navigator, Vasco da Gama, anchored his ship at the Kerala coast in South India in 1498. In consequence, conceptually, in the Indian eyes, Europe remains the hub of the West. A home of many great civilizations and cultures, a cradle of many epoch making revolutions and political movements, a continent of great seafarers who engendered an outward looking tradition, a region which made outstanding contributions to the world thought, science and technology, art, architecture and sculpture, and at the same time remained a theatre of prolonged and intermittent bloody and destructive wars, born out of internecine quarrels and aggressive nationalisms, and a scene of horror under leaders like Adolf Hitler, is the complex picture that comes before one's mind when one ventures to have a comprehensive view of the West in historical perspective. That view of the West is superimposed by many distinguishing features of positive developments in the post-war period which witnessed the launching of European reconstruction around a community concept. Following the rationale provided by a French genius, Jean Monnet, European nations chose to give up their traditional approach towards each other based on mutual suspicion and distrust, which caused wars and destruction in the past, and adopted a joint approach for growth and development, and established new and effective instruments of cooperation based on community concept. The revolutionary change it brought about in the general psyche of Europe and in the threat perception of European nations, and the collective prosperity it propelled everywhere in Europe, have been looked upon in India with great admiration. This successful experiment in the West has demonstrated how Europe could reap, during the last five decades, all the benefits countries can hope to have from an environment of prolonged peace, tranquillity and stability.

Another admirable feature of the present day West is its distinction as the pioneer of the welfare state system. Indeed, many countries of the developing world have drawn inspiration from the welfare state experiment of the West and tried to emulate it, depending upon the extent to which they could mobilize resources for the purpose. Besides, during the last two decades, the West has shown greater vigil against the emerging global challenges like the environmental degradation and damages to the ecological balance, the absence of a stable security system for maintenance of peace everywhere, and against the dangers of preserving unequal societies, both nationally and globally. Programmes of how to meet this engulfing challenges have come in the form of recommendations made by various expert commissions, chaired by eminent social democratic leaders of the West like Willy Brandt, Olof Palme, Gro-Harlem Brundtland, etc. The Brandt Commission Report on North-South Cooperation, Palme Commission Report on Common Security and the Brundtland Commission Report on environmental protection and sustainable development which also focussed on the common future of mankind, contained practical propositions to meet these challenges.

This current positive image of the West is overshadowed by its many negative features. One such negative feature pertains to the directions in which the Western societies, at a macro level, move on. One of the most fundamental negative feature of the Western societies today is the atomization and steady erosion of the social fabric. It is vividly manifest in the highly impersonal human relationship, growing permissiveness, high rate of divorces, the growing number of single parents, alienation or virtual segregation of the old people from the young, and in the permeation of a throw away culture in large parts of the West. Indeed, all post-industrial societies suffer from these maladies. When uncontrolled material acquisitiveness and insatiable consumerism become all pervading objectives of life, it is inevitable that human psyche will tend to increasingly lose its human touch — emotional bonds between humans become very thin. Those essentials of a meaningful life are tended to be viewed as old fashioned, and therefore to be discarded. In consequence, life inevitably becomes increasingly sterile and atomised, generating a lot of frustration in the midst of prosperity and plenty. The West seems to be under the grip of such an undercurrent.

Similarly spectacular is the ongoing demographic change in the West, due to a declining trend in population growth, which can have far-reaching socio-economic consequences for many societies there. As the size of the old people is constantly expanding, the size of the younger people, particularly of the working age, is steadily shrinking. Whatever may be the reasons of this phenomenon, the implications of this revolutionary change in the composition of the population are many — both domestically and internationally. Domestically, this would, no doubt, significantly change the market structure and consumption pattern in the West. In concrete terms, it would mean that a smaller number of people in the working age group will have to shoulder the responsibility of the unkeep of an ever increasing number of the older people — a situation in which eventually about one-third of the population will have to look after two-thirds of the people. If it is coupled with a free market approach, it can have tremendous social implications. As it would radically alter the consumer market potential of Europe, it can reduce the West's import market potential as well. It has already been noted in India that the import market potential of the European Union, a major constituent of the West, is shrinking. The import pattern of the European Community between 1981 and 1990 showed that the total share of EC imports got shrunk from 52 per cent in 1981 to 40 per cent in 1990. Of this, the share of class-2 imports of the EC, a category in which much of the developing countries' exports, including Indian exports, belong to got shrunk from 40 per cent in 1981 to 31 per cent in 1990. Therefore, in realistic terms, the West's market potential for the developing countries is progressively shrinking, though it will still remain an important market for quite some time. In addition, there is apprehension that more and more refined methods of protectionism are likely to be introduced in the West in the coming years to increasingly ebb out developing countries' products from the Western markets. This trend, coupled with the ongoing demographic change, can cut down the consumer market potential of the West in general for the outside world.

The irony is that while the consumption capacity of the consumers of the West is fast reaching a saturation point, a large number of consumers in the developing world who still have enormous potential to consume, are unable to do so far want of the needed purchasing power. This phenomenon, if not remedied suitably through international efforts, can become a source of tension and instability in the West as it can fuel recession and unemployment there, with all the adverse social and political consequences accompanying it. Despite this dim prospects, the West has not yet heeded the wise counsels of eminent world statesmen of European origin, like Bruno Kreisky and Willy Brandt, that the long-term interests of the developed countries lay in the development of the developing countries. Their pleas for a new Marshall Plan for third world development and for a meaningful North-South cooperation have fallen so far on deaf ears.

One is also struck by the fact that Europe is in the throes of an unemployment crisis. The current level of 20 million unemployed in Europe can have unpredictable consequences for the region. A free market approach, anchored purely on profit motive, coupled with the indiscriminate adoption of job displacing technologies to maximize that profit, has created an in-built fast breeder of unemployment in Europe which can take the crisis to dangerous and explosive levels. However, the fact remains that the more the governments of the West move away from a full employment strategy for ideological reasons, the deeper will be the crises in which they would be plunging into. There are indications that the struggle between the full employment strategy and free market approach will resurface when the social cost of the free market approach becomes more manifest. It may be recalled that in the inter-war period, fascism in Europe grew with unemployment as its midwife. Today, Europe is once again witnessing the growth of xenophobia and right-wing extremism, reminiscent of Europe of the early 1930s. It is manifest in Germany, France, Austria, Spain, etc. The xenophobic elements have unleashed violent attacks on foreigners, including on people from less developed European nations, which have sent shockwaves all over the world. The silverlining in the darkening sky is that all major democratic parties everywhere have publicly opposed it and held huge rallies in many parts of Europe, including in Germany, against the xenophobic and neo-fascist elements. Yet, it causes concern as some of these extreme right wing elements have made electoral gains in the local elections in many countries of the West. However, one consequence stands out. It has made the life of immigrants in Europe increasingly miserable. On the one hand, the neo-nazis perpetuate violence against them; on the other, it is complemented by some governments, like Austria in

1993 for example, which have taken measures to tighten the residence rules of the immigrants.

Today, the West is credited with policies which perpetuate the drain of resources from poor countries to the rich. In addition, it is viewed as making concerted efforts to suck many developing countries, like India for example, which have the potential to emerge as competitors to the West commercially in certain fields, into debt traps to undermine their potential capabilities. There is also a strong feeling in the developing world that many Conservative regimes of the West are turning decisively anti-poor in their global strategy. Their drive for globalization of markets and prices, without simultaneous drive for globalization of incomes, is seen as a recipe to affront the poor everywhere. The globalization of prices of essential life saving products, like medicines for example, under a free market system can only make these items beyond the pale of the poor people, which in effect would be seen as a policy designed to heighten the mortality rate among the poor people. The worst victims of this enhanced incapacity of the poor would be the children and the aged belong to this category. Could this be a covert hidden agenda of the present policies of the West? Could this be a methodology of the West, apart from the profit part of it, to reduce the population of the poorer people in the developing world? These are mind boggling questions, for which there cannot have any satisfactory answer at the moment. But, future will tell.

However, there is also a strong feeling that the selfish oriented business nationalism which many western countries assiduously practice today is undermining the economic security of many developing countries. The feeling is also strong that the West is still engaged in building up structures of domination and exploitation of the developing countries. Through various multilateral institutions like the WTO, World Bank and IMF, and through the Western multinational companies, the developing countries are progressively, reduced to client states of the West. Indeed, today these institutions have become partners of an ideological drive and have become instruments of a concerted move to coerce the developing countries to accept damaging conditionalities to promote the interest of the West. They forced many developing countries to restructure their domestic economies to promote a free market approach, detrimental to their own nascent industries, and open up their domestic markets to Western multinationals, before they were granted loans, etc. Obviously, more subtle and sophisticated methods of exploitation and instruments of domination are being employed to bleed the developing countries white.

On trade matters, the West has been found assiduously practising protectionism against exports from developing countries to their markets. At the same time they do not fail to resort to applying all sorts of pressures on the developing countries to force them to throw their markets open and expose their infant industries to unfair competition from the developed countries through the creation of a market anarchy in the third world. The mayhem that can follow in the Third World markets would have twin effects: (1) It can destroy the small and medium level labour intensive indigenous industries of the developing countries, with inestimable potential for generating social unrest; and (2) the Western exports can capture the markets in the developing countries, at the cost of indigenous manufactures, with little reciprocity obligations. It can lead to the re-establishment of a new pattern of colonial type relationship between the West and the developing countries.

How still alive is the West's colonial attitude is discernible in the last WTO "agreement" and in the arm-twisting and other methods employed to force the developing countries to take GATT negotiations beyond its original parameters of goods, and extend its ambit to new areas like agriculture, services, insurance, banking, patents, medicines, investments, insecticide, etc., which could cause severe damage to their national interests and curtail their freedom to manage their economies for the benefit of their people. The scope in the WTO treaty to practice cross-sector retaliation makes the poor countries vulnerable to the pressures of the powerful West, including the United States, which is now functioning as a cartel against the poor countries to continue the exploitation of the third world's weak position and maximize their profits. Instead of promoting a just world order, the West seems to be straining every nerve to promote and stabilize the present unjust world order based on inequity.

Therefore, from India, the view of the West remain complex and generates hopes and anxieties. It appears that after the 1989 revolution in Europe, the West has not stabilized itself with a coherent approach.

It is once again in the melting pot. From a regional angle, the West is resurgent. The benefits it drew from the community approach in the post-war period is inspiring. But, from a global angle, its parameters remain exploitative and suppressive of the developing countries. The picture is not promising and it must change. The political arena of the West today is experiencing a void of great personalities with global vision. It is hard to see in the political horizon of the West, men of Willy Brandt's or Bruno Kriesky's calibre who could rise above their provincial cocoon and think about the wider world as well and try to reconcile the interests of the rich and poor countries through meaningful initiatives. But the bane is that in many important countries of the West, provincial minded politicians, sans wider vision, happen to be in the helm of affairs.

Notes on Contributors

Professor Ankush B. Sawant
Former Director, Centre for African Studies, University of Bombay.

Professor B. Vivekanandan,
Professor and former Chairman, Centre for American and West European Studies, School of International Studies, Jawaharlal Nehru University, New Delhi.

Dr. D.K. Giri
Senior Researh Fellow, Institute of Social Sciences, New Delhi.

Professor Hartmut Elsenhans
Professor, Institute for Political Science, University of Leipzig, Germany.

Professor Mario Telo
Jean Monnet Professor and Research Director, Institute of European Studies and Institute of Sociology, Free University of Brussels, Belgium.

Dr. Mick Wilkinson
Lecturer, University of Hull, United Kingdom.

Dr. Nimmi Kurian
Research Fellow, Centre for Policy Research, New Delhi.

Dr. O.P. Sharma
Advisor, Planning Commission, Government of India, New Delhi.

Professor Paul K. Sutton
Centre for Politics and Asian Studies, University of Hull, United Kingdom.

Professor Purusottam Bhattacharya
Joint Director, School of International Relations, Jadavpur University, Calcutta.

Tom Burden
Principal Lecturer of Political Science, Leeds Metropolitan University, Leeds, United Kingdom.

INDEX